NEW PROCLAMATION

New Proclamation
Year C 2013

Advent through Holy Week
December 2, 2012—March 31, 2013

G. Lee Ramsey Jr.

Joni S. Sancken

L. Susan Bond

Jonathan Linman

David B. Lott, Editor

Fortress Press

Minneapolis

NEW PROCLAMATION
Year C 2013
Advent through Holy Week
December 2, 2012—March 31, 2013

Illustrations: Joel Nickel, Margaret Adams Parker, Robyn Sand Anderson, Margaret
Bartenstein Bussey, M.P. (Paula) Wiggins
Cover design: Laurie Ingram
Book design: Sharon Martin

Library of Congress Cataloging-in-Publication Data
The Library of Congress has catalogued this series as follows.
New Proclamation: Year C 2013 Advent through Holy Week
      p. cm.
    Includes bibliographical references.
    ISBN 978-1-4514-0259-9
        1. Church year. I. Moloney, Francis J.
    BV30 .N48 2001
    2511.6dc21 2001023746

Library of Congress Cataloging-in-Publication Data
ISBN 978-1-4514-0259-9

Manufactured in the U.S.A.
16   15   14   13   12   1   2   3   4   5   6   7   8   9   10

Contents

Epiphany—Time after Epiphany / Ordinary Time
Joni S. Sancken

Lent
L. Susan Bond

Holy Week
Jonathan Linman

Preface

For nearly four decades Fortress Press has offered an ecumenical preaching resource built around the three-year lectionary cycle, a tradition that this latest edition of *New Proclamation* continues. *New Proclamation* is grounded in the belief that a deeper understanding of the biblical pericopes in both their historical and liturgical contexts is the best means to inform and inspire preachers to deliver engaging and effective sermons. For this reason, the most capable North American biblical scholars and homileticians are invited to contribute to *New Proclamation*.

    New Proclamation has always distinguished itself from most other lectionary resources by offering brand-new editions each year, each dated according to the church year in which it will first be used and featuring a fresh set of authors. Yet each edition is planned as a timeless resource that preachers will want to keep on their bookshelves for future reference for years to come. In addition, *New Proclamation*, true to its ecumenical scope, has traditionally offered commentary on all of the major lectionary traditions. Now, reflecting changes in practices among the mainline Protestant denominations, those number just two: the *Revised Common Lectionary* (RCL) and the Roman Catholic *Lectionary for Mass* (LFM).

    New Proclamation is published in two volumes per year. This first volume covers all the Sunday lections and major festivals from Advent through Easter Day. The second volume, which will be published later this year, begins with new commentary on the Easter Vigil and covers the remaining Sunday lections and major festivals through Christ the King Sunday. For those churches that celebrate minor feast days and solemnities, including saints' days, denominational days such as Body and Blood of Christ (Corpus Christi) or Reformation Day, and national days and topical celebrations, a separate volume covering the texts for those days is available: *New Proclamation Commentary on Feasts, Holy Days, and Other Celebrations* (ed. David B. Lott; Fortress Press, 2007).

    Longtime users of *New Proclamation* will note that this latest edition adopts a fresh look, which ties the series in visually with Augsburg Fortress's popular worship resource *Sundays and Seasons*. We hope that this change not only makes the text more readable and accessible, but also encourages readers to use these fine resources in tandem with each other. We also invite you to visit this volume's companion Web site, www.NewProclamation.com, which offers access not only to this book's contents, but also to commentary from earlier editions, up-to-the-minute thoughts on the connection between texts and current events, user forums, and other resources to help you develop your sermons and enhance your preaching.

What has not changed with this edition is the high quality of the content that *New Proclamation* provides to preachers and those interested in studying the lectionary texts. Each writer offers an introduction to her or his commentary that provides insights into the background and spiritual significance of that season (or portion thereof), as well as ideas for planning one's preaching during that time. In addition, the application of biblical texts to contemporary situations is an important concern of each contributor. Exegetical work is concise, and thoughts on how the texts address today's world, congregational issues, and personal situations have a prominent role.

This latest volume brings together four writers who are making their series debuts. Lee Ramsey, a professor of both pastoral care and preaching who most recently has explored the depiction of the preacher in southern literature, brings his wide-ranging knowledge and imagination to the texts for Advent and Christmas. A first-time author, Joni Sancken, draws on her Mennonite roots to contemplate how preachers might bring a fresh word during the Time after Epiphany. Susan Bond, who has written a highly regarded volume on preaching in the African American tradition, writes passionately and thought-provokingly on the season of Lent. And liturgical scholar Jonathan Linman takes us on a spiritual journey through Holy Week, leading us into a joyful celebration of Easter. All four breathe new life into the lectionary texts and will help preachers do the same as they proclaim the gospel within the congregations they serve. We are grateful to each of these contributors for their insights and their commitment to effective Christian preaching, and are confident that you will find in this volume ideas, stimulation, and encouragement for your ministry of proclamation.

David B. Lott

Advent

G. Lee Ramsey Jr.

The Christian year begins not with arrival but anticipation. Though the great celebration of Christmas beckons, especially the deeper the calendar rolls toward December 25, these next four Sundays of the lectionary accent preparation for the arrival of Jesus. Such waiting is particularly difficult to preach within the Western context because all around us the culture gallops toward Christmas Day. Malls are jammed with Christmas goods. Carols announcing Jesus' birth float across the airwaves beginning in November. Everyone scurries to scoop up Christmas foods and to decorate the house from porch to patio. "Why wait?" a consumerist society asks us. We can all start Christmas with the gong of the shopping bell on Black Friday following Thanksgiving Day, if not before.

These cultural impingements upon Christian faith and worship provide all the more reason for the preacher and worshiping community to attend carefully to the biblical and theological themes of Advent. For in this season of Advent (the word *Advent* derives from the Latin meaning "to come"), the church prepares itself to receive the central mystery of the Christian faith—the incarnation of God, "Immanuel," God with us. It is time to slow down, pray, fast, wait, watch, and ponder along with Mary and Joseph as we anticipate the birth of God in human form. "People look east," the Advent hymn invites the church, for "love the guest is on the way." The lections for the four Sundays of Advent help us to remember to watch, wait, and look east until the fullness of time has come.

But Advent is much more than silent waiting. The Scripture lessons of the season sound sharper notes. From the prophecies of the second coming of Jesus on the first Sunday to the shrill calls of repentance of John the Baptist on the second and third Sundays, the lessons awaken us to *now* time. *Now* is the time to put our houses in order. *Now* is the time to scrape away from our lives the accretions of sin in its many forms. *Now* is the time to prepare the way of the Lord! No one knows the time or the hour that the Son of God will return. Advent urges us to stay on the alert, ready to receive him.

Preachers will feel the push and pull of these polarities of Advent—the second coming of the resurrected Christ juxtaposed with the first arrival as a newborn baby.

Luke and the other Gospel writers understood the tension. We preach the whole gospel even when focusing upon certain seasonal themes. Advent looks back to the birth of Jesus as an infant (incarnation) even as it looks forward to his return in triumph at the end of days (eschatology). But whether the biblical readings direct us forward or backward, anticipation marks this season of preaching and worship. Preaching through these four Sundays, the astute preacher understands that anticipation is a good location from which to look in both directions.

December 2, 2012
First Sunday of Advent

First Reading
Jeremiah 33:14-16 (RCL, LFM)

From a Hebrew prophetic book that often dwells on lament, we find these powerful three verses of hope. The prophet Jeremiah projects hope for Israel, whether it is through return from Babylonian captivity or restoration of the Davidic dynasty. Either way, the prophet points Israel toward a future in which a "righteous Branch" (an anointed one, a messiah) will spring up to guide the disheartened nation (v. 15). God will make good on the promise to sustain Judah and save Jerusalem from destruction.

Since scholars are uncertain about the dating of this passage, preachers need not dwell on whether the situation is pre- or post-exile. Clearly, the Davidic kingship has not yet been restored, and earlier verses in chapter 33 indicate that Jerusalem lies in ruin (vv. 4-11). Israel's sins have piled in upon them, but God is now ready to relieve the people of their guilt (v. 8).

This passage can be preached with conviction on the First Sunday of Advent without interpreting it as an anticipation of the birth of Jesus of Nazareth. God's promise is to execute justice and righteousness in the land through the hand of the anointed one. The promise grows out of Judaism's central commitment to justice and righteousness. These are social values stressing financial equity and political fairness within the nation. Salvation comes to the land not only from beyond time but within human history. Justice is not something that happens only at the end of time but is most needed here and now within every tribe and nation. A messiah in the line of

David will be the one to carry out God's justice and to rule fairly among the people. Fulfillment of this promise has always been at the heart of Jewish faith.

Such striving for justice was heard clearly in the Middle East and Northern African nations during the "Arab Spring" of 2011. There the world watched whole nations of people—whether Jews, Muslims, or Christians—publicly yearning, calling out for Jeremiah's prophesied justice and righteousness. It was heard again in the "Occupy Wall Street" protests of 2011–2012 in the United States and around the globe. What better season than Advent to proclaim the coming of God's righteousness upon the earth? As we watch and wait for those days that are "surely coming" (v. 14), Christians can join hands with Jews and Muslims throughout the world to anticipate and to help usher in the day of the Lord.

Psalmody
Psalm 25:1-10 (RCL)
Psalm 25:4-5, 8-9, 10 + 14 (LFM)

Taken as a whole, Psalm 25:1-14 speaks in two distinct voices: the voice of the individual petitioner of God (vv. 1-8, 11), and the voice of a worship leader or priest, addressing the congregation (vv. 9-10, 12-14). Between the two emerges an important message for Advent. The individual in prayer waits upon the Lord (vv. 3, 5) while requesting that God not remember his or her sins of the past (vv. 7, 11). In response, God hears the waiting pleas of the one who prays and, through the voice of the priest, offers redemption "for those who keep his covenant and his decrees" (v. 10). Advent would be a bleak season indeed if at the end of all our waiting and prayer there was only silence. But as the psalmist reassures us, "The friendship of the LORD is for those who fear him, and he makes his covenant known to them" (v. 14).

Second Reading
1 Thessalonians 3:9-13 (RCL)

This earliest of the New Testament Christian letters features Paul and Timothy sending a note of strong encouragement to the fledgling Christian congregation at Thessalonica along with instructions about Christian eschatology (4:13—5:11). Apparently the congregation has experienced persecution by nonbelievers (2:13—3:5). Paul wants to assure them that he understands what it is like to be persecuted and to encourage them to remain steadfast in the face of trials. He rejoices upon learning that the congregation has not wavered in its faith (3:7), and he offers prayers and blessings on their behalf (vv. 10-13).

A mood of anticipation marks this portion of the letter as Paul waits for the day when he can see the congregation "face to face" (v. 10). Surely this human longing for connection with those we love is an important feature of Advent. While we wait for the coming of the Lord, we also long to be united with family and friends among both the living and the dead. Such reflections may prompt the preacher to draw sermon analogies between anticipation of Christmas and anticipation of reuniting with loved ones. Longing and hoped-for fulfillment reside in both.

In verse 13 Paul begins to address the eschatological concerns of the Thessalonians. Expecting the imminent return of Christ, Paul pushes the congregation to remain holy and blameless until Christ comes again. He addresses the matter more fully in succeeding verses (4:13—5:11), assuring them that those who have died before the return of Christ will be the first to be resurrected by him (4:16). This concern is important for Christians in Advent, though it is doubtful that many in our congregations would intentionally choose this season to reflect upon it. What makes the coming of Jesus at Nazareth so important is that he comes again as the resurrected Christ beyond the grave at Jerusalem. In Advent, we do not simply await the hush of the manger but the trumpet call of resurrected glory for all who live and die with Christ. Playing this note on the first week of Advent invites the congregation to ponder the mystery of birth and death, of sin and salvation, on a personal and cosmic scale.

Then come two of the most-often-quoted verses from Thessalonians: "Now concerning the times and the seasons, brothers and sisters, you do not need to have anything written to you. For you yourselves know very well that the day of the Lord will come like a thief in the night" (5:1-2). This passage sets the stage for the day's lectionary reading in Luke's Gospel.

1 Thessalonians 3:12—4:2 (LFM)

Another potential avenue for preaching from this text during Advent is suggested by the first two verses of chapter 4. The accent here is upon sanctification of the believers who wait upon the return of Paul and upon the return of the Lord. Paul's instructions are very specific in the following verses: avoid fornication (v. 3), do not exploit one another (v. 6), live quietly (v. 11), and so forth. Like the season of Lent, Advent is a good time to take personal stock of our own morality (or lack thereof). Reflected in the mirror of the returning Christ, our own character often needs some deep polishing. Even if we are mature in Christ, as Paul says to the Thessalonians, we ought to be and "do so more and more" (v. 1). A sermon along these lines need not be "moralistic" to get the point across, especially if the preacher places himself or herself in the pews along with the congregation to hear the Advent summons to personal and congregational righteousness in preparation for the coming of the Lord.

Gospel
Luke 21:25-36 (RCL)
Luke 21:25-28, 34-36 (LFM)

If there is any thought that the Gospel reading for the First Sunday of Advent will provide a gentle stroll toward the warm and loving embrace of Christmas, Luke 21 quickly dispels such notions. This apocalyptic passage broadcasts an urgent alarm. Heavenly eclipses stir cosmic turmoil. Earthquakes and tsunamis batter the earth. Famines and plagues eviscerate the nations. Jerusalem, the holy city, will be surrounded by foreign armies bent on destruction (21:20). "These are days of vengeance," warns Luke (v. 22). "People will faint with fear and foreboding of what is coming upon the world," the writer prophesies (v. 26).

Little wonder that some Christian groups turn to Luke 21 and its Gospel parallels (Matthew 24; Mark 13), along with the book of Revelation, to explain the end of days as an apocalyptic clash between the forces of light and darkness. The wildly popular novels of Hal Lindsey (*The Late Great Planet Earth*) and Tim LaHaye with Jerry Jenkins (the "Left Behind" series) build upon literal interpretations of passages such as Luke 21 to spin out their fictional accounts of the last days. Certain denominations such as Jehovah's Witnesses espouse that we live in just such times as described in New Testament apocalyptic literature and are experiencing the unfolding of the final worldwide tribulation in our own time. The cosmic battle is already under way, and those who put their full trust in Christ will be redeemed or raptured away by the returning Son of Man (v. 36).

The preacher has some work to do to clear away these misleading interpretations of Luke 21 while retaining the passage's promise and urgency for contemporary hearers during Advent. The language is highly symbolic and metaphorical though nonetheless vital for Christian faith. The first-century persecutions of Christians that gave rise to this particular apocalyptic passage were real, as they were for the hearers of Paul's letter to the Thessalonians previously discussed. In extremity, humans stretch language and imagination to combat fear and to instill hope. Think of the poetry of T. S. Eliot following the devastation of World War I ("The Wasteland"), the soaring hopefulness of Martin Luther King Jr.'s "I Have a Dream" speech, the challenging rhetoric of Sojourner Truth in the mid-1800s of the United States ("Ain't I a Woman?"), or the poetic preaching of Bishop Desmond Tutu in apartheid South Africa. Apocalyptic speech colorfully and dramatically names the current social and political struggle as a way to empower the hearers to trust in the promised liberation that is boldly proclaimed as the result of the struggle. "Now when these things begin to take place, stand up and raise your heads, because your redemption is drawing near" (v. 28).

Undergoing persecution at the hands of the Romans, uncertain about their own survival, fearful of the consequences of swearing loyalty to Christ against Caesar, the hearers of Luke's Gospel, in particular of chapter 21, needed strong reassurance that if the world was coming to an end, at least their understanding of it, still God would not abandon them. With the Jerusalem temple in ruins, all that Jesus warned about in earlier verses of the passage seemed to have come to pass (vv. 20-24). Luke says to them, "Hold on! Christ is coming." "When these things begin to take place, stand up and raise your heads, because your redemption is drawing near" (v. 28). Following that speech-act, you can almost hear the first-century Christians breathing deeply and see them standing tall, facing into the uncertainty of the future with hope.

The challenge for preachers in the Western world is how to make sense of this hope-saturated language that is clearly more applicable in a culture of struggle, deprivation, and religious and political oppression than in a culture of ease and accommodation. As scholars suggest, Christianity's peculiar apocalyptic appeal reaches non-Western hearers with a great deal more force than it does us.[1] Our hearers may be either puzzled by the strangeness of the passage and its placement in Advent or uncertain of what to do with its frightening images. But for many, at least among the middle and upper classes of established Christians, the sharp edges of the passage will be difficult to convey. This is in part because faith has become so privatized in the Western world that it is hard to read the Scripture through social and global lenses. But as Fred Craddock says about this passage, "The human heart is too small a screen on which to cast the grand scene. . . . The church cannot continue to permit, much less endorse, a subjective captivity of the gospel."[2] We will need to challenge our hearers pastorally to see the national, international, even cosmic scope of this grand passage as it speaks to us in Advent.

In some congregations, of course, there will be hearers who are experiencing the loss of jobs in a stalled economy. Many know the fear and pain of enduring illness without adequate health-care treatment and coverage. Among immigrant populations, the fear of deportation, poor education, and mistreatment looms large. Conditions are oppressive for some of our hearers, and the passage offers a strong dose of hope to those whose backs are bent. The preacher who pastors among such a congregation will pull out the strands of hope that wind through this Advent passage and offer them as promise to the listeners. After all, Christians do worship a God whose "words will not pass away" and whose kingdom is "drawing near" (vv. 28, 31).

As for the many who because of privilege and comfort find it difficult to comprehend the social implications of Luke 21, a slightly different direction might be helpful. The passage ends on a note of exhortation for Luke's hearers: "Be on guard so that your hearts are not weighed down with dissipation and drunkenness and the worries of life, and that day does not catch you unexpectedly, like a trap. For it will come upon all who live on the face of the whole earth" (vv. 34-35). The passage cautions us not to sleep through the drama of redemption that is humanity's hope. Let's face it, for many life is long on drudgery and short on joy. Something about daily existence drains the zest out of life. Call it the dullness of routine, or maybe the tendency of things to become static. Call it the drag of sin. We set the clock, shuttle the kids off to school, grind our way through phone calls, meetings, maybe a little time for study or reviewing the numbers, and then, at night, sink down into oblivion hoping that a day off will bring some small moments of rest if not pleasure. Even our entertainments seem more and more burdensome as we crank up the fun machine, ever more fearful that we may indeed, in writer Neil Postman's evocative phrase, be "amusing ourselves to death."[3] Technology snags us in its electronic force field and we fritter away hours lost in the invisible nets of cyberspace. Seasons turn. The earth moves, like the fig tree in verses 29-30, from blossom to fruitfulness to harvest, but we barely note its changing. The person in the mirror looks distracted or tense, putting on a good face that doesn't quite seem to connect with the more authentic, more hopeful and trusting person buried deep inside. We do have a tendency to sleep through large parts of the drama of creation and redemption that is our life, regardless of how many times we hear the good news.

Luke says to those of us who are walking in our sleep, "Wake up!" The day of redemption draws near. And it's far larger than our own individual selves. Sun, moon, stars, the starving of Africa, the oppressed of Latin America, the impoverished, unemployed, and even the wealthy of North America—all are being reclaimed by God's anointed one, the Son of Man (vv. 28, 36). We can snooze through the action if we choose. But God's redemption of all creation is just too good of a show to miss. Hence, for all who hear this passage—rich and poor, possessing and dispossessed— the final note is fulfillment and joy, the joy of God's own coming to their senses, found and claimed by the God who comes in the beginning and at the end.

Notes

1. See Philip Jenkins, *The Next Christendom: The Coming of Global Christianity* (New York: Oxford University Press, 2002).
2. Fred B. Craddock, *Luke*, Interpretation: A Bible Commentary for Teaching and Preaching (Louisville: John Knox, 1990), 247.
3. Neil Postman, *Amusing Ourselves to Death: Public Discourse in the Age of Show Business* (New York: Viking, 1985).

December 9, 2012
Second Sunday of Advent

First Reading
Malachi 3:1-4 (RCL)

We know very few specifics about the prophet Malachi based upon this book at the end of the Hebrew Bible. On textual grounds, scholars believe that he wrote the book during the postexilic period of Israel's return from enslavement to the Babylonians, but even this is not certain. If, in fact, the book was written during this period, the writer addresses a relatively stable community after the Jerusalem temple has been rebuilt, sometime around 450 BCE—hence Malachi's concern with temple practices and the practices of the priests in particular.

In this reading, words of caution shadow the hope of Advent. The Lord will send a messenger to the people in the temple who will speak on behalf of God's covenant with Israel. This messenger is one in whom the nation "delights" (v. 1). Such an arrival is good news for those who wait upon the Lord. But the messenger will not only bring comfort. He will be "like a refiner's fire and like fullers' soap . . . he will purify the descendants of Levi and refine them like gold and silver, until they present offerings to the LORD in righteousness" (vv. 2-3).

Malachi's sharp call to self-examination of the worshiping community, especially its priests and pastors (Levites), comes as an important warning to us as we move more deeply into Advent. The God who comes will not tolerate false worship, mistreatment of the stranger, and oppression of the hired workers, the widow, or the orphan (v. 5). For us to receive the God of the covenant, our own lives must demonstrate justice and righteousness. Malachi makes this requirement plain while he points the way to another messenger, John the Baptist, whom we will encounter in the upcoming Gospel reading.

Baruch 5:1-9 (RCL alt., LFM)

Scholars have not been able to determine the authorship or time period of the composition of Baruch. Among Protestants it is collected in the Apocrypha because it is not included among the Hebrew Scriptures. The book of Jeremiah states that Baruch was a scribe of the prophet Jeremiah (see Jer. 32:12; 36:4; 45:1), but much of the material found in Baruch appears to be written closer to the time period of Isaiah 40–55 (c. 539 BCE). Some even date the book to the period following the fall of Jerusalem to the Romans in 70 CE.

Uncertainty of dates notwithstanding, this prophetic book addresses a people who are either in exile or on the verge of recovery from exile and destruction. The poetry of 5:1-9 is part of a larger section (3:9—5:9) that offers hope for restoration. With Israel's confession of guilt behind them (1:15—3:8), the writer turns to the hope of what lies ahead, and a glorious hope it is. Israel and Jerusalem can remove the "garment of sorrow and affliction" and "put on forever the beauty of the glory from God" (v. 1). God will show Israel their splendor "everywhere under heaven," and God will call Israel "Peace of righteousness and glory of godliness" (vv. 3-4 RSV). From slavery, they will emerge as a free people. From the destruction of war, they will enter a period of justice and peace.

Echoing Isaiah (42:16-17), the writer prophesies that the mountains will be "made low" and the "valleys filled up" to make level ground (v. 7). The sons and daughters of the nation will return from their exile. "God will bring them back to you, carried in glory, as on a royal throne" (v. 6). These themes of restoration from Isaiah and Baruch are picked up in the Gospel reading for the day as well. The hammer of war and slavery will be lifted. A period of peace and prosperity awaits the faithful remnant.

Perhaps at Advent, these hopeful verses will stir anticipation among the congregation. Whether our exiles are personal and familial—poor health, addictions, abusive relations, emotional depletions—or social and communal—unemployment, hunger, poor education, upward-spiraling costs of health care—these words offer comfort. They promise warmth in the depth of winter; return for the lost; renewal for the defeated; "joy in the light of God's glory" (v. 9).

The preacher will need to work at making such promises real for a people who frequently live, as Henry David Thoreau said, "lives of quiet desperation." Often we mask our brokenness behind a shallow response and a forced smile. We hide our various addictions for years, sometimes decades. Enslaved to personal debt, we work harder to try to win a race where the finish line keeps moving. The hope of Advent promises an end to such captivity. But how does the preacher make such hope real for the hearers?

It will not happen by simply proclaiming, "Hope is on the way." Optimism is not the same as hope, and everyone knows it. The preacher will need to offer close-to-the-ground images and stories of fulfilled hope and restored joy that will connect with the congregation and that faithfully illuminate the word of God in the text. Where is hope being rekindled in your own community, congregation, and in the wider world? What are the actual and believable events that have recently happened or are happening right around or within the congregation? Tell those stories as if the lives of the people depend upon them. Bring the images of hope within your own congregation into the awareness of the people. Paint for your hearers word pictures that parallel those which Baruch placed before the Hebrews. Then pray mightily and look closely for the fresh sparks of hope within the lives of the people.

Psalmody
Luke 1:68-79 (RCL)

In this Sunday's Revised Common Lectionary reading, Luke 1:68-79 is substituted for a reading from the Psalter. This substitution is fitting for the day because in it John the Baptist's father, the elder priest Zechariah, offers a psalm-like blessing and prophetic utterance upon the birth of the infant John. This well-known passage of Scripture is usually referred to liturgically as the *Benedictus* because of the first word of the passage in the Latin translation: "Blessed." In verses 68-75 Zechariah offers a blessing to God for the birth of "a mighty savior for us in the house of his servant David." And in verses 76-79, Zechariah prophesies that John will become the one who prepares the way for the savior who will give light to those who sit in darkness. When we turn to the Gospel reading for today, we will see that Zechariah's prophecy does, indeed, come to pass.

The utterances of Zechariah are forceful because they come after nine months of silence during the pregnancy of Elizabeth. Zechariah has been mute for many days while awaiting the birth of John. Upon writing for the people that the infant's name is John (as instructed by the angel Gabriel in verse 13), Zechariah's tongue is freed for him to offer songs of praise to God (v. 64). The *Benedictus* flows out of Zechariah's gratitude to God. At the same time, Zechariah announces that John will be the "prophet of the Most High," who "will go before the Lord to prepare his ways" (v. 76).

Luke has carefully crafted this story of John's birth as a parallel to the birth of Jesus. Gabriel announces the births to both sets of parents. Elizabeth and Mary, kinfolks, wait together for the arrival of their sons. Elizabeth and Zechariah's son will be a mighty prophet in the line of Hebrew prophets. Mary and Joseph's son will be the redeemer, the anointed one of God. Together, the births of these foretold infants will fulfill Jewish expectations of the coming of the Messiah.

Since upcoming lections will focus more on Jesus' birth and the adult John the Baptist, it is important this Sunday to stay focused on Zechariah, Elizabeth, and the birth of the infant John, if preaching from this text. Several directions are possible.

Since Advent's primary theme is waiting, the sermon could explore the faithful waiting of Elizabeth and Zechariah. As Abraham and Sarah were surprised in their later years, so, too, Elizabeth and Zechariah conceive a son in their later years after Elizabeth was considered barren (1:7). God comes to Israel and all of humanity especially in our waiting periods marked by barrenness. The joy of new birth in old age, imaged by the smiling faces of Zechariah and Elizabeth, is the deep joy of fulfillment. Through them, God has chosen to announce a new thing. Among our listeners, the sermon can explore the nature of waiting and the announcement of hope that God may be doing a new thing in our own lives.

The sermon might also explore the significance of covenant and its fulfillment between God and God's people. Verses 72-73 speak of God's promises to Israel. "He has remembered his holy covenant," Zechariah sings. Zechariah's name means "God remembered." A sermon might engage the congregation around the question of what it means to be remembered by God, the God who makes good on promises even when we do not.

Finally, requiring additional creativity, the sermon might develop in the form of a blessing for the congregation. Since Zechariah's speech is a blessing of God and John the Baptist, the sermon could unfold as a blessing of God and the congregation. Those who wait in Advent are not always barren or on guard. While we are not yet ready to sing "Joy to the World," there is much to be grateful for in Advent. God's promise is on the way. Anticipation is a blessing in itself.

Psalm 126:1-2a, 2b-3, 4-5, 6 (LFM)

Psalm 126 is apt for the Second Sunday of Advent with its movement back and forth between then in times of sorrow and now in times of restoration, then in tears and now with shouts of joy. Advent prompts this kind of deep reflection upon wastelands of loss—personal, congregational, and communal—relieved by fountains of God's mercy yielding joy. Just as Zechariah sings of new life in the Lukan passage above, the psalmist here sings of restoration from devastation. The psalm is chock-full of imagery that invites homiletical treatment: fortunes of Zion, dreamers, mouths filled with laughter, tongues with shouts of joy, rivers in the desert (watercourses in the Negeb), sowing in tears, harvesting the sheaves of joy. When looked at together, most of the images point toward a central and eternal claim within Judaism and Christianity among those who trust God. It is succinctly expressed in Psalm 30: "Weeping may linger for the night, but joy comes with the morning" (30:5 NRSV). It is appropriate in Advent to repent of those sins that have isolated us from God and one another, causing tears of remorse; it is also appropriate to anticipate that at the end of our crying time, we "will return with cries of joy" (v. 6 NAB).

Second Reading
Philippians 1:3-11 (RCL)
Philippians 1:4-6, 8-11 (LFM)

Paul opens this letter to the Philippians in typical fashion with a lengthy statement of thanksgiving. Following writing conventions of his day, he begins by recalling all for which he is thankful between himself and the congregation at Philippi: their partnership in the gospel (v. 5), their good work on behalf of Jesus Christ (v. 6), their prayers for each other that bind them together in heartfelt communion (v. 7), and their common experiences of imprisonment and persecution (v. 7). Similar to the epistle reading for last week, 1 Thessalonians 3, Paul is writing to encourage the Philippians during difficult times and to urge them on to greater faithfulness as they await the return of Christ (vv. 9-11). These are the themes that Paul develops throughout the letter.

Although we do not know Paul's geographical location at the time of the letter (some scholars say Rome, others argue for Ephesus or elsewhere), which makes precise dating difficult, we do know his existential location. He is in prison (vv. 7, 13). Paul interprets his imprisonment for the "confirmation of the gospel," as additional parts of the letter explain. Some take Paul's witness seriously and are thereby introduced to Christ. Others ridicule and mock him. But either way, Paul states, Christ is "proclaimed in every way, whether out of false motives or true; and in that I rejoice" (1:18).

The lectionary offers this text during Advent because in two verses Paul mentions "the day of Jesus Christ" (vv. 6, 10). Paul and the followers of Christ at Philippi anticipated the imminent return of Jesus. Eschatology pressed in upon them (as I noted during the first week of Advent, above). Readiness to greet Christ was crucial for the nascent Christian community; hence Paul offers words of instruction about righteous living in these verses and the ones that follow (vv. 9-11). The church still waits for that second coming of Christ who is both among us by the power of the Holy Spirit here and now (realized eschatology) and yet to come in final glory (future hope). Some days as Christians we live into the present reality of Christ, and other days we yearn for the fullness of redemption, groaning like a mother in childbirth (cf. Rom. 8:22-24). Paul's wise words to the Philippians do translate into our time as well. Live today, he admonishes, as if Christ is already among you; live today as if he will arrive at any minute.

What makes this passage even more compelling at Advent is Paul's location in prison. This love letter to the Philippians, filled with longing, remembrance, exhortation, and hope, is written by a prisoner on death row. The Philippians are not reading pious reflections of a well-to-do Christian basking on the warm beach sands of the Mediterranean. He is not writing pithy insights born out of lengthy and sublime ruminations on the life of Jesus. No. Paul writes from a cramped, filthy, mean, dank jail cell. He is alternately mocked by other prisoners (1:15) and threatened for his life

(1:20-24), so much so that he bursts through to a theology of suffering that causes him to seriously weigh whether to live or die in Christ promises the most gain, ending in the triumphant hymn of the self-emptying Christ (1:23—2:11).

Set within this context, the words of thanksgiving in verses 3-11 might uniquely wake up our listeners on the Second Sunday of Advent. Paul is undergoing all of this, and he is still thankful; yes, even more thankful. He sees the gospel in a new light because for him light and life are precious in their absence. As Bishop Desmond Tutu of South Africa is reported to have said upon a visit to North America, "It must be difficult to be Christians in this country because they will not imprison you for your beliefs." Seen in this light, the real difficulties and challenges of life are not a hindrance to the gospel but a way to deepen and solidify faith. "Nobody knows the trouble I've seen; nobody knows like Jesus," the African American spiritual says. What Paul offers to his readers in Philippi and to us today is the confidence that when the waters are deeply troubled, Jesus is surely near.

If we interpret the passage in this fashion, it also points us toward one another. For as Paul tries to convey, we find a balm for suffering among the fellowship of believers: "And this is my prayer, that your love may overflow more and more with knowledge and full insight to help you to determine what is best" (vv. 9-10). Prisons of all kinds clarify what really matters. As the imprisoned minister Rev. Joe Pike Moseley says in Robert Inman's delightful novel *Dairy Queen Days,* "I'm not ready to leave the jail yet. You can find all sorts of riches if you take long enough to think on it."[1] One of the things imprisonment of all kinds makes clear is how much we in the Christian community really need each other. As Paul says, "You share in God's grace with me" (v. 7). We matter to each other, on both sides of the jail—jails of steel and jails of emotional, physical, and financial captivity. We wait *together* for the day of Jesus Christ. That is at the heart of what it means to be the church united in fellowship with Christ and for each other.

Gratitude can arise out of the darkest of circumstances. When it does, it surely depends upon the active love of others and the awareness that Christ is coming to meet us. This is good news for Advent and any season of the church year.

Gospel
Luke 3:1-6 (RCL, LFM)

John, the son of Zechariah, has grown into adulthood. Just as his father prophesied in Luke 1:68-79, the word of God has come upon John and he has gone forth to prepare the people to receive the Messiah through "a baptism for the repentance of sins." He stands in the line of the Hebrew prophets whose words we have been hearing— Jeremiah, Malachi, Baruch, and now Isaiah, whom he quotes in verses 4-6: "The voice of one crying out in the wilderness: 'Prepare the way of the Lord, make his paths straight. Every valley shall be filled, and every mountain and hill shall be made low, and the crooked shall be made straight, and the rough ways made smooth; and all flesh shall see the salvation of God'" (cf. Isa. 40:3-5).

John's prophetic ministry occurs at a particular time and place in history: "In the fifteenth year of the reign of Emperor Tiberius" (c. 26–29 CE). God's call comes to John in the wilderness or desert and he "goes in all the region around the Jordan" (vv. 1-3). He is not speaking just anywhere at any time. He prophesies during a particular time in political and social history when Judea and Galilee were under the constant thumb of Rome, and when the people of Israel were ready to hear news of a messiah, a savior, an anointed one. John begins in the desert, evoking Israel's days in the desert during the exodus and recalling that God is the one who leads the people out of the wilderness. John is not the Savior, but he points the way to the one who is (cf. Matt. 3:1-12; Mark 1:1-8; John 1:6-9, 14-18). As promised, Luke's account is orderly (1:1-4). So it is important for the writer to identify John's historical, political, social, and geographical location.

The work of John, however, occurs because of God's initiative. God is the one who announces John's birth, sets John's ministry in motion, and comes to Israel in the person of Jesus of Nazareth. As Fred Craddock comments, "Both the Lord's coming and the preparation for that coming are the initiatives of a gracious God."[2] God's work is unfolding in human history. As the gospel expands from Nazareth to Jerusalem and then Rome, "The gospel will encounter not only the poor, lame, halt, and blind, but also high priests, synagogue rulers, city officials, leading women, ship captains, imperial guards, governors, and kings."[3] Luke seems to be saying to his readers, "Please do not spiritualize this message." John announces in the course of real human time that Jesus is coming in the fullness of time to bring the salvation of God to *all* flesh (v. 6). If we miss this historical punctuation of Luke's Gospel, spelled out in the introduction of the adult John, then we miss one of the primary themes of the narrative.

Why is this important for us today as readers and hearers of Luke 3? Because John's ministry begins surrounded by two types of social and political authority. As Sharon Ringe points out, "The relevant context of his [Luke's] account is the double system of authority—Empire and temple—that prevailed in Palestine. . . . Luke alerted his readers to pay attention to how his story came to bear on historical circumstances in Jesus' day, and, by extension, in their own specific context as well."[4] Without this recognition of political and ecclesial location, we run the risk of privatizing the gospel. Uncoupled from the political and priestly forces that press in upon Jesus as the story unfolds, we miss the radical claims of the story. Jesus' life, death, and resurrection, as foretold by John the Baptist, were not simply for the saving of *souls* but for the redemption of the whole world—Jews and Gentiles, nations and empires. "And *all flesh* shall see the salvation of God," John says while quoting Isaiah (v. 6). All flesh includes the Roman governors, the high priests, and the blind, poor, lame, and outcast who cross Jesus' path.

John proclaims that this salvation begins with "a baptism of repentance for the forgiveness of sins." This baptism was not the customary purification ritual of

Judaism; rather, it was most likely a onetime event linked to repentance on the part of the believer and to the beginning of a new life.[5] Such a baptism, however, will put John, Jesus, and their followers smack in the path of the powers and authorities of the rulers of church and state. Those who follow Jesus and who are baptized into his way through repentance and forgiveness of sin will join a movement peopled by the poor, the blind, and the social outcast that will subvert and threaten the dominant powers of the age. Luke is not sanctifying the status quo when in chapter 3 he introduces the politicians and ecclesial leaders of John's day. Rather, he is saying these are the very forces that John and Jesus will meet and challenge on the way from Bethlehem to Jerusalem.

The preacher might develop a sermon on this Second Sunday of Advent that demonstrates the countercultural nature of the gospel and the unexpected scope of salvation. Our tendency during Advent and pre-Christmas is to anticipate a celebration of Jesus' birth that blesses our own personal comfort and sanctifies both the personal and political status quo. But God does not come to the powerful of Rome or Jerusalem, Washington, D.C., or Berlin. God comes to John, the son of Zechariah and Elizabeth, in the frightening and eventful desert. God does not come to bless our personal, national, or ecclesial power but to make the crooked straight and the rough smooth. When that message takes hold of us, it will call for our own repentance as we prepare the way of the Lord.

Notes

1. Robert Inman, *Dairy Queen Days* (Boston: Little, Brown, 1997), 237.
2. Fred B. Craddock, *Luke*, Interpretation: A Bible Commentary for Teaching and Preaching (Louisville: John Knox, 1990), 46.
3. Ibid., 47.
4. Sharon H. Ringe, *Luke*, Westminster Bible Companion (Louisville: Westminster John Knox, 1995), 49–50.
5. Ibid., 52.

December 16, 2012
Third Sunday of Advent

Revised Common Lectionary (RCL)	Lectionary for Mass (LFM)
Zephaniah 3:14-20	Zephaniah 3:14-18a
Isaiah 12:2-6	Isaiah 12:2-3, 4, 5-6
Philippians 4:4-7	Philippians 4:4-7
Luke 3:7-18	Luke 3:10-18

First Reading
Zephaniah 3:14-20 (RCL)
Zephaniah 3:14-18a (LFM)

On this Third Sunday of Advent, many preachers will probably gravitate to the Gospel reading. The strident call of John the Baptist begs for interpretation by the preacher who is following the lectionary and successfully resisting the appeal to rush to Christmas. But this text from Zephaniah can either be read without comment during the service and allowed to proclaim Advent hope on its own, or interpreted along with the Gospel lection as a strong statement of coming good news. Should the preacher decide to address the passage directly, a couple of lively possibilities emerge.

First, Zephaniah was active during the reign of Josiah of Judah, 640–609 BCE (see 1:1). This places the prophetic material during the Assyrian control of Judah and surrounding nations. Most of the book, therefore, addresses Israel's oppression under foreign domination as the judgment of God. This is a common theme in Hebrew prophecy and literature. For example, chapter 3 begins, "Ah, soiled, defiled, oppressing city! It has listened to no voice; it has accepted no correction. It has not trusted in the LORD; it has not drawn near to its God" (vv. 1-2). Therefore, "every morning he [God] renders his judgment, each dawn without fail; but the unjust knows no shame" (3:5). Israel is reaping the consequences of its faithlessness. It experiences the hammer blows of a righteous God. Understanding this context is essential for homiletical treatment of the closing verses of Zephaniah. For when we arrive at 3:7-18, the promises of restoration ring out against a backdrop of destruction. Forgiveness follows judgment. God's hand of justice is stayed by God's hand of mercy.

Second, given that it is likely that Zephaniah's concluding verses (today's lection) were a later addition to the book, either exilic or postexilic (perhaps this is why the Roman Catholic lectionary omits the last two verses of the passage), the verses cast our eyes toward a longer horizon of hope. God will "remove disaster" from us (v. 18) and bring us home (v. 19). But this apocalyptic hope is out on the distant horizon of our lives, beyond whatever current personal, congregational, national, or international distress threatens human wholeness. Our hope in God may not be confirmed by immediate circumstances, but God's promises are sure. As Paul says in the New Testament, "Now faith is the assurance of things hoped for; the conviction of things not seen" (Heb. 11:1).

Psalmody
Isaiah 12:2-6 (RCL)
Isaiah 12:2-3, 4, 5-6 (LFM)

The lectionary for this Third Sunday of Advent substitutes this joyful reading from Isaiah for a reading from the Psalms. The responsorial structure of the passage and its hymn-like nature make it a logical choice for the psalmody reading. The passage breaks into two structural units, verses 1-3 and verses 4-6, both introduced by the phrase, "You will say." The chapter concludes the first section of Isaiah, ending on a note of joyful worship based upon the anticipation of restoration and provision of messianic leadership found in the earlier chapters of the book (see 11:1-10). The last three verses strongly echo Zephaniah 3, suggesting a further reason for pairing these texts on this Sunday.

As the congregation hears these words or recites them antiphonally, two important themes emerge for Advent. First, God delivers us from distress (vv. 1-3). Second, our response is to offer praise and thanksgiving (vv. 4-6). What are the situations of distress that members of our congregations are facing? Here is the assurance that God will not stand idly by as we suffer debilitating illness, joblessness, or fear. God is our salvation, our strength and might (v. 2). Knowing that God delivers us, the only proper response is to "sing praises to the LORD" (v. 5), preferably with Advent hymns appropriate to the theme.

Finally, it is important to note that God's deliverance is not simply for our personal benefit. The Holy One of Israel is the one whose deeds are "known in all the earth" (v. 5). This God, as Charles Wesley's Advent hymn puts it, is the "desire of every nation," the "joy of every longing heart" ("Come, Thou Long Expected Jesus"). Individual rescue is too small a hope to place upon the altar at Advent. We join our voices and prayers to thank God for the redemption of all creation.

Second Reading
Philippians 4:4-7 (RCL, LFM)

A quick review of last week's comments on Philippians reminds us that Paul writes to the Philippians from an undisclosed geographical location but a very clear existential one: prison. The brief benediction and invitation to "rejoice in the Lord always" of 4:4-7 are the imprisoned Paul's words to some of his most beloved partners in the gospel. Out of captivity, he writes to them of joy in the Lord. Out of a situation that threatens death, he writes to them of resurrection through sharing in the suffering of Christ (3:7-11). Out of a period of deprivation, he offers the Philippians a benediction: "And the peace of God, which surpasses all understanding, will guard your hearts and your minds in Christ Jesus" (4:7). The letter flows over with Paul's pastoral concern for the Philippians. As it moves to a close, he seals it with a note of joy in these four verses for today's lection.

Coupled with the readings from Zephaniah and Isaiah, this passage for the Third Sunday of Advent urges us forward in anticipation of the joyful arrival of Christ. But the passage is best preached through keeping Paul's context before the congregation. As with Isaiah and Zephaniah, Paul's hope grows out of turmoil, captivity, destruction, and death. Paul, like the nation of Israel in exile, bears the word of God within himself as he undergoes captivity. It stirs him to pray, to remember better days, to impart hard-earned wisdom, and to encourage the surviving Christian community to be steadfast in the faith. His location in prison makes his encouragement all the more powerful and convincing. Meditating upon the life and death of Jesus, united in suffering with him, Paul says that he presses "on toward the goal for the prize of the heavenly call in Christ Jesus." He encourages his readers to do the same and to "hold fast to what we have attained" (3:14-16).

How will contemporary Christians during the third week of Advent hear this passage? With the great Western Christmas machine moving into high gear, what sights and sounds from this first-century Mediterranean world of prisons and struggling Christian communities can our people see and hear? To what end?

This may be just the Sunday to invite our listeners to pull up short. Slow down. For a few moments of authentic worship we can leave the consumer lists and the frayed nerves, the mounting tension and the compulsive shopping, outside the door. Stepping inside the sanctuary can liberate us from the various captivities of the season. The chains of cultural Christmas no longer bind us. In sacred space we can breathe again. We can open ourselves to the new mind of Christ Jesus, who "though he was in the form of God . . . emptied himself, taking the form of a slave" (2:6-7).

Now we are getting closer to the riches of Advent, to wait expectantly for the one who is "born to set the people free" ("Come, Thou Long Expected Jesus"). Now, having left aside the cumber that engulfs the season, we can hear Paul's life-giving words. "The Lord is near," he says. So be gentle to everyone (4:5). "Do not worry about anything." But in prayer and petition "let your requests be made known to God" (v. 6). Then the peace of God will surround your hearts and minds (v. 7). So rejoice; again I will say, Rejoice (v. 4).

Perhaps some folks in the congregation are wondering what else they need for Christmas. What will really bring the family and church together? What will put our personal and communal priorities in order? Paul has a list for those who believe that God is near. It is a simple list consisting of goods of infinite worth. Thanks to Jesus Christ, the items on the list are free through all the seasons of life: gentleness, contentment, prayer, thanksgiving, peace. And the final one, the one thing that Paul through Jesus Christ really wants to give us—joy.

Gospel
Luke 3:7-18 (RCL)
Luke 3:10-18 (LFM)

It is not clear to this interpreter why the LFM reading for this Third Sunday of Advent would omit verses 7-9 of the passage, unless economy of space is a consideration. Dropping verses 7-9 takes the harsh edge off of John the Baptist's sermon, which may make the passage more palatable to contemporary listeners who would rather not be confronted so close to Christmas by John's stridency. But dulling the edge of John's ax (v. 9), or hiding the ax altogether, may in the long run make it harder to receive and respond to the full message of the sermon. Thus I will treat the passage in its entirety and leave it up to the preacher to decide which version to use for his or her preaching context.

John's righteous indignation has been looming in the background of Advent for the past couple of weeks. It always does because one or the other of the Synoptic Gospel parallels of this passage is used in each of the three years of the lectionary for Advent. Last week we heard John calling for a baptism of repentance for the forgiveness of sins and reciting Isaiah 40:3-5. That was the introduction to his sermon. With verses 7-18, he unloads.

His words are harsh—then and now. To the crowds who came to hear him and be baptized, he shouts, "You brood of vipers! Who warned you to flee from the wrath to come? . . . Even now the ax is lying at the root of the trees; every tree therefore that does not bear good fruit is cut down and thrown into the fire" (vv. 7, 9). Can't you hear a defensive, comedic response: "Well, that's not very nice"? Indeed, it is shrill, judgmental, angry, and threatening. Why on earth would anyone want to listen to such a harangue; even more, why would anyone consent to be baptized by him?

John thunders with the righteousness of God like his Hebrew prophet predecessors. It is time, he announces, for the people and the nation to repent. Time to turn around (convert), confess, and receive forgiveness of sins or else. And then John throws in a kicker. And you think I am tough. I only baptize with water. The one who is coming will baptize with the Holy Spirit (the holy breath of God) and fire. "His winnowing fork is in his hand to clear his threshing floor and to gather the wheat into his granary; but the chaff he will burn with unquenchable fire" (vv. 16-17). So just in case we thought Jesus would make things easier, take that, John seems to say, before he stomps out into the river to begin the baptisms.

When Luke finally gets through the sermon, and adds his concluding comment, we can hardly believe it. "So, with many other exhortations, he [John] proclaimed the good news to the people" (v. 18). If this has been good news, I sure wouldn't want to hear the bad news. But there it stands at the end of the reading—"good news to the people."

What makes this call from John good news, gospel? How can we hear it on the Third Sunday of Advent, especially along with much more positive passages announcing joy (Philippians 4), hope (Isaiah 12), and promise of restoration (Zephaniah 3)? The preacher must decide whether or not to tackle the passage in its entirety. The decision may be to leave alone Luke 3 and focus on one of the other passages. If so, there is plenty to preach about already. But if we decide to wade into the baptismal water with John, where is the good news?

First, the middle section of the passage, verses 10-14, suggests moral responsibility that is both bad news and good news. John claims that God is not interested in shallow repentance that leads to easy faith. The bad news for those who feel convicted by John is that God desires an ethical response befitting forgiveness. Let those who have two coats give one away. Let the tax collectors charge only what is legally due. And let the soldiers cease taking advantage of their subjects. In other words, those who hear and respond to God must clean up the house. Otherwise, our faith is void. This is really good news because it calls for social and economic justice, a hallmark of Luke's Gospel. The one who is coming, God's beloved, will put the world to rights, and those who repent and believe will take part in that righteousness. As Isaiah has said, "the crooked shall be made straight, and the rough ways made smooth" (Isa. 40:4; Luke 3:5). Especially during Advent, when it is all too easy for greed and wanton materialism to blind us to the needs of others, this passage comes as good news.

Second, while it hurts to admit our sin and unrighteousness, confession opens us and our social world to new life in God. Like the self-righteous character Ruby Turpin discovers at the end of Flannery O'Connor's short story "Revelation," even her "virtues were being burned away," or those things that she thought were virtuous.[1] Submitted to God, our virtues and vices become cleansed and refined. We get ready, finally, to participate in the new life that Advent promises. Though the passage is filled with images of winnowing and cleansing, burning and refining, God is ultimately concerned about the good grain rather than the chaff. John's call to repentance is harsh, but he voices the desire of God to move through judgment to forgiveness. The passage ends not on bad news but on good news. Like Robert Duvall's character, Felix Bush, in the remarkable movie *Get Low,* repentance before God and the community is the next to the last thing that matters. Following repentance, forgiveness in full measure flows forth from God and the community. After coming clean, tears of relief are as fresh as baptismal waters. The arms that embrace us are as sturdy as those of John the Baptist and as tender as those of Jesus.

If our listeners really want to get ready for Christmas, invite them to listen to the sermon of John the Baptist. Then invite them to take their place in the line of those who want to be baptized. They will find Jesus standing right beside them (vv. 21-22).

Note
1. Flannery O'Connor, "Revelation," in *The Complete Stories of Flannery O'Connor* (New York: Farrar, Straus and Giroux, 1986), 508.

December 23, 2012
Fourth Sunday of Advent

Revised Common Lectionary
Micah 5:2-5a
Luke 1:46b-55 or Psalm 80:1-7
Hebrews 10:5-10
Luke 1:39-45 (46-55)

Lectionary for Mass
Micah 5:1-4a
Psalm 80:2-3, 15-16, 18-19
Hebrews 10:5-10
Luke 1:39-45

First Reading
Micah 5:2-5a (RCL)
Micah 5:1-4a (LFM)

The designation of these verses is different in the RCL and LFM lectionaries due to the fact that the LFM lectionary follows the New American Bible based upon the Vulgate and the RCL follows the New Revised Standard Version. Neither lectionary reading for today includes what is actually verse 1 of the passage in the NRSV and 4:14 in the NAB. But it is important to include this verse since it establishes the context of oppression and exile to which the subsequent verses provide a response. And verse 4a (or 5a) carries the passage to its completion in designating the anointed leader as the harbinger of peace, a key theme of Advent and Christmas.

By this Sunday in Advent, only two days away from Christmas, the congregation is fully geared to celebrate the day of fulfillment, both religiously and culturally. Christmas is practically upon us, and the pastor or worship committee that resists singing Christmas hymns on December 23 will surely hear some grumbling from the congregation. They are ready to break forth with "O Little Town of Bethlehem," "Hark! the Herald Angels Sing," and "Silent Night," even if the lectionary says, "Not quite yet." The Gospel passage for today will help with its focus upon the expectant Elizabeth and Mary. Similarly, this passage from the eighth-century prophet Micah, who sounds very much like Isaiah, will help carry the congregation to the brink of fulfillment without having us cross the finish line prematurely.

While scholars agree that much of the first four chapters of Micah address the period of Assyrian domination of Israel and Judah, hence the oracles of woe in these chapters, there is uncertainty about chapter 5 and the verses of today's lection. These verses may have foretold recovery from Assyrian control, but they sound either exilic or postexilic in nature, which would place them later in history. They strike a resounding note of hope for the coming of a promised leader, who in the line of David will, shepherd-like, feed his flock and restore their security "to the ends of the earth" (v. 4). So significant was the promise as read by the early church that Matthew incorporates a version of this passage into his Gospel (cf. Matt. 2:6) as a reference to the birth of Jesus.

The passage prophesies that one of the lesser tribes of Judah, Bethlehem of Ephrathah, will be the birthplace of the next great leader. The new ruler will start from humble origins, as those of ancient days (v. 2). Though an earlier ruler has been defeated (v. 1) and the city or nation walled around, this new ruler will govern in the strength and majesty of the Lord (v. 4). From the insignificant will come one who will do great things. Among a people who have brought destruction upon themselves, and who have been beaten back by the enemy, new life will spring forth.

Most significantly for this Advent and Christmas season, "he shall be the one of peace" (v. 5). The message is unmistakable. With the arrival of the anointed one, a new day will begin, a day in which this ruler of peace will lead the people to "beat their swords into plowshares, and their spears into pruning hooks; nation shall not lift up sword against nation, neither shall they learn war any more" (4:3). The Lord will deal justly and gently with the beleaguered people, requiring only that they "do justice, and love kindness, and walk humbly with God" (6:8). These are some of the most poetic renderings of peace with justice found in Scripture, and they surround the prophetic pronouncement of chapter 5, pointing the way to a new day for Israel.

The message could not be more relevant in a world where nations continue to clash over territory, economic gain, religious differences, and power. From the modern-day Holy Land to the United States and Pakistan, from the Sudan to North Korea, wars rage and simmer. The radical nature of the message of peace has not yet been fully heard and heeded by Jews, Christians, or Muslims. War will not be ended by more war. We cannot fight our way into God's reign of peace. In this season of hope and expectation, we wait and pray for the one whose message of peace will be lived "to the ends of the earth."

Psalmody
Psalm 80:1-7 (RCL alt.)
Psalm 80:2-3, 15-16, 18-19 (LFM)

Parsing of this psalm into either the first seven verses (RCL) or separate verses of the entire chapter (LFM) is not a particularly helpful use of the passage. Either selection truncates the importance of the psalm for Advent. The psalm is both a lament and a plea for restoration. The Hebrews feel abandoned by God (vv. 4-6, 12-13, 16). At the same time, they plead with God for a return to redemptive relations (vv. 1-3, 7, 14, 17-19). They pray, as Micah prophesies, for a leader who will execute God's favor toward the nation: "But let your hand be upon the one at your right hand, the one whom you made strong for yourself" (v. 17). Tying this passage to Advent proclamation, we recognize that distress on a social and personal level still plagues all of us and all of creation. We yearn now, with Christmas just days away, for the God whose face will shine "that we may be saved" (v. 19).

Luke 1:46b-55 (RCL)

See comments below on the Gospel reading.

Second Reading
Hebrews 10:5-10 (RCL, LFM)

On first reading this passage strikes us as a peculiar one for the Fourth Sunday of Advent. Here we are ready to sing Christmas carols of praise to God for Jesus' birth while the epistle reading focuses upon his death. And not just his death but the very nature of his death as sacrificial atonement for the sin of humankind. Are we mixing Lent into Advent here?

The preacher who decides to unpack this passage on December 23 can be helped by a couple of observations. First, we recognize that while the Christian calendar carries the church in a more or less linear progression from Christ's birth through his life, then on to death and resurrection, the meaning of Jesus Christ can only be understood by looking at the whole picture. His first coming at birth anticipates his second coming at the end of time, as we have noted in various Advent texts. His birth at Bethlehem carries within it the seeds of his death at Jerusalem. This is so because Jesus comes to do God's will (v. 7). That will is not simply to be born or to die but to be born, to die, and to be resurrected. Even though Advent stresses anticipation of Jesus' first and second coming, his death cleaves the two. Admittedly, this is a sober reminder so close to Christmas, but the theological truth is that the body of the baby Jesus becomes "the body of Jesus Christ [offered] once for all."

The second angle directs us toward sin and forgiveness. Though the authorship and date of Hebrews are not known, it is clear from this and the rest of the letter that the writer is preoccupied with the priestly sacrificial system, either before or after the fall of the Jerusalem temple in the first century CE. The practice of ritual sacrifice that leads to cleansing of sin has been an ongoing and controversial practice within Judaism throughout its history. Hebrews 10 draws on Psalm 40:6-8 to establish the point that God desires purity of heart and life rather than animal sacrifices and burnt offerings. Relying upon the Greek translation rather than the Hebrew original of verse 5, the passage reads, "Sacrifices and offering you have not desired, but a body you have prepared for me," rather than "Sacrifice and offering you do not desire, but you have given me an open ear." Since Jesus is the speaker of this part of Hebrews 10, the body he refers to is his own. It is the body that he will submit to God's will later in his own life, saying, "See, God, I have come to do your will" (v. 7; cf. Luke 22:42; Mark 14:36; Matt. 26:39). Jesus wills to do the will of God. This is why he came (and comes still) into the world (v. 5).

John the Baptist has already worked us over pretty well about confession of sin as preparation for salvation. But the message here has a slightly different edge. Advent is a good time to admit to ourselves and God that all our efforts at repeated self-justification cannot succeed. If we think that we alone can come up with a worthy enough sacrifice to please God, we are only fooling ourselves. "It can never, by the same sacrifices that are continually offered year after year, make perfect those who approach" (10:1). We cannot appease God's judgment upon the sin of our lives and within creation. Indeed, the good news of Advent, Lent, and Easter is that God's mercy has overruled God's judgment. Born in Bethlehem, crucified in Jerusalem, and resurrected on Easter, grace—in the form of Jesus—triumphs.

Gospel
Luke 1:39-45 (46-55) (RCL)
Luke 1:39-45 (LFM)

Of these two slightly different lectionary texts, we will take the full passage, 1:39-55, for comment. Since the last verses (46-55) do not appear elsewhere in the lectionary readings for Advent and Christmas, it is appropriate to cover them now, especially given their importance in understanding Mary's role in the birth of Jesus and their powerful message of redemption.

The Gospel reading takes us right to the edge of birth with the joyful meeting between the expectant mothers, Mary, who has just heard and humbly received the angel's announcement that she will be the mother of Jesus, and Elizabeth, who is now six months pregnant with the baby John, who will be the forerunner to Jesus. The narrative is rich with allusions to other parts of the Bible. With Elizabeth's baby's recognition of Mary's voice ("For as soon as I heard the sound of your greeting, the child in my womb leaped for joy," v. 44), this story recalls Rebekah's giving birth to Esau and Jacob; the struggle within her womb; and the outcome that the "elder shall serve the younger" (Gen. 25:21-23), just as John will serve Jesus. Mary's song of gratitude, the *Magnificat* (vv. 46-55), alludes to and draws parallels from Hannah's song as she thanks God and makes a gift of her son, Samuel, to the service of God (1 Sam. 2:1-10). The birth of John to Elizabeth and Zechariah, following years of barrenness, is another allusion to the birth of Isaac to Abraham and Sarah.

Luke uses these allusions to establish Jesus' story within the larger framework of covenant and redemption. He is the fulfillment of Jewish history and prophecy that in Bethlehem (recall Micah 5:2-5a) an anointed one will be born, who will be the "Son of the Most High" (1:32). Through him God will show "mercy . . . for those who fear him from generation to generation . . . according to the promise God made to our ancestors, to Abraham and to his descendants forever" (vv. 50, 55). All of this occurs through the faithfulness of two women, one who never expected to give birth (Elizabeth) and who makes the first profession of faith in Jesus according to Luke's Gospel, when she calls him "my Lord" (v. 43); and one who from humble beginnings listens faithfully to God's promise and says with all the strength of her womanhood, "Let it be with me according to your word" (v. 38).

It may take a female preacher to understand fully and interpret the unique bond between these two expectant mothers who dance on the edge of hope with all the fear that also accompanies pregnancy and childbirth. But anyone, male or female, who has seriously contemplated or experienced the promise and danger of childbirth can come close to imagining the connection between Mary and Elizabeth. It is this mood of hope touched by fear that the preacher might want to evoke for the day. From each other the women draw strength as they go through the days of waiting. To each other they offer restrained joy as they await the arrival of their children. Making these emotions real on the last Sunday of Advent will help place the congregation where they need to be as Christmas arrives.

The *Magnificat* (so named because it is the first word of the Vulgate translation) is one of the most sublime passages in all of Scripture. Mary's song reaches back to Hannah and forward to every person, congregation, and nation that has longed for God's day of justice and deliverance. The passage nearly stops our hearts—its beauty and simplicity, the final trust of Mary, the letting go to God, the prophetic prayer like that of her ancestor Hannah in 1 Samuel, exalting the lowly, bringing down the proud in the imagination of their hearts. Mary is the one mother willing to believe that she among women is singled out for this moment in the human–divine story, in which as she yields to interruption in her own life, God joins her story to the story of the whole creation. In Mary, through Mary, God risks it all for love's sake.

We sing so many songs about her. In Bach's *Magnificat* we sing her song embroidered with classical melodies. And in powerful spirituals, we sing, "Mary had a baby, yes, Lord," and "Oh Mary, don't you weep, don't you moan." Mary is the very human us in the story—wonderstruck, interrupted, questioning, quiet, yielding, then singing, "Let it be with me according to your word." A sermon could be quite appealing that simply invites the congregation to sing with Mary.

But further homiletical grounding can be found in this passage beyond its invitation to the congregation to join Mary in song. Notice that verses 46-55 are cast in the past tense, as if the foretold Savior has already come. "My soul magnifies the Lord, and my spirit rejoices in God my Savior, for he *has looked* with favor on the lowliness of his servant" (v. 46); "He *has brought down* the powerful from their thrones, and *lifted up* the lowly" (v. 52 [emphasis mine]). Salvation has already come. The wholeness of God's reign, where the hungry will be filled with good things and the rich sent away empty, has already happened in Mary's song. There is here supreme confidence that what God has done in the past, God will do in the future. Time collapses in God's reign to the present moment where God is all in all. As Fred Craddock puts it, the past tense is "a way of expressing the confidences and the certainty as though they already were. So sure is the singer that God will do what is promised that it is proclaimed as accomplished fact."[1]

We tell this story in Advent not only to be drawn along by its narrative details and its compelling poetry. We tell it to proclaim theologically that God's favor, past, present, and future, is always upon those who believe. Therefore, with Mary, our souls can magnify the Lord.

Note

1. Fred B. Craddock, *Luke*, Interpretation: A Bible Commentary for Teaching and Preaching (Louisville: John Knox, 1990), 30.

Christmas

G. Lee Ramsey Jr.

We have crossed from Advent's anticipation of Jesus' birth and second coming to the moment of his arrival as an infant in Bethlehem. For those who have been able to refrain from jumping over Advent, the fulfillment of Christmas is that much more joyful. Now the time has come. Now the one who saves—Jesus—is born among us. God's good news has come again into the world, just as foretold by the prophets and John the Baptist. Our hearts quicken at the news. We raise our voices in praise or still them in silent wonder. "Christ the Savior is born; Christ the Savior is born."

The lectionary passages for these six services of the Christmas season offer a rich smorgasbord of options for the preacher. Indeed, they are so packed with familiar (Luke 2) and not-so-familiar texts (Titus 2–3) that the preacher may be easily overwhelmed by the choices, coming as they do amid a full set of congregational worship services and the many activities that occur with families, friends, and strangers at Christmas. How does the preacher stay focused upon the essential proclamation of the gospel amid the heightened excitement within church and society that accompanies Christmas?

Here is a suggestion. Let the preaching based upon these familiar and unfamiliar texts revolve around three simple themes, all of which are organically rooted in the Christmas story and the good news of God's salvation. First, there is the *wonder* of Christmas and the responses of awe that arise when remembering and witnessing again the birth of the child. Here Mary and Joseph are our companions as we revivify the Christmas story and find our own places at the manger, adoring the "wondrous gift given" at the "little town of Bethlehem."

Second, we preach in Christmastide so to evoke the *joy* that flows in response to the birth of Jesus. We turn to the angels and the shepherds, spreading "good news of great joy." We join our voices to the natural and heavenly choruses toward which the psalms point in the season (Psalms 96–98). Heaven and earth cannot contain the exuberance that arises when the King of creation descends from the throne to dwell among the poor and lowly, the broken and bereaved. The Savior has come; the day of liberation has arrived. Surely our preaching and worship will do no less than lead the congregation to sing "Joy to the World."

Finally, the seasonal texts, especially those of December 30 and January 1, gently *instruct* the hearers regarding the "so what" of Christmas. With Hannah and Samuel, Mary and Jesus, as our guides, we learn what it means to belong to God's family. We discover again the importance of our names—Christians, sons and daughters of God. Claimed by God through the birth, life, death, and resurrection of Jesus Christ, we know our names and to whom we belong. The baptismal waters are deep and clear that first named Jesus and now name us. It will take a lifetime even to begin to understand fully the significance of Jesus' birth for all of us, but thank God he is born among us, our family and next of kin.

December 24 & 25, 2012
Nativity of Our Lord I (RCL) /
Christmas: Mass at Midnight (LFM)

Revised Common Lectionary (RCL)

Isaiah 9:2-7
Psalm 96
Titus 2:11-14
Luke 2:1-14 (15-20)

Lectionary for Mass (LFM)

Mass at Midnight
Isaiah 9:1-6
Psalm 96:1-2a, 2b-3, 11-13
Titus 2:11-14
Luke 2:1-14

At the Vigil Mass
Isaiah 62:1-5
Psalm 89:4-5, 16-17, 27-29
Acts 13:16-17, 22-25
Matthew 1:1-25 or 1:18-25

First Reading
Isaiah 9:2-7 (RCL)
Isaiah 9:1-6 (LFM, Mass at Midnight)

The familiar words from Isaiah 9:2-7 (9:1-6 NAB) flow perfectly into the celebration of Christmas Eve and the birth of Christ. They may have been written as accolades for a recently elected Judean king, for they bear strong resemblance to similar passages extolling Davidic kingship. The verses outline the virtues of the ideal king: he brings light to the people (v. 2), multiplies the nation (v. 3), and breaks the rod of the oppressor (v. 4).

Christian appropriation of the text focuses upon verse 6: "For a child has been born for us, a son given to us; authority rests upon his shoulders and he is named Wonderful Counselor, Mighty God, Everlasting Father, Prince of Peace." The epithets sound powerfully mysterious and hopeful as we read them in the candlelit sanctuary of Christmas Eve. The child who comes, whom the church knows as Jesus, will be full of wisdom, might, and eternal loving-kindness and will rule in peace.

While we should not overlook the passage's possible meanings in its original context, it is easy to see why the church has historically read the passage as a foretelling of the birth of Jesus as Messiah. Isaiah speaks as if a child king has been given to protect and restore Israel to a reign of peace with justice. "There shall be endless peace for the throne of David and his kingdom. He will establish and uphold it with justice and with righteousness from this time onward and forevermore" (v. 7). The church sees Jesus the newborn baby as the fulfillment of this hymn-like prophecy. Whether Jews or Christians, the faith proclaimed here is that the most vulnerable of humans—a baby—is the one who brings peace.

Isaiah 62:1-5 (LFM, At the Vigil Mass)

The Roman Catholic Lectionary for Mass begins with a different reading from Isaiah that will be continued through the second service of Christmas (see Proper II, below). The focus here is upon the glory of Israel as a whole rather than upon the coming Prince of Peace as in Isaiah 6. But the message is equally joyful. "For Jerusalem's sake I will not rest, until her vindication shines out like the dawn, and her salvation like a burning torch" (v. 1 NRSV). God will restore Israel from her oppression and exile. She will become as a light to the nations. She will be "a crown of beauty in the hand of the LORD" (v. 3 NRSV). Whatever losses have befallen the chosen people will now be regained. In the foretold day of glory, God shall call Israel, and specifically Jerusalem, "My Delight Is in Her" (v. 4).

Christian interpretation of this passage is clearly possible. Whether or not the preacher wants to read the passage through the bright lens of Jesus' birth is another question. Most preachers will probably focus upon the Gospel reading for the Christmas Eve service anyway. But Isaiah's note of joy and delight can support and enhance the birth narrative of Jesus without being forced to be a direct and literal prophecy of it. Even some of the language of Isaiah 62 could be borrowed for the Christian homily ("the LORD delights in you," v. 4) without pressing the passage too far. The theological stake in the service is upon the mysterious and joy-making revelation of God: redemption and wholeness have come to all the world. Isaiah 62:1-5 certainly affirms that message.

Psalmody
Psalm 96 (RCL)
Psalm 96:1-2a, 2b-3, 11-13 (LFM, Mass at Midnight)

This enthronement psalm is an obvious choice of the lectionary committee for Christmas Eve. It is triumphant and full of praise for the Lord, the heavenly king. "Say among the nations, 'The LORD is king!'" (v. 10). "Honor and majesty are before him; strength and beauty are in his sanctuary" (v. 6). Just as the national kings rule over their nations, Yahweh is the ruler who leads with glory and strength (v. 7).

While one may not choose to preach directly from this psalm on Christmas Eve, important elements within it can contribute to the Christmas Eve sermon. The psalm invites us to bless the congregation's desire to sing. Finally, *we* can sing the Christmas hymns that have been rendered in a million different ways in a million different malls over the past several weeks. Now the people of God can sing until our hearts are full: "O Little Town of Bethlehem," "In the Bleak Midwinter," "Silent Night." The psalm says, "Sing to the LORD a new song, sing to the LORD, all the earth" (v. 1). The preacher who forgets that the congregation wants to sing on Christmas Eve can find the reminder right here.

The psalm recognizes that God's reign extends beyond humanity. All of creation is the site of God's handiwork. Heaven, sea, field, creatures of the field, and trees of the forest sing for joy. God bends toward all of creation on this holy night. Many stories, songs, and poems come to mind that imagine the natural world responding with praise to God who judges the world with righteousness and the people with God's truth (v. 13). The preacher will want to avoid oversentimentalizing the night, but there is a place for those creative stories or songs that align with Psalm 96 and Luke 2. For example, the beloved medieval French carol, "The Friendly Beasts," or even an artful retelling of the legend of the poinsettia, can be a way to point toward creation's response to the glory of God.

One additional note for consideration is the psalm's universal reach. Some may be tempted on Christmas Eve to see the incarnation as a special act of divine gift for the select few—those who call upon the name of Jesus. But a broader view of Jewish and Christian relations with the rest of the world can be inferred from the passage. The text instructs us to declare God's glory "among all the peoples" (v. 3) and asserts that God will judge the "world with righteousness" (v. 13). This story that began in creation and covenant and continues to be fulfilled in the birth of Jesus the Messiah extends God's justice and grace to all the world. If God wants to save the world, who are a few Christians to try to stop it?

Our response is more properly centered upon thanksgiving. Come to the sanctuary. Give thanks to God. Offer our gifts. Worship the Lord in awe (v. 8). Any sermon that flows through these themes will be heard as good news.

Psalm 89:4-5, 16-17, 27-29 (LFM, At the Vigil Mass)

This psalm affirms the covenant that God has made with Israel (vv. 4-5 NAB). The covenant will be fulfilled through the kingship of David. "Forever will I keep my steadfast love for him, and my covenant with him will stand firm. I will establish his line forever" (vv. 29-30). Including this psalm among the lections for the Vigil Mass calls to mind that Jesus is born in the lineage of David (cf. Matt. 1:1-17). While David was the earthly king who ruled with righteousness, Jesus will be the heavenly king who will fulfill God's reign in heaven and earth. Our tendency at Christmas is to preach the gentle, incarnational message of God wrapped up in the flesh of a human baby. But this psalm invites preacher and congregation to consider Jesus as king, son of the Lord whom the very "heavens praise."

Second Reading
Titus 2:11-14 (RCL; LFM, Mass at Midnight)

The preacher who focuses upon Titus on the night when the entire Christian world is listening to either Luke or Matthew's version of the birth of Jesus has an uphill climb to make. Titus's core proclamation is certainly the heart of the gospel. "For the grace of God has appeared, bringing salvation to all" (v. 11), or as the New English Bible helpfully translates it, "For the grace of God has dawned upon the world with healing for all [humankind]." That is precisely the message of Christmas and precisely the act of God that we recall, relive, and renew on Christmas Eve. If nothing else, the preacher could include this verse in a homily based upon the Gospel reading.

If the preacher decides to address Titus in a significant way, he or she will want to avoid moralizing on Christmas Eve. This is the night in which we bend before the mystery of God with us. The hymn "Let All Mortal Flesh Keep Silence" establishes the right tone for Christmas Eve worship and preaching (so let the preacher beware on Christmas Eve: less is more). Because so much of Titus addresses Christian behavior, it would be easy to slip into moralizing or didacticism when what is called for is proclamation and praise.

The key is grace. Verse 11 says it plainly: "The grace of God has appeared." All behavior is in response to God's grace. James may say that faith without works is dead (James 2:17), and the anonymous writer of this pastoral epistle, Titus, may readily agree. But faith based in God's grace is the source of all human response. The writer can urge Titus to tell the congregation how to live as self-controlled, upright, and godly because the grace of God has dawned upon them and they await the final manifestation of God's glory (v. 13).

A sermon that heads in this direction could establish an important theological claim for all who gather on Christmas Eve—the devout Christian, the occasional visitor, the obligatory attendee. What shall we do with this God dwelling among us? How do we respond to this baby who saves the world? We respond with our lives. Sometimes events conspire to get our attention, to wrest us free from all the little gods that we idolize in a largely secularized world (cf. Ps. 96:5), as happens in that old Christmas movie, *It's a Wonderful Life*. And sometimes the birth of Jesus, told truly and gracefully, sets us on a new path. Either way, we begin the first steps toward holiness of life (personal and social holiness) as grace leads us forward.

Acts 13:16-17, 22-25 (LFM, At the Vigil Mass)

This reading from Acts narrates a part of Paul's sermon in the Jewish synagogue in Antioch during his missionary travels into Asia Minor. It offers a concise summary of Paul's understanding of the coming of salvation through the covenant made with

Israel, reaffirmed in David, and fulfilled in Jesus. "Of this man's [David's] posterity God has brought to Israel a Savior, Jesus, as he promised" (v. 23). John the Baptist foretold the coming of Jesus, as we have seen in the Advent passages, and now Paul proclaims the promise has come to pass (vv. 24-26). The passage may not be well known to many of the hearers on Christmas Eve. It may not be the central text of the worship service. But preachers can find here a succinct retelling of the good news by Christianity's earliest interpreter. The worship service points to the baby Jesus as Savior of the world. Paul joins us in pointing in the very same direction.

Gospel
Luke 2:1-14 (15-20) (RCL)
Luke 2:1-14 (LFM, Mass at Midnight)

Because for many Protestant congregations, only one worship service will be held on either Christmas Eve or Christmas Day, we will look at the entire passage suggested in the RCL, 2:1-20. For Roman Catholics, or those who will be leading multiple services over the course of the two days, you may wish to break the passage into two or more sections. This central narrative within the larger Christian story certainly bears multiple homiletical treatments.

The danger of preaching on this text on this night or on Christmas Day is to try to say too much. For some preachers, especially loquacious ones, the better part of wisdom may be to read the passage within a rich liturgical setting and sit down. In one sense, there is little more that we can say as preachers to open up the mystery of the incarnation. With all the cultural renderings and misrenderings of the story, it can be a huge relief to the congregation to hear it straight without any chaser. Ponder the mystery, sing the songs, eat the bread and drink the wine, express love to friend and stranger, and go home.

Still, the story is so central. The moment is so high. The occasion is so sublime and pregnant with meaning that the preacher will usually want to hazard a word or two of interpretation. After all, if faith comes through hearing, as Paul says, how shall they hear unless someone proclaims (Rom. 10:14-17)? But where to land in this overflowing text set within an overflowing moment of the year?

There is a sermon to be preached (many in fact) that proclaims that the birth of Jesus occurs within historical time. "In those days a decree went out from Caesar Augustus," Luke says in verse 1, "while Quirinius was governor of Syria" (v. 2). We know that Luke wants his hearers to understand that these things that have happened and are happening occur within specific moments in human time. God comes among human and political history in the form of an infant. Ironically, this little child born to parents of humble origin will be the salvation of the world. He, as Mary has already sung, will fill the hungry with good things and send the rich away empty, bringing down the powerful from their thrones and lifting up the lowly (1:52-53). Whoever is governor or ruler will certainly be threatened by this birth, as Luke will show us later in his Gospel, because he offers a new kingdom that subverts all earthly loyalties and orients its followers to a new way. The message is scandalous, which makes it hard to preach and hear on Christmas Eve or Day. This sermon proclaims the countercultural and liberating message of God with us. But preached convincingly, hearers may choose to rethink their priorities and figure out who is really Lord of their lives.

Another sermon might invite the congregation to see the story from the point of view of the shepherds, who against the advice of the angels are certainly afraid. And why shouldn't they be when all heaven breaks loose? Luke and the other Gospel writers have all these characters in their stories who keep telling people not to be afraid at the very moment when fear is an understandable reaction, like at the birth of a king or the resurrection of a savior. It is one small step from fear to awe, and in biblical terms, the words are frequently interchangeable. Awe is where we want to help people arrive at Christmas. The shepherds hear awesome news! They respond with eagerness and testimony. They return to their fields glorifying and praising God. These are the postures of worship that the sermon can encourage among our hearers.

There is also the sermon that explores our kinship with Mary, the mother of Jesus. She is the one who treasures the words of the shepherds and ponders them in her heart (v. 19; see the comments below on January 1, Mary Mother of God). Mary along with Joseph take their place in the inn (v. 7) and there give birth to the infant Jesus. Outside of normal comforts, while seeking to fulfill their political obligations to a foreign power to be registered for taxation, Mary and Joseph give birth to the Son of God. They will name him Jesus, "the name given by the angel before he was conceived in the womb" (v. 21). A sermon can invite the congregation to dwell with Mary and Joseph upon this mystery. This night we remember and celebrate that God comes among us through the faithfulness of Mary and Joseph. There he lies in the manger. "Let all mortal flesh keep silence," we sing.

Stories, songs, images, and experiences all come rushing in to fill out the Christmas sermon. The preacher will want to sift them carefully for that which is theologically fitting, faithful to the biblical text, and socially engaging. As already stated, less is usually more in the Christmas sermon.

Occasionally human experience lines up so closely with the biblical story that it can be prudently shared in the sermon without a great deal of additional interpretation. Like the time shortly after I graduated from seminary. My first pastoral appointment was to a Latino congregation in Atlanta, Georgia. Just before Christmas of my first year, I received a call from a North American woman who was in the process of "releasing" a domestic helper, Maria, who was Venezuelan. They wanted to know if our congregation could help Maria get back home since her visa was about to expire and she had recently had a baby boy, whom the employer family was not willing to support. Basically, they had decided to boot the mother and infant out of the house, but they at least were decent enough to call a few of the Hispanic churches and community agencies that might assist.

It's a lengthy story, as you can imagine. But the end result was that Maria and her infant son wound up in the apartment of my fiancée, Mary Leslie. They would remain there for a couple of days until our congregation could pull together funds and secure the necessary papers for Maria to return home. Mary Leslie was not entirely happy with the arrangement, since she was busily involved in a night-shelter ministry in another congregation during the coldest month of the year. Having a houseguest who did not speak English, with a newborn child, sleeping on her couch in a small apartment, was not her idea of fun. I understood that, but it was the best option that I could come up with at the time.

Mary Leslie relates that on the first night when she got home late from the night shelter, she begrudgingly prepared a meal for herself and Maria. She attempted to communicate with Maria, but the language barrier was pretty tough. After a great deal of sign language and broken English and Spanish, they began to make some headway. Mary Leslie discovered that she actually liked Maria. Her patience and kind disposition under extreme circumstances were moving. The young mother clearly adored her child, and she was desperate to get him home to Venezuela where they would be among family. Mary Leslie asked Maria the name of the baby. When she replied, Mary Leslie could not understand the name because of the Spanish pronunciation. So Maria dug through her bags and proudly produced the birth certificate. She passed it over to Mary Leslie. And then Mary Leslie saw the baby's name: *Jesus*. The baby was named *Jesus*.

You can make the connections for yourself. It is Christmas, a foreign mother is homeless, and in a cramped apartment she cradles an infant child whose name turns out to be Jesus. Every now and then in the church we stumble upon (are confronted by?) people and situations that are so analogous to the core elements of the Christian story that the two stories merge into one. We realize that the Christian narrative does indeed interpret our world and us, and it gives us new eyes to see and hear the gospel that Christ is among us. Often this good news comes through the presence of strangers, foreigners in our midst who beckon us to be who we are, communities deeply formed by the hospitality of Jesus Christ. Jesus is the unexpected stranger who turns out to be host of the unending banquet where bread and wine run clean out into the streets. Preach that message however you can on Christmas, and let the gospel find a hearing.

Matthew 1:1-25 or 1:18-25 (LFM, At the Vigil Mass)

The stage has been set. We have heard John the Baptist crying in the wilderness. He has urged us to repent of our sins and prepare to receive the Lord, the bringer of salvation. We have listened to the prophets of the Hebrew Scriptures announce that redemption and restoration are at hand. The psalmist has proclaimed that a new king is ready to ascend the throne. All signs point toward the climax of the story. What does Matthew give us? A list. He gives his readers a genealogical list.

The list is important, especially if we couple it with the following verses in which Matthew tells of the holy conception and birth of Jesus. The list is important because through the recital of Jesus' genealogy Matthew ties the bringer of salvation to the entire history of Israel. This Gospel writer in particular wants to depict Jesus as the fulfillment of all the hopes of the nation of Israel. Naturally, he draws upon the prophet Isaiah to support his claim. "'Look, the virgin shall conceive and bear a son, and they shall name him Emmanuel,' which means God with us" (v. 23; see Isa. 7:14). The list is not incidental but determinative of the arrival of Jesus the Messiah, who is "the son of David, the son of Abraham" (v. 1). Those who do not like lists, or who would rather not struggle in the pulpit with all those names, could leave off the first eighteen verses of the chapter, but in doing so will run the risk of cutting Jesus off from his family roots.

This may be a compelling angle to preach during the Christmas Vigil mass. We learn from these twenty-five verses a great deal about the family of Jesus. We know who his ancestors are, who his grandparents and parents are, and we learn how God places him right in the lap of a chosen family and a chosen people to become God with us. Take a look around the sanctuary on Christmas Eve. Who is there? Families. Or pieces of families. Or those who are longing to be with their families. Or those who are hungry to be a part of a family that they never really had. On this of all nights, roots are important.

The good news is that with the birth that we celebrate on this night Jesus adopts us into God's family. We needn't be alone. God claims us personally while claiming the whole world on this night of nights. The church is the vehicle through which every person present can experience a part of what it means to be enfolded by God and redeemed by Christ. People bring a world of loneliness and heartache into the sanctuary on Christmas Eve. The preacher should not forget it. Proclaiming the good news according to Matthew can restore some of those broken people to the family that they might have lost, the family that is broken, or the family they never had. It is, of course, God's family, and Jesus is the baby who draws everyone in.

December 25, 2012
Nativity of Our Lord II (RCL) /
Christmas: Mass at Dawn (LFM)

Revised Common Lectionary (RCL)	**Lectionary for Mass (LFM)**
Isaiah 62:6-12	Isaiah 62:11-12
Psalm 97	Psalm 97:1 + 6, 11-12
Titus 3:4-7	Titus 3:4-7
Luke 2:(1-7) 8-20	Luke 2:15-20

First Reading
Isaiah 62:6-12 (RCL)
Isaiah 62:11-12 (LFM)

Readers may wish to look at Christmas: Mass at Midnight (LFM, At the Vigil Mass) above for comments about the first five verses of this chapter of Isaiah. In these verses, 6-12, the writer continues to ring an eschatological note of hope as Jerusalem anticipates its salvation and restoration by the hands of God. In the day of the Lord, the foreigner will no longer dominate Jerusalem. It is time to announce to the people, "See, your salvation comes" (v. 11). In a poetic turn of phrase, the writer says that redeemed Jerusalem "shall be called, 'Sought Out, A City Not Forsaken'" (v. 12). This is the message of Advent and Christmas: God has not forsaken the creation. As Christmas Day dawns, we peer around all the familial and cultural traditions that surround the day to see a dayspring of hope. God has not forsaken creation.

The writer is so convinced of God's promised fulfillment that he instructs the faithful in postexilic Jerusalem to remind God of the divine promises, just in case God forgets. "You who remind the LORD, take no rest, and give him no rest until he establishes Jerusalem and makes it renowned throughout the earth" (v. 6). Since God is the primary actor in the biblical drama of salvation, why would God need reminders of what God has already promised to do—namely, redeem all of creation? It is a curious notion, but one that might yield important homiletical insight for Christmas Day. This kind of appeal to God's memory is based in the Hebrew lament tradition in which the faithful plead with God, express anger to God, and urge God to deliver them from suffering or captivity. It may seem odd, but this kind of theological urging has its place at Christmas. We do sing joyfully of the arrival of Jesus the infant king. But even as we sing, we know that the world piles up suffering upon God's doorstep—from the hungry of southern Africa to the violated and abused of North America, brokenness remains and often seems to be on the increase. Since God through Christ is the deliverer, isn't it important to say to God, especially on the high holy days, the work is not yet complete? And so we pray to the God who delivers good news on Christmas Day, "We hear your promise." Along with Mary and Isaiah, we implore, "Let it be so according to your word" (Luke 1:38).

Psalmody
Psalm 97 (RCL)
Psalm 97:1 + 6, 11-12 (LFM)

Like Psalm 96 (see Christmas: Mass at Midnight, LFM, above), this enthronement psalm affirms the kingship of the Lord. From its opening verse, "The LORD is king! Let the earth rejoice," to its closing line, "Rejoice in the LORD, O you righteous, and give thanks to his holy name!" the psalm invites the congregation to give thanks for God's righteousness and justice (v. 2) and for God's protection from evil (v. 10).

The images within the psalm seem more appropriate to the second coming of Christ, as anticipated in Advent, than the first coming of the infant Jesus celebrated at Christmas. Clouds and darkness, fire and lightning cause the earth to tremble and the mountains to "melt like wax" before the Lord. This is no gentle baby lying in a manger. This is a righteous Lord striding across heaven and earth to root out idolatry (v. 7) and wickedness (v. 10). For those who are faithful to this God above all gods, there is great joy. Light will dawn upon them and joy will take root in their hearts (v. 11).

It is important on Christmas Day to retain these images of the creating and righteous God alongside those of the baby in the manger. This will help us push back the tendency to sentimentalize Jesus on Christmas Day. Preachers most likely will not choose to use this as their primary text for the day's sermon. But the theological affirmation here is that the righteous God of Psalm 97 who approaches in power and glory is the same Lord who stoops low to meet the world through a baby in Bethlehem. Advent meets Christmas when we read Psalm 97 along with Luke 2. A scene from C. S. Lewis's *The Lion, The Witch, and the Wardrobe* speaks to this dual identity of God. When Susan asks Mr. Beaver about Aslan the lion, who is the symbolic Christ figure of the story, "Is he—quite safe?" Mr. Beaver replies, "'Course he isn't safe. But he's good. He's the King, I tell you."[1] The mighty Lord hides within himself the *peace* that passes understanding, while the gentle Jesus bears within himself the *power* of peace.

Second Reading
Titus 3:4-7 (RCL, LFM)

Readers may wish to consult earlier comments on Titus, since this passage connects logically with that selected for Nativity of Our Lord I (Titus 2:11-14), above. Here the writer of the letter to Titus (scholars debate if the letter is actually Pauline) continues to exhort Titus to teach the congregation how to live a righteous life *in response* to the grace of God offered through Jesus Christ. The verses selected for Christmas Dawn crystallize the core beliefs of the church from the first century until today. God redeems humanity through a Savior who embodies God's goodness and loving-kindness (v. 4). This salvation is not a result of our righteousness but of the mercy and grace of God received through the baptism of water and Spirit (v. 5) poured out by Jesus Christ (v. 6). Recipients of that grace may anticipate a full inheritance of the hope of eternal life (v. 7). Then, if we extend the limits of the passage to verse 8, the writer caps off this summary statement of the Christian story with an affirmation—"The saying is sure" (v. 8a).

We gather to worship Jesus, the infant Christ, Son of God, Savior, on Christmas Day. "To you is born this day in the city of David a Savior, who is the Messiah, the Lord" (Luke 2:11). The church witnesses this miraculous birth and quickly runs from the manger to tell the entire world—from Rome to Corinth, from Thessalonica to Crete (whom Titus seems to be addressing)—that this one indeed enfleshes the goodness and loving-kindness of God. It is no fable. The Messiah is born and he redeems the world from sin.

Stirring underneath this summary of the good news in Titus are baptismal waters. Some scholars suggest that these verses may directly refer to baptism and spiritual cleansing.[2] If that is the case, the preacher may want to consider how to tie baptismal theology and imagery into the Christmas Day sermon. We might recall from Advent that John announced Jesus' baptism (Luke 3). The one who is born on Christmas is the one who will grow to be baptized by John. We could allude to the key moments in Jesus' life as markers for the Christian way—birth, baptism, witness, death, and resurrection. And we could celebrate the purity of the moment of Jesus' birth as the promise of our own rebirth in Christ.

Gospel
Luke 2:(1-7) 8-20 (RCL)
Luke 2:15-20 (LFM)

For a more complete treatment of this text, readers should consult the comments on the Gospel for Nativity of Our Lord I, above. Here we can add that as we move from Christmas Eve to Christmas Dawn, a mood shift in the spirit of worship is expected. Preached on Christmas Eve, Luke 2:1-20 might stress the mystery of the incarnation; the wonder of Mary, Joseph, and the shepherds; and the remarkable silence that accompanies the birth of the one who is the new king. The hymn "O Little Town of Bethlehem" captures the spirit that the Christmas Eve sermon can evoke, with its memorable phrases "How still we see thee lie" and "Yet in thy dark streets shineth the everlasting light."

Preached on Christmas Dawn, Luke 2:1-20 shifts our religious affections from awe to joy.[3] We shift the camera a little more toward the angels and the shepherds and a little less toward Mary, Joseph, and the baby Jesus. Jesus is, of course, the reason for the shepherds and the angels, but the Christmas sermon can takes its cue from their actions and responses. The angels make their announcement of the birth of Jesus with a multitude of heavenly hosts, singing, "Glory to God in the highest heaven, and on earth peace among those whom he favors" (v. 14). The shepherds hurry to see Jesus, then return "glorifying and praising God for all they had heard and seen" (v. 20). The preacher does not so much aim to explain all of these joyful responses by shepherds and angels as to craft a sermon and worship service that evoke such responses within the congregation. After all, our place in the story is more likely to be with the shepherds or with all who hear what the shepherds tell (v. 18). Their response is most properly our response. So we sing "Hark! the Herald Angels Sing" and "Joy to the World" to add our praises to those found in the text.

This is the time to name within the congregation the small and large ways that joy is occurring in our midst. Lift up those events where people are experiencing the joy of Christ among us, and invite them to give God thanks and praise. For example, a new birth to a congregation or community member, good news of someone's restoration to health, a triumph in social or personal reconciliation that might have happened in the community or within the world, a positive development in securing environmental health. The goal is to point toward salvation *now*, to paint a word picture of what God's in-breaking looks, sounds, and feels like for those who gather on Christmas Day. Then invite the congregation to raise its voice in singing, "Repeat the sounding joy. Repeat the sounding joy. Repeat, repeat the sounding joy."

Notes

1. C. S. Lewis, *The Lion, the Witch, and the Wardrobe: A Celebration of the First Edition* (New York: HarperCollins, 2009), 77.

2. James G. D. Dunn, "The First and Second Letters to Timothy and the Letter to Titus," in *The New Interpreter's Bible: Second Corinthians—Philemon*, ed. Leander Keck et al. (Nashville: Abingdon, 2000), 11:877.

3. For an excellent study of the religious affections in worship, see Kendra G. Hotz and Matthew T. Mathews, *Shaping the Christian Life: Worship and the Religious Affections* (Louisville: Westminster John Knox, 2006).

December 25, 2012
Nativity of Our Lord III (RCL) /
Christmas: Mass During the Day (LFM)

Revised Common Lectionary
Isaiah 52:7-10
Psalm 98
Hebrew 1:1-4 (5-12)
John 1:1-14

Lectionary for Mass
Isaiah 52:7-10
Psalm 98:1, 2-3a, 3b-4, 5-6
Hebrews 1:1-6
John 1:1-18 or 1:1-5, 9-14

First Reading
Isaiah 52:7-10 (RCL, LFM)

This joyful passage from Second Isaiah centers on the good news that Israel will be redeemed from her exile to the Babylonians and restored to her life in Zion. Preceded by verses (vv. 3-6) that summarize the history of Israel's captivity by the Egyptians and the Assyrians (later still the Babylonians), these four verses announce a glorious reversal as God returns to the throne of Zion.

The messenger of verse 7 is the one who runs from desert to village to town carrying the good news. The messenger is a text message on feet, a newspaper hand delivered, a radio and TV address delivered with personal strength and jubilation, a phone call made person to person. Those on the watchtower ("the sentinels," v. 8) see the messenger coming across mountain and valley. His feet are beautiful, though they may be scarred by callus and blister, for they are feet that deliver the best news possible. Israel's hope shall be fulfilled; their salvation has come.

A remarkable image sits in the middle of these four verses: "Break forth into singing, you ruins of Jerusalem; for the LORD has comforted his people" (v. 9). What do singing ruins look and sound like? What would be the biblical and contemporary analogies for singing ruins that would bring this passage to life for the Christmas Day congregation? Ezekiel's vision of the dry bones comes to mind (Ezekiel 37). The valley of death in the passage becomes a garden of life when the bones put on flesh and sinew. So, too, God puts on flesh on Christmas and enters our valleys of death with the gift of new life. Into our ordinary and routine dying, bit by bit, day by drab day, a new day dawns as we see "the salvation of our God" (v. 10). Contemporary analogies may be found among the survivors of natural disasters such as Hurricane Katrina or tornadoes in the United States (especially in 2011), or after the tsunamis of Japan (2011) and Indonesia (2006). In each of these instances, we find stories of hope and joy that arise straight from the ruins of flood and fire.

Out of the ruins, people express hope through singing. Think about the importance of song for slaves in North America, and later, during the difficult days of the civil rights struggle, we know of the crucial role of singing to express and sustain the hope of the people. Songs like "We Shall Overcome" and "Ain't Gonna Let Nobody Turn Me Roun'" became rallying songs for the entire movement as African Americans rose up out of the ruins of slavery and Jim Crow to sing and march their way into liberation from captivity.

Such themes are crucial to keep in mind as we preach on Christmas Day. Isaiah reminds us that the salvation of God is all tied up with social, political, and economic liberation. Our tendency to sentimentalize Christmas, if we are not careful, will cause us to miss the wholeness of salvation (peace = *shalom*, v. 7) as promised by Isaiah and affirmed by the Gospel writers. Jesus does not come into the world on Christmas only to redeem us from personal sin. He comes to set the captives free and to inaugurate the reign of the Lord (cf. Luke 4:18-19). The reign of the Lord that begins in Jerusalem among the singing ruins of Zion shall be shown to "the ends of the earth" (v. 10). This is the truly good news of Christmas Day.

Psalmody
Psalm 98 (RCL)
Psalm 98:1, 2-3a, 3b-4, 5-6 (LFM)

Psalm 98 continues the triumphal notes sounded in the previous lections of Psalms 96 and 97. Taken together, they offer a poetic symphony on Christmas Day in praise of God who has "remembered his steadfast love and faithfulness to the house of Israel" (v. 3). After reciting God's marvelous deeds of salvation (vv. 1-3), the psalmist urges (note the imperative form) the congregation to "make a joyful noise," "break forth into song," "sing praises to the Lord" (vv. 4-6). Preachers will want to think creatively about how best to encourage the congregation to sing boldly and joyfully on Christmas Day with lyre and trumpets (vv. 5-6). For many, this will be their natural inclination. For others, who are not feeling as much joy on Christmas Day, perhaps because of grief or illness or discouragement over world affairs, it will be important to proclaim that their situation is precisely what the God of the psalmist and Jesus of Bethlehem come to redeem. Even out of sadness and captivity, as we saw with Isaiah 52, we can find the power to sing our way toward hope, because the Lord has come to "judge the world with righteousness and the peoples with equity" (v. 9).

One similarity between this psalm and Psalm 96 is the response of the nonhuman world. All creation breaks forth in song on the day of the Lord. The sea, the hills, the floods all "sing together for joy." It will add beauty and spice to the Christmas Sunday service if the preacher finds a way to help the congregation hear the singing of the humpback whale, the clacking of the African gray parrot, the beeping of the bat, the braying of the donkey, the stirring of the waves, and the swaying of the trees upon the mountain as they join their natural voices to the human ones that sing the songs of Zion in praise of the newborn king.

Second Reading
Hebrews 1:1-4 (5-12) (RCL)
Hebrews 1:1-6 (LFM)

When we join this text from the anonymous epistle of Hebrews with the reading from the Gospel of John that is forthcoming on Christmas Day, we encounter two readings that share many of the same theological concerns. Both assert high christological claims for the divinity of Christ. Both articulate the preexistence of Christ, who from the beginning is with God and who co-creates with God through speech. And both claim that the fullness of God's image dwells within the incarnate Christ.

The text can seem abstract for Christmas Day. With the above-mentioned themes, and its later interest in establishing the divine priesthood of Jesus, the one who "made purification for sins," it seems a long way from the birth narratives of Matthew and Luke that our hearers are accustomed to on Christmas Day. If the theological emphasis on Christmas is upon the mystery and joy of the incarnation, this passage pulls in a direction that risks losing sight of the vulnerable baby in the manger, the shepherds croaking out their songs of joy.

A strong homiletical hook will be needed to keep this passage and a sermon based upon it tethered to the ground. The preacher will want to do the necessary homework to understand the various arguments and exhortations of the writer as he claims the superiority of Christ to all previous revelations, the superiority of Christ to the Levitical priesthood, and the superiority of Christ's sacrifice to the animal sacrifices of the Levitical priests. But most of this background work can remain in the background on Christmas Day. The meaning for this high holy day hangs upon verses 2 and 3: "God has spoken to us by a Son . . . [who] is the reflection of God's glory."

Christmas is a time when words matter. We reach across space and time through Internet, Facebook, cell phone, Skype, Christmas cards, and text messages to say words that really matter: "We love you"; "We miss you"; "We wish you were here, we really do"; "We are saying a prayer for you." Words at Christmas can bind up wounds, restore relations, connect us with loved ones miles away. Just so, God speaks a love-filled word to us on Christmas. God speaks hope into our fear and promise into our longings. That word, God speaks to us "by a Son" (v. 2); the very Son through whom God created all the world (cf. John 1).

That Son comes to us on Christmas and at the end of days bearing the exact imprint of God, a reflection of God's glory (v. 3). What more important can be said on Christmas? Look at the baby Jesus, that vulnerable child. He is the reflection of God for all the world. See in his face the face of God who stoops low to raise the world on high. See in his vulnerable body the fullness of God whose glory spills over into human form, and who does not remain distant, but comes to us in the form of a servant (cf. Phil. 2:5-11). In the word made flesh (cf. John 1), God pours God's self into all of creation. Find a way to tether the lofty rhetoric of Hebrews 1 and John 1 to the sleeping infant of Luke and Matthew's birth stories, and the congregation will want to sing, "O come, let us adore him, Christ the Lord."

Gospel
John 1:1-14 (RCL)
John 1:1-18 or 1:1-5, 9-14 (LFM)

With this final reading for Christmas Day, we arrive at one of the most soaring passages of the New Testament, the prologue to the Gospel of John. We will briefly explore the entire prologue for preaching on Christmas Day, verses 1-18, though preachers may choose to accent one or another of the suggested approaches for the day.

As discussed in the commentary on Hebrews 1, John shares that writer's concern to proclaim the preexistence of Christ. Jesus Christ is the *logos*, the Word, which from the beginning was with God and was God. All things come into existence through this Word and nothing exists apart from the Word's creative action (vv. 1-3). As with the Hebrews passage, the preacher will need to work to tie this lofty, theo-philosophical claim with its Greek influences close to the ground of the Christmas story that hearers bring with them into the sanctuary on Christmas Day. There is room for a sermon that ponders the grand mystery that the Christ who joined God in making the heavens and the earth comes in the fullness of time in human form. He was before us, yet he comes to us clothed in our very flesh. He was above us, yet he bends low to us. The Parent of all the universe reaches out through the Son to touch the world: "And the Word became flesh and lived among us, and we have seen his glory, the glory as of a father's only son, full of grace and truth" (v. 14).

Another of John's beloved themes that emerges in the prologue is light and darkness (vv. 4-5). For many, Christmas does come in a dark season. At least in the Northern Hemisphere, Christmas may arrive with foul, bitterly cold weather and long nights. Depression hangs in the air for many. As the bereaved parents realize in Oscar Hijuelos's novel *Mr. Ives's Christmas,* the jangly carols that we hear in every store and coffee shop remind many that Christmas is not always cheerful. Despite consumerism's best efforts to drape the buying public in tinseled joviality, in many places and in many hearts, darkness rages on. There is a reason that on Christmas Eve and Christmas Day we light candles as we sing "Silent Night" or "It Came upon the Midnight Clear." And the reason is not to manufacture false feelings of seasonal coziness. The reason is that the darkness is real. And there is only one light that can illumine the evil and sin that howl around the corner. That is the Christ. "The light shines in the darkness, and the darkness did not overcome it" (v. 5). Wherever light is breaking in upon human suffering and natural degradation, point that way on Christmas Day and light a candle for hope.

John testified to this hope in the dark. He said that the light was coming (vv. 6-8). And on Christmas Day we proclaim that he did indeed come, that he dwells among us now, and that he will come again. The passage clearly links the coming of Jesus to the announcement of John. In this way, the Fourth Gospel shares theological concerns with Matthew and Luke. Verses 6-8 and 15 all hearken back to John. Jesus does not appear unexpectedly. He comes as previously announced. He is the fulfillment of Israel's hopes and dreams.

The problem, of course, is that often in church and world we fail to recognize the presence of God among us. We mistake darkness for light and light for darkness. "He came to what was his own, and his own people did not accept him" (vv. 10-11). Even though the world's rejection of Jesus is not the dominant theme of the day, the theological fact is that the one who lies in the manger will be the same one who hangs on the cross. We often fail to recognize the one who has surrendered glory to live in humility.

Some will feel convicted of ignoring or denying Christ on Christmas. This can be a day to start again. It may stir our ethical sensibilities to listen and look more deeply for Jesus where he is always found among the poor, the broken, the hungry, the enslaved. We might allude to Matthew 25:31-46 in response to John 1:10-14. To divorce the birth of Jesus from his radical ethic of love and his repeated identification with the poor would be to sentimentalize the very one who stands firmly in the breach, holding the door open against the darkness and welcoming *all* into the kingdom of light. Christmas is the right day to proclaim that message with love and humility.

Finally, the preacher can find solid ground for the Christmas sermon based upon John's prologue by highlighting verses 16-17: "From his fullness we have all received grace upon grace. The law indeed was given through Moses; grace and truth came through Jesus." We want to be careful here not to fall into a triumphalist or supercessionist reading of the passage. John affirms what Moses and the Hebrew ancestors have offered to faith—the gift of the law and the prophets. Jesus extends that gift by filling it with grace and truth. For Christians, we affirm that we know God through receiving the entire package—law, prophets, and the grace of Jesus Christ. We can do this without disparaging Jewish faith or that of any other faith group. God's righteousness always exceeds our own. God's grace extends to all whom God intends. Believing in the incarnation of God in Jesus Christ does not put us above or beyond others. It leaves us with grateful, open hands, receiving the grace upon grace that God extends on Christmas to those who believe in his name (vv. 12, 16). Like a friend and fellow church member who, battling with life-threatening pancreatic cancer, said, "I do not know about others, but in my life, with all the good that has happened, I have received grace upon grace." Whether he lives or dies, he knows that he has been on the receiving end of Christmas.

The preacher will want to find the right stories and images that will flesh out this powerful Christmas text regardless of which part of the pericope he or she chooses to address. As stated in an earlier lection, on Christmas Day less is usually more. If preaching from this text, restraint is the better part of wisdom. But when you find that fitting image or story of light and darkness, of glory revealed in unexpected ways, of grace pouring out in full measure, place it gently beside John's glorious words. The Christ child will come shining through.

December 30, 2012
First Sunday of Christmas (RCL)

Revised Common Lectionary
1 Samuel 2:18-20, 26
Psalm 148
Colossians 3:12-17
Luke 2:41-52

First Reading
1 Samuel 2:18-20, 26

This first Sunday after Christmas traditionally recognizes the childhood and the family of Jesus. The reading from 1 Samuel connects with the Gospel reading from Luke via verse 26. "Now the boy Samuel continued to grow both in stature and in favor with the Lord and with the people" (cf. Luke 2:52). Both Samuel and Jesus are growing boys, attending the priests and talking with the elders in the temple. And both are growing in favor with God and the people.

Samuel's story comes at a critical time in Israel's history as they shift from a loosely connected group of tribes to an organized nation under divinely appointed kingship. Samuel attends Eli, the chief priest whose leadership will come to an end because of the sins of his sons, Hophni and Phinehas. The lectionary passage for today omits the verses that describe their sinfulness, but their lack of faithfulness to God and disrespect of their father are in clear contrast to the virtues of Samuel (1:22-25). Samuel will be the bridge between the fall of the tribes of Israel and the rise of the monarchy. He will be the one to help select and anoint both Saul and David as the future kings.

Samuel's faithfulness and action are based upon the commitment of his mother, Hannah, and his father, Elkanah. Since Hannah is barren, she prays for the gift of a son whom in turn she will dedicate to God to become a Nazirite, one who is consecrated to God (1:10-11). Eli hears Hannah's prayer and blesses her to find favor with God. Hannah conceives the child, Samuel, and as she promised, when he is old enough to be weaned, she offers him to God. "Therefore I have lent him to the Lord; as long as he lives, he is given to the Lord" (1:28).

Samuel grows up in the temple in the service of (ministering to) the priests and God (v. 18). He wears an ephod, a sort of linen apron that was apparently part of the temple garments and rituals. Each year Hannah and Elkanah return to the temple to offer their yearly sacrifice and to give to Samuel the new clothing that he needs as a growing boy (v. 19). Eli recognizes the faithfulness of the mother and father and even extends his blessing that they might have more children as a sign of God's favor (v. 20).

This is a good Sunday to focus upon the meaning of family and raising children within the context of faith. Most of the Christmas fanfare is receding. Many in the congregation have inundated one another with material gifts and feasted to the point of satiation. In these annual Christmas rituals of gift giving, consumption of special foods, traveling across great distances by car and plane, we have tried to express familial love and affection. Among it all has been the presence of God, but often as an afterthought. We might not have stopped to wonder, So what does God have to do with the raising of children? How do we as believers express our deepest commitments to God through our very own families?

Hannah offers us an ancient story with immediate contemporary application. Hannah recognizes that from the beginning Samuel is a gift from God. God blesses Hannah and Elkanah, as they had prayed, with a son. But Samuel is not really theirs to keep. As in Christian baptism today, Hannah dedicates the son to God; she gives him up to the Lord. In doing so, she demonstrates her own faithfulness to God. The child's future, just as his birth, resides in God.

Notice, however, that Hannah and Elkanah do not then sever ties with the young Samuel. They keep the faith, observing their annual religious practices, while at the same time supporting Samuel in his growing ministry. Samuel's identity is first as God's child and second as the son of Hannah and Elkanah. This is as it should be for faithful parents. When we baptize our children into the life and death and resurrection of Christ, we commit them to their true identities as sons and daughters of God. Their family is wider than blood kin; it extends to the whole body of Christ, the church. But they remain our children of flesh and blood. Naturally, we care for them as they grow into the people whom God desires for them to become.

Such a view of parenting as stewardship sounds countercultural in today's world. Many parents either abandon their children to the tides of a frequently indifferent and hostile culture or cling to them way past the point of necessary separation. With Hannah and Elkanah as guides, we can see another way to be family. A family that places God in the center is a family that says that when the time comes, the child will reach out and take God's hand and will walk with God and our ongoing prayers of support into God's future. When that happens, hopefully we can say along with the writers of Samuel and Luke, "Now the boy [or child] continued to grow both in stature and in favor with the Lord and with the people" (v. 26).

Psalmody
Psalm 148

Like Psalm 98 from the Christmas Day (Proper III) psalmody, above, this psalm invites praise of God from both the natural world and humanity, only more so. Psalm 148 extols everything to praise the Lord, animate and inanimate—heavens, angels, sun, moon, stars, waters, monsters of the deep, fire, hail, snow, wind, mountains, fruit trees, wild animals, cattle, flying birds, and, finally, all peoples, princes and rulers, young and old, women and men—let them all praise the Lord together. If anything or anyone has been left off of this list, it is not for lack of trying on the part of the psalmist.

What a grand vision the writer places before the congregation on the Sunday following Christmas! Christ has come among us, sent from and embodying the God who makes all heaven and earth. This is the God we praise with all our voices, joining human to natural choruses to praise the Lord whose glory "is above earth and heaven" (v. 13).

That the psalmist seems to single out Israel in verse 14 as the people whom God most favors and who, therefore, should sing the loudest, does not actually contradict the universal scope of the psalm. Israel is the representative among all of creation to lead the praise, but Israel points toward the God who redeems humanity, the earth, and the cosmos.

A sermon based upon this text will attempt to open the gates of joy within the congregation. Sing the Christmas hymns again—this time like we really mean it. Lift our voices in poetry and song for the new day that has come, the new year that awaits, full of God's glory. For one thing is sure: if we find a way to offer God our full-bodied thanks and praise, all other things will find their proper place within the world that God creates and sustains.

Second Reading
Colossians 3:12-17

As we continue to think about the emphasis upon the family of Jesus and the family of the church into which we are baptized, Colossians 3 provides important guidance. These verses are among many in Colossians that instruct the readers about the disciplines of Christian living based solely upon the lordship of Jesus Christ. The chapter begins with the writer's reminder that Christian faith and living depend entirely upon the believers' participation in the life, death, and resurrection of Jesus Christ. "So if you have been raised with Christ, seek the things that are above . . . for you have died and your life is hidden with Christ" (3:1, 3). Then follows a laundry list of those things that Christians do not practice because Christ is our life—anger, wrath, malice, slander, impurity, evil desire, greed, and so forth.

Verses 12-17 flip the instruction around from the negative to the positive. In these verses the writer, who may or may not have actually been Paul, reminds the congregation of those virtues that we should uphold. Compassion, kindness, meekness, humility, patience, forgiveness of one another, love, and peace—these are the fruitful traits of those who truly worship (serve) Jesus Christ.

The language of the passage is baptismal. The follower of Christ takes off the old clothes and puts on the new. "As God's chosen ones, holy and beloved, clothe yourselves with compassion, kindness . . . " (v. 12). Taking on Christ through baptism, we die to ourselves that we might live to the Lord. We join our body to his body, the church, and so live by the standards of Jesus Christ.

The virtues that the writer commends, and the practices that he lifts up for the people of Colossae, are not primarily personal virtues. Yes, each individual must take responsibility for his or her own life and behavior. But we do so as mutual members within the body of Christ. The instructions are intended to guide the members of the church in how to live together truthfully and harmoniously. For wherever two or more attempt to occupy the same place at the same time, conflict is sure to occur. This is normal within the church, the writer says. And the way forward is not to pretend that we are always happy with each other. Rather, we must "bear with one another and, if anyone has a complaint against another, forgive each other; just as the Lord has forgiven you" (v. 13). Here are the practical theological instructions for how the church can continue to be the church, even when members disagree.

The only way such mutual forgiveness and love can occur within the church is if we recognize that Christ is the one who "rules in our hearts." He was given to church and world at Christmas by God the Creator. So just as we saw in Titus 3:4-7 (Nativity of Our Lord II/Christmas: Mass at Dawn, above) and John 1:16 (Nativity of Our Lord III/Christmas: Mass During the Day, above), the faithful practices of the church grow straight out of the grace of God through Jesus Christ if they grow at all.[1] We are recipients of God's grace upon grace. That means that our proper response, even beyond the virtues outlined in the passage, is gratitude. We give thanks to God because we have been overwhelmed by grace. We live our lives by the power of that grace within the Christian community, and we offer our thanks to God for that grace.

Gospel
Luke 2:41-52

As with the passage from Samuel, Luke places us with the main character of the story in the temple. The birth of Christ has come and gone. The crowds have all dispersed. The festivities are over and everyone has gathered their poinsettias and donkeys and headed home. Only, Jesus remains in the temple, in his "Father's house," listening and learning from the elders and asking them questions. It's a good time for reflection within the congregation. It may be that now that the fuss of Christmas is behind us, the few who are sticking around on the Sunday after Christmas are ready and able to learn more deeply about who Jesus is and who we are in the light of his identity.

One matter that can trip up hearers of this passage is how Mary and Joseph could leave Jesus in the first place and not miss him until late in the day. Apparently for the Passover festival, the families traveled in large groups to and from the temple in Jerusalem. It is likely that Mary and Joseph were among their extended kin. They assumed that Jesus would be in the group as well as they headed out of Jerusalem. This was not parental neglect but a simple case of relying upon the family network to watch out after all the children and youth. Of course, when the parents discover his absence, their natural anxiety rises to the surface (v. 48). The search is on, and the parents do not rest until on the third day they find Jesus in the temple.

His abrupt response to Mary may be more about Luke's theological intent than an actual exchange between a frightened mother and an impertinent son. When Jesus says to Mary, "Why were you searching for me? Did you not know that I must be in my Father's house?" Luke is pointing us toward the importance of the temple in his story and the supreme value of Jesus' sonship to God. As with Samuel, Jesus' loyalty is first to God and secondarily, though nonetheless really, to his own flesh and blood. In fact, Luke points out that following this exchange in the temple, Jesus was obedient to his parents (v. 50).

Lining this story up with that of Samuel, the preacher may want to offer them both as ways for the congregation to think about how parents do or do not entrust their children to God. When children make real their declarations of faith, how do parents take the next steps to entrust them to the wider church? We affirm in the baptismal rituals in many congregations that the child, youth, or adult is now a member of Christ's body, having been washed in water and blessed by the Holy Spirit. The child must and can learn that faith is corporate, that there are many other wise teachers for the child to encounter, and many other spiritual mothers and fathers who can help nurture the son or daughter as he or she matures in faith.

Mary's response to Jesus, after her initial puzzlement, is a cue for the Christian parent. Just as in her response to Jesus' birth (2:19), Mary "treasured all these things in her heart" (v. 51). Whatever else Luke might be suggesting by this repetition of Mary's response to her own son, it is at least an affirmation that Mary the mother *wonders* at the mystery of her own child, as do all parents. Where did this child come from, anyway? Why does she say the things she says? What will she possibly do in the future? What kind of person will he become? Even more, will he know God? Will she know to give God thanks for life itself? When things go downhill, even spiraling into tragedy, will he still rely upon the Lord? Now these are the questions that keep parents up at night, wondering, watching, waiting, hoping.

Mary has asked them already. Thank God she had enough faith to trust that Jesus was not only her son but God's Son. Thank God that Mary was mature enough in her faith and her motherhood to allow Jesus to increase in wisdom and in divine and human favor.

Note

1. On Christian practices as response to God's grace, see Dorothy C. Bass, ed., *Practicing Our Faith: A Way of Life for Searching People* (San Francisco: Jossey-Bass, 1997).

December 30, 2012
The Holy Family of Jesus, Mary, and Joseph (LFM)

Lectionary for Mass (LFM)
    1 Samuel 1:20-22, 24-28
    Psalm 84:2-3, 5-6, 9-10
    1 John 3:1-2, 21-24
    Luke 2:41-52

First Reading
1 Samuel 1:20-22, 24-28

For this passage readers may wish to consult comments on the first reading for the First Sunday of Christmas (RCL), above. These verses precede those of the RCL, but each reading relates part of the same story of Samuel's birth and dedication to God through the temple.

One angle that was not touched on in the preceding commentary is the name of Samuel, given to him by Hannah. The name Samuel probably means "name of God," according to biblical scholars. Hannah asked God for a son. She literally begged or borrowed the child from God. After the child was given, she then lent him back to God. "Therefore I have lent him to the LORD; as long as he lives, he is given to the LORD" (v. 28 NRSV).[1] Thus by name and the actions of his mother, Samuel is tied directly to God.

For preachers, the point here is direct. Are not all our lives and the lives of our children gifts from God? Do we not all bear the imprint of God's image and God's name upon our lives since God is the source of our being? When we dedicate ourselves and our children to God, we are really giving back to God what God has already given to us. Here, just a few days after Christmas, with gift giving still happening in many families, this gift exchange between God and humanity is most notable in the premier gift of Jesus Christ to the world. He is the one who shows us what it means to carry the "name of God."

Another possible approach to this passage is to note the obvious parallels between the birth of Samuel and the birth of Jesus. God blesses both Hannah and Mary with a miraculous birth. Both Hannah and Mary sing songs (poems) of thanksgiving to God for this wondrous reversal of fortune. Both fathers, Elkanah and Joseph, accept their responsibility to support mother and child as the birth and early caretaking occur. As Elkanah says to Hannah, "Do what seems best to you, wait until you have weaned him; only—may the LORD establish his word" (v. 23 NRSV). The mothers and fathers both dedicate their children to God at the temple. And both young Samuel and young Jesus grow and mature in service of God at the temple.

To what extent Luke intended to draw *fully* from the earlier Hebrew story is hard to say, but that he did is clear. The later story does not supersede the importance of the former. Both are stories of good news to Israel and to the early church as God does a new thing. Christians can find great joy in reading 1 Samuel as confirmation that as God has done in the past, so God continues to do in the present and future—bring forth new life from barrenness, "raise up the poor from the dust," and "guard the feet of the faithful ones" (2:8, 9 NRSV).

Psalmody
Psalm 84:2-3, 5-6, 9-10

This pilgrimage psalm is one of the most beautiful in the book of Psalms. It seems to reflect the anticipation and joy of a group of worshipers who are on their way to the temple to worship God. As with other such psalms, it may have been part of a processional liturgy during a fall harvest festival at the temple. The worshiper's "soul yearns and pines for the courts of the LORD," as he or she almost envies the sparrows and swallows who find a permanent home among the altars in the sanctuary (vv. 3-4 NAB). The comfort, security, and beauty of the temple cause the psalmist to exclaim, "Better one day in your courts than a thousand elsewhere. Better the threshold of the house of my God than a home in the tents of the wicked" (v. 10 NAB).

The preacher may find in this joyful psalm at least two directions for preaching. The obvious one is that the joy of Christmastide, and the fulfillment of the promise of birth to Mary and Joseph, finds voice in the jubilant mood of this psalm. There is reason to journey to worship on the Sunday after Christmas. For "blessed is the [one] who finds refuge in you [God]" (v. 6 NAB).

Another approach to the sermon is to think of this psalm as giving voice to either Samuel's or Jesus' dedication to God through the temple. It is easy enough imagining either of them chanting this psalm as they go about serving the temple priests (Samuel) or learning from the elders in the temple (Jesus). As Samuel and Jesus "go from strength to strength" in dedication to God, they do indeed encounter the living Lord. "They will . . . see the God of gods on Zion" (v. 8 NAB).

What this particular verse suggests is that Yahweh will from time to time visit, or tabernacle, or tent among the people. While the temple is not literally the dwelling place of God, through the use of God's name in the temple, God's presence is recognized and invoked.[2] Who better to invoke that presence than Jesus? For he is the one in whom we fully know God, in whom we fully behold God's glory (cf. John 1:14-18).

Second Reading
1 John 3:1-2, 21-24

Writing to a community that is misunderstood by at least some within the synagogue and some within the wider culture, the anonymous writer of 1 John seeks to shore up the faith of his readers and congregation with a foundational understanding of belief. The epistle is not really a letter but more a sermon or treatise on Christian belief to a group of Christians who are associated with the Johannine circles that apparently formed around the teachings of the writer of the Gospel of John. This epistle, like 2 and 3 John, may be from a different hand than John's, but it reflects many of the same themes as that Gospel (light and dark, body and spirit, love, being born again from above, and so forth).

One distinction, however, that arises in today's passage is the writer's eschatological concern. Whereas the Gospel of John seems primarily concerned about present revelation of God through the incarnate Jesus Christ, the epistle writer (referred to as "the elder" by scholars) is equally concerned about the future of those who believe in Jesus Christ. As the first century drew to a close and the return of Christ was delayed, this new generation of Christians began to wonder what the future would bring.

Thus verse 2 for today states, "Beloved, we are God's children now; what we will be has not yet been revealed. What we do know is this: when he is revealed, we will be like him, for we will see him as he is." We know who we are, the elder states. We are the children of God. Our identity as God's children leads us to live moral lives empowered by Christ. But, even more, as we hope for the future we know that in the fullness of time we will be more and more "like him" (v. 2). In other words, to live *by Christ now and for Christ in the future* is to live as Christ always. Our actions reflect the depth of our faith and commitment to Christ. Through him we are becoming a new creation that will be fully realized in God's future.

This leads the elder to then instruct the faithful in the virtues of Christian living within the Christian community. "And this is his commandment, that we should believe in the name of his Son Jesus Christ and love one another, just as he has commanded us. All who obey his commandments abide in him, and he abides in them" (vv. 23-24). This is the elder's core ethic centered on Christian love. Similar to Paul's instructions in 1 Corinthians 13, the members of the church are instructed to love one another. And in loving one another, we come to know God. "Everyone who loves is born of God and knows God," he says in 4:7. This is what it means to abide in Christ. By loving one another, we abide in him and he abides in us.

There is, of course, much to work out when it comes to Christian love. The word *love* is easy to say and hard to live. As Lucy says to Schroeder in the *Peanuts* comic strip, "That's the problem with you. All you do is talk about love. But you never show it. Your love sure looks good on paper!" Love entails great patience, honesty, humility, acceptance of oneself and the other, willingness to ask for forgiveness, and willingness to forgive. Anyone who thinks that sentimentality or romance is the same as love has not really attempted to love. The elder does not give us details on how to enact Christian love within community. Those lessons come over the course of a lifetime. But he does give us the key for the basis of love. "That we should believe in the name of his Son Jesus Christ and love one another" (v. 23). Jesus Christ is the bedrock upon which Christian love is founded. Without him, love is impossible. Through him, love is our practice and our aim.

Gospel
Luke 2:41-52

See the comments on the Gospel for the First Sunday of Christmas, above.

Notes

1. See note, 1 Samuel 1, in *The New Oxford Annotated Bible: An Ecumenical Study Bible,* New Revised Standard Version, ed. Bruce Metzger and Roland E. Murphy (New York: Oxford University Press, 1991), 342.

2. Bernhard W. Anderson, *Out of the Depths: The Psalms Speak for Us Today,* rev. and exp. ed. (Philadelphia: Westminster, 1983), 197–98.

January 1, 2013
Name of Jesus (RCL) /
Mary, Mother of God (LFM)

Revised Common Lectionary (RCL)	**Lectionary for Mass (LFM)**
Numbers 6:22-27	Numbers 6:22-27
Psalm 8	Psalm 67:2-3, 5, 6-8
Galatians 4:4-7 or Philippians 2:5-11	Galatians 4:4-7
Luke 2:15-21	Luke 2:15-21

First Reading
Numbers 6:22-27 (RCL, LFM)

The church has traditionally celebrated the first day of the new year as a day to remember the naming of Jesus on the eighth day following his birth and a day to commemorate Mary, the mother of Jesus. While many worshipers on this day may expect a sermon that discusses new beginnings, that particular theme can be woven into the traditional theological emphasis of naming and Mary.

The Numbers passage occurs within the broader context in the Pentateuch of the giving of the law at Sinai and its interpretation (Exodus 19 through Numbers 10). It includes the blessing that God gives through Moses to Aaron and all succeeding generations. This is one of the most familiar of the biblical benedictions to Jews, Protestants, and Roman Catholics. "The LORD bless you and keep you; the LORD make his face to shine upon you, and be gracious to you; the LORD lift up his countenance upon you, and give you peace" (vv. 22-26). This blessing has been set in a variety of choral scores and arrangements and often occurs as a final benediction in Christian worship.

The thematic tie for today's sermon comes in verse 26 where God says to Moses, "So they shall put my name on the Israelites, and I will bless them." Naming carries major significance in Jewish and Christian tradition, indeed, in most religious and cultural traditions. God gives Abraham and Sarah new names as they respond in faithfulness to the covenant and call of God (Genesis 17). After struggling all night with the divine stranger, Jacob receives a new name, Israel, which means "the one who strives with God," even though the stranger will not reveal his name to Jacob, because the name holds power (Gen. 32:27-29). And here in Numbers 6, the name of God is conferred upon Israel, assuring them of God's blessing.

We know the power of naming in our own lives. Some of us carry the name of our parents, grandparents, beloved family friends, biblical characters, or saints. New parents deliberate over what to name a child, recognizing that the name itself will affect the child's future in untold ways. As we grow and mature, we cannot separate ourselves from our names. We respond when friends and loved ones call our names, and we may bristle when others forget or mispronounce our names. In a very real sense, we are the names that we have been given.

The importance of God's bestowing the name upon Israel cannot be overestimated. Israel strives with God and so God names Israel. The people are permanently tied to the God who made heaven and earth and who redeems humankind through covenant and fulfillment. This naming God provides protection (v. 24), grace (v. 25), and peace or wholeness (v. 26). Even when Israel forgets or denies its relation to God, as it frequently does while wandering in the wilderness, God does not forsake the people. "[I] will be your God, and you shall be my people," says God in Leviticus 26:12. And that is exactly what God upholds for the ones whom God names.

Perhaps this is the Sunday to remind the congregation that as we begin a new secular calendar year on January 1, we carry into our new beginnings an ancient name: the people whom God loves. Each of us bears the image of that God. God knows each of us by name.

Psalmody
Psalm 8 (RCL)

This beloved psalm is the first of the praise psalms in the book of Psalms. It begins and ends with praise of the sovereign God and glorification of God's *name* (vv. 1, 9). In between, humanity's glory and responsibility are placed within the context of God's glory: "Yet you have made them a little lower than God, and crowned them with glory and honor" (v. 5). As humanity reflects the glory of God, we share in God's care of all creation, not through domination but through loving dominion. We are the caretakers on behalf of God for "the beasts of the field, the birds of the air, and the fish of the sea" (vv. 7-8). No wonder this psalm has the distinction of being the first biblical text to reach the moon, having been placed there by the members of the Apollo 11 mission.[1] It extols the glory of God and humanity from heaven to earth, and invites the congregation on the first day of the new year to praise God's name in all things.

Psalm 67:2-3, 5, 6-8 (LFM)

Verse 2 (NAB) of this psalm recalls the divine blessing of Numbers 6 that we discussed earlier. From there the psalm leads the people in praise of God for God's saving power.

The refrain is a familiar one to Jew and Christian alike. "May the peoples praise you, God; may all the peoples praise you" (vv. 4, 6 NAB). But we praise God for salvation not only of the chosen nation, Israel. Through Israel God blesses "all nations," and "all the ends of the earth revere" God (vv. 3, 8). This universal note echoes throughout the Hebrew and Christian Scriptures, as we have seen in other passages during Advent and Christmas. We do not guard the name of God for ourselves as a personal and private deity. No, those who call upon and worship the name of God do so within the company of the whole human race and all of creation. This God is above all gods, and is the one who makes all "nations be glad and rejoice" (v. 5). On the first day of the year, it will be important to remind the congregation that the God we worship and serve is Lord *every* day of the year for *all* people in all times and all places.

Second Reading
Galatians 4:4-7 (RCL, LFM)

Galatians 4 connects with the day's traditional emphasis upon Mary, the mother of God, because of verse 4: "But when the fullness of time had come, God sent his Son, born of a woman, born under the law." Mary is the woman to whom Jesus is born. Mary and Joseph scrupulously live their lives devoted to the law of Moses (cf. Luke 2:39-51). Since Jesus completes the law of Moses in every way (Matt. 5:17), he redeems the Jews and through them extends God's grace to the Gentiles. We note again, as with Psalm 67, the universal reach of salvation proclaimed here by Paul in his letter to the Galatians. Through the Son, born to Mary the mother, we all become heirs of God.

The preacher might take this passage in a couple of related directions. There is the primary theme of God's adoption of the entire human family. No one gets left out. No one gets thrown off the bus. Since none of us is worthy, broken as we all are by sin, all of us are dependent upon God's searching and forgiving love. Friend and foe, citizen and immigrant, Jew and Gentile, God's love through Jesus Christ covers us all. Mary gives birth to an ordinary child who, as the story unfolds, bears the complete and extraordinary fullness of God. Through that fullness of God, in the fullness of time (v. 4), Jesus reaches out to all the world ("For God so loved the world," John 3:16) to adopt every last one of us into the household of God. As N. T. Wright says, commenting on Luke's Gospel, "When Israel's history comes to its God-ordained goal, then at last light will dawn for the world. All the nations, not just the Jews, will see what God is unveiling—a plan of salvation for all people without distinction."[2] That is the core of the Christian message and the core of our faith. It bears proclaiming on the first and every day of the year.

A related theme could lead to a sermon that focuses upon the human family as an image of the divine family, albeit a flawed one. Our views of family are sometimes too narrow, fixed upon blood relations and ancestry rather than upon our relatedness in God. The truth is that families take many shapes. Some bonds within families can be stronger than blood, based within genuine love, appreciation, and respect. Some families are remarkably open to God's wide-ranging love, even though the members may not all share the same gene pool. Adoptions occur within human families that create bonds every bit as strong and creative as those that exist between blood kin. For example, one family in my own community that already had a seven-year-old son and a five-year-old daughter was going through a legal adoption of their third child, an eleven-year-old son. The eleven-year-old had lived with the family for about a year, and during that time the entire family had forged new bonds with him and each other. When the judge turned to the seven-year-old and asked him what he thought about the adoption, that boy, understandably frightened by the experience, began to cry quietly but managed to say to the judge, "He's my brother. You're not going to take him away, are you?" At our best, our human families reflect the inclusive family of God, the one who adopts us all into the divine household and who would never let anyone take us away.

Philippians 2:5-11 (RCL alt.)

Here at the end of the Christmas season and the beginning of the new year, the lectionary reaches back to pick up Philippians with a slightly different accent than it did in the Second and Third Sundays of Advent. This passage appears as an alternative reading for this Sunday because it also stresses the name of Jesus in verses 9-11.

The passage is memorable among Paul's letters, both for its hymn-like quality (it possibly was used as an early Christian hymn or creed) and for its poetic rendering of the image of Christ as the suffering servant. Born in human likeness, he humbled himself and "became obedient to the point of death—even death on a cross" (v. 8). The words are haunting, especially when we consider that Christ's suffering becomes the means of his glorification (v. 9). The one who was with God becomes fully obedient to humanity, subject to our very own death. *Therefore,* God highly exalts him and gives him "the name that is above every name."

Meditating upon the entire story of "Jesus," we discover the very features that Philippians 2 voices. It is a proclamation of the gospel in succinct form. Paul links his own suffering and that of the Philippians to the suffering of Jesus. Jesus is the one who, being of God, should not suffer but indeed does. Through his suffering with all of humanity, God exalts (raises) him that we should all confess him as Lord.

A sermon rooted in Philippians 2 takes the congregation deep into the soil of the Christian faith and theology. We cannot recite this name lightly or use it sentimentally. Jesus is the "one who saves"; that is what his name means. In how many ways do we yearn for the salvation of Jesus—from our own self-centeredness, our own vanities, greed, exploitation of each other, various kinds of idolatries, the hunger of millions, the violence of war, the injustice of global economics, and the spoiling of the earth? Yes, it will take the suffering love of Jesus, born in human form, to raise us and all of creation to the glory of God. January 1 is a good day to make sure we know the full meaning of that name.

Gospel
Luke 2:15-21 (RCL, LFM)

In the Gospel reading we return one final time to the birth narrative of Jesus. The spotlight shines on Mary, the mother of God, and it shines on the naming of Jesus at his circumcision.

If Protestants are sometimes critical of the Roman Catholic emphasis upon Mary, the reverse criticism could be offered by Roman Catholics toward Protestants for not stressing Mary enough. It is true that Luke's Gospel, like all of the four Gospels, tells the story of Jesus who is Lord, Savior, and Messiah. When we read these Gospels, it is to learn of the primary character—Jesus—and of the movement and character of God through Jesus and the Holy Spirit. Neither Roman Catholic nor Protestant would disagree with this.

But Mary's role is crucial to the story. According to Luke, she is the one who accepts the angelic announcement that she will give birth to the Savior. She is the one who journeys to her kinswoman, Elizabeth, and shares with her the expectation of new birth. She is the one who sings a song of how God is doing a new thing to bring about justice and wholeness in all the earth. And she is the one who journeys with Joseph to Bethlehem after nine long months of waiting to give birth to the Son of God, to place him in a manger where shepherds would know and adore him, and to ponder his birth and future within her mother's heart. At the end of all that, Mary fulfills Jewish law and the angelic prophecy by having him circumcised on the eighth day and naming him Jesus, "the one who saves."

I suppose it would be possible to tell the bare bones of the Christian story without including many of the details regarding Mary and Joseph. But who would want to? We would wind up with a message without the story that gives it meaning in the first place. Even more, we would miss one of Luke's primary theological concerns. Jesus is born to Mary and Joseph in Bethlehem. Shepherds met the mother and saw the infant son. They "oohed" and "aahed" over him and hurried back to tell the good news to others. Mary, exhausted by labor and birth, marveled at what had happened. With all mothers everywhere, she pondered in her heart the miracle that she was looking at, a baby, a son named Jesus.

In a very real sense, up until the birth, and for many years later, everything depends upon Mary and Joseph. She is the chosen vessel of the Lord. She is the mother who will raise the infant to adolescence and then adulthood when he will fully take up his ministry of life, death, and resurrection. The only way to tell this world-altering story of God's incarnate (enfleshed) love is to place a mother and father right in the center of the story along with the child. That holy family mirrors the holy love of God for the whole human family. Seeing them in the story, we see the face of God shining through not just the baby Jesus but through his loving mother and faithful father. The preacher who can bring this holy mother, father, and son to life for the congregation on Sunday will be the preacher who watches the congregation members ponder all these mysteries in their hearts.

Notes

1. J. Clinton McCann Jr., "The Book of Psalms," in *The New Interpreter's Bible*, ed. Leander Keck (Nashville: Abingdon, 1996), 4:711.
2. N. T. Wright, *Luke for Everyone* (London: SPCK, 2001), 26.

Epiphany—Time after Epiphany / Ordinary Time

Joni S. Sancken

We experience Advent as a season of waiting for God to break into our world, a season of darkness moving to light. Christmas joyfully commemorates God's in-breaking and the incarnation of God enshrouded in mystery. These veiled and mysterious seasons build to a glorious triumph in the celebration of Epiphany and the Sundays following, which offer us the brilliance of revelation. Jesus' divine identity as Son of God and Savior is made known among us.[1] Epiphany represents the earliest celebration of the incarnation. In fact, the early church celebrated the birth of Christ on the feast of Epiphany, and the thrust of Advent pushes us toward Epiphany as the liturgical peak of the season. In the midst of busy celebrations surrounding Christmas and the new year, however, our congregations today seldom attend to the theological and liturgical significance of Epiphany and the Sundays that follow.

Unlike the many texts where Jesus' identity is purposely hidden or obscured, the Gospel texts for the time after Epiphany allow us to claim boldly the fullness of revelation, of who Christ is as God among us. Drawing from Matthew and John as well as Luke, in the coming weeks we see explicit signs ranging from cosmic to miraculous, from joyful to threatening. We begin with Epiphany Sunday itself and the visit of the magi in Matthew's Gospel, wise men cosmically drawn to the toddler Jesus by a new star in the heavens and warned in a dream to avoid Herod. This is followed by Luke's rendition of the "theophany" of Jesus' baptism, where a heavenly voice explicitly identifies him as God's Son, and then we hear John's account of Jesus' first miracle at Cana. We return to Luke to hear Jesus' self-revelation as fulfillment of Isaiah's prophecy of good news, liberation, and healing. This is followed the next week by Jesus' rejection and his former friends and neighbors nearly throwing him off a cliff, a blatant sign that Jesus' version of good news will shake up the status quo and that proclamation of God's presence among us will cost Jesus dearly. For those following the Revised Common Lectionary (RCL), the season ends with another fantastic theophany from Luke 9. Jesus, gloriously transfigured and engaging with Moses and Elijah about the coming events in Jerusalem, is announced from heaven as Son of God and Chosen One. The Lectionary for Mass (LFM) focuses on a miraculous catch of fish in Luke 5 that inspires a group of disciples to follow Jesus and become fishers for people. The clarity of Christ's identity and purpose in the texts of Epiphany and Transfiguration serves as theological nourishment and inspiration for the church, living into its calling to be Christ's body in the world as we end the time after Epiphany and turn toward the long journey to the cross in the coming season of Lent.

While we bask in what Scripture reveals to us during the time after Epiphany, the complexity of revelation means that much is still hidden from view. Many texts during this season deal with God's glory. The Hebrew word for glory has "heaviness" or "weightiness" as part of the definition—the weightiness of God's glory reminds us that the full brilliance of God's revelation is too much for us to take in at one time. We proceed with reverence, hope, and trust that the Holy Spirit will continue to make God's presence known to us.

Note

1. Robert E. Webber, *Ancient Future Time: Forming Spirituality through the Christian Year* (Grand Rapids: Baker Books, 2004), 76.

January 6, 2013
Epiphany of Our Lord

There is nothing subtle or private about these texts for Epiphany Sunday. God's glory shines among us in Jesus Christ with vivid signs that move heaven and earth. Isaiah boldly proclaims that God's light and glory have come to Israel; Psalm 72 prays for God to bless a mighty and just king; Ephesians speaks of God's revelation culminating in Christ and of God's good purposes for creation spreading through the church to the Gentiles and "the rulers and authorities in the heavenly places" (3:10); and Matthew tells us of wise men following a star, seeking to pay homage to a new King whose birth shakes the foundations of earthly rulers.

First Reading
Isaiah 60:1-6 (RCL, LFM)

These verses, situated within the third major block of material in the book of Isaiah (also called Third Isaiah), reflect the situation of exiled Israel's return to Jerusalem under the protection of Persia and the challenges of reshaping and restoring the community of faith.[1] While the first chapters of this section of Isaiah, 56–59, tend to address divisions, difficulties, and ethical demands, following the announcement that God will redeem Israel and will never depart (59:16-21), the tenor of chapter 60 is triumphant and confident that God is working out God's salvific purposes and is fulfilling God's good promises to Israel. While God is spoken of in the third person, some scholars classify these poetic verses as an oracle of God—God's words of blessing and hope spoken directly to God's people.[2]

The language of light connects to imagery used earlier in Isaiah: "The people who walked in darkness have seen a great light; those who lived in a land of deep darkness—on them light has shined" (9:2) and "I will turn the darkness before them into light" (42:16). Preachers and liturgists should be careful in their appropriation of light and dark imagery apart from the text itself. Assigning only negative traits to darkness can underscore latent racism against people of color. For Israel, darkness was not a literal darkness but a poet's metaphor for continued experiences of despair and defeat and a longing for a ray of hope to show them the future God promised. To proclaim God's overwhelming glory as light shining in darkness is to confess God's sovereign power as able to overcome every obstacle. God bursts forth as a righteous deliverer, bringing hope and sustenance for people struggling in the midst of a wide range of circumstances.

For Israel, these verses speak of the return of those still in exile and of gifts of material goods that will help restore Israel in visible ways that bear witness to the presence and power of God.[3] Where Israel was formerly under the thumb of powerful empires and required to serve and pay taxes to other nations, God has reversed Israel's fortune. Other nations will be drawn to Israel's buoyant prosperity, bringing lost children home and bearing valuable gifts as tributes and taxes.[4] The specific gifts of gold and frankincense mentioned in verse 6 will spark a connection for listeners with the gifts of the wise men from other nations offering valuable gifts to Jesus in today's Gospel reading.

Psalmody
Psalm 72:1-7, 10-14 (RCL)
Psalm 72:1-2, 7-8, 10-11, 12-13 (LFM)

Psalm 72 serves as an intercession for the king. It envisions a reign lived out in harmony with God's intentions for Israel: justice for the poor, prosperity for all, deliverance to the needy, peace, and respect and honor from other rulers and nations. Those who live under the rule of such a just and righteous king will enjoy peace, protection, and deliverance in times of need. For Israel, a just and righteous earthly king served as intercessor at times and direct advocate for the people before God. A righteous king was a tangible link and witness to God's own righteousness and justice. Interestingly, portions of today's psalm are also read for the second week of Advent in Year A. The theme of promise and fulfillment is present in both seasons of Advent and Epiphany, with Advent emphasizing the desire for God's promised arrival and Epiphany celebrating God's glorious presence and promises fulfilled.

Second Reading
Ephesians 3:1-12 (RCL)
Ephesians 3:2-3a, 5-6 (LFM)

This text from Ephesians continues the themes of revelation and God's glorious provision. The blessing that begins Ephesians sets a theological tone, emphasizing

God's gracious actions as prior to human response, a theme that is carried through the whole letter.[5] Along with a focus on God as central actor in human history and humanity's call to respond as members of Christ's body the church, there is a sense of eschatological in-breaking here, of mystery giving way to revelation, part of God's plan for the "fullness of time, to gather up all things in him, things in heaven and things on earth" (1:9-10). These themes come to the fore in today's lections from chapter 3.

While Ephesians was likely not written by Paul, having significant language differences from his other letters, and may not have served as a true letter addressing a specific context or congregation, chapter 3 begins with a reference to Paul's work among Gentiles that has led to imprisonment and suffering. Verse 2, which starts the LFM selection, implies that the audience might not be completely familiar with Paul's work and ministry.[6]

Nevertheless, the Gentile audience toward whom Ephesians is directed is graciously taken up into God's unfolding revelation. The RCL treats a larger portion of chapter 3, addressing Paul's work as a central figure or "guide" in the midst of this unfolding revelation through his calling and role as servant within God's plan, which includes the church—made up of diverse peoples, Jew and Gentile.[7]

Part of the calling of the church is to participate in God's revelation by bearing witness to the "rich variety" present in the wisdom of God before the powers and authorities on a cosmic scale.[8] Quite a fantastic and inspiring destiny for the church! In spite of our weaknesses and shortcomings, this witness is made possible as a continuation of the work of Christ through whom we have access to God. The tension between diversity of witness and unity of calling as members of Christ's one body will continue into chapter 4. Interestingly, the RCL selection ends at 3:12, but verse 13 nicely wraps up the pericope with symmetry, drawing us back to verse 1, picking up on the mysterious and sometimes troubling connection between suffering and glory—a common theme in Pauline epistles and a strong impulse in the epistolary reading for Transfiguration Sunday, which ends this time after Epiphany and prepares us for Lent.

Gospel
Matthew 2:1-12 (RCL, LFM)

Matthew's Gospel gives us our only access to the story of what tradition calls the "three wise men" or "three kings" who followed a star, carrying gifts from a great distance to offer to a newly born king. These gifts offered to Jesus as well as Jesus himself, as gift from God, lie at the roots of Christian gift giving during the Christmas season. The term *magi* is connected to the Greek root and could also be translated as "astrologers."[9] While the text does not tell us how many wise men visited Jesus, the three gifts given led to the inclusion of three figures in our nativity scenes and Christmas pageants. These same manger scenes and pageants falsely distort Matthew's timetable by having all the players—shepherds, angels, the holy family, and the wise men—show up at the same time. The fields of astrology (finding relationships between human activities and the stars) and astronomy (study of the stars) were linked in the ancient world.[10] The wise men noticed the star around the time of Christ's birth, began tracking it, and first arrived in Bethlehem some months after Jesus' birth, making Jesus more of a toddler than an infant in swaddling clothes. At the time of the writing of the Gospel, cosmic events were often seen as accompanying the birth of a powerful leader, but Matthew's account of Jesus' birth causing a new star to rise also picks up on a prophecy from Numbers 24:17, "A star shall come out of Jacob, and a scepter shall rise out of Israel."[11]

Matthew's Gospel is a rich theological feast, and today's verses are no exception. The Epiphany doctrinal emphases of God's glory and revelation radiate from today's verses from Matthew 2. The birth of the infant Christ has moved the cosmos and inspired wise people from a distant land to pay homage. However, what may appear obvious to outsiders can confound those close at hand. The wise men were not Jewish themselves, yet they recognized God's power made manifest in Jesus Christ.[12] In fact, they enact the promise of Isaiah 60:3, "Nations shall come to your light, and kings to the brightness of your dawn." The brightness of unveiled revelation is most evident after the veil is drawn again. This tension between those who recognize Jesus for who he is and those who do not recognize or understand him accompanies the entire Christ event. The word used for paying homage to Christ by the wise men in chapter 2 is the same word that will be used at the end of Matthew in chapter 28 for the disciples worshiping the risen Christ. Indeed, even in the final scene of Christ's earthly ministry when the disciples are commissioned, Matthew tells us that some worshiped (paid homage) and some doubted (28:17). The magi introduce revelation on many levels. God's power is manifest in nature through the star they followed to Jerusalem that subsequently led them to Jesus (2:1-2, 9-10). God is revealed in the Jewish scriptural tradition, interpreted for Herod by scribes and priests that led them to Bethlehem—the city of messianic hope (2:4-5). Finally, God is revealed in the person of Christ (2:11). Bearing witness to the confounding tension of God's incarnation, the magi pay homage to Christ who is both a vulnerable toddler and a king.

While government officials and religious leaders do not join the wise men in bowing before Christ, his birth not only affects the cosmos but also shakes the foundations of seats of power. The text tells us that Herod and all of Jerusalem were frightened when the magi arrived looking for "the child born king of the Jews." Herod's reaction to the news of a new king is contrasted to the behavior of the magi. While the magi seek Jesus to worship him, Herod and his soldiers seek Jesus to kill him. Herod was a leader desperate to retain his throne, and it is likely that when Herod was not at peace, the whole of Jerusalem could not be at peace. Herod killed three of his own sons to prevent any threat to his own power.[13] When the visiting astronomers arrive inquiring after the birth of a new king, Herod calls together Jewish leaders, priests, and scribes who draw on Micah to name Bethlehem as the probable location of nativity. This first meeting of civic and church leaders to discuss Jesus so early in his life foreshadows later meetings, just as Herod's deadly course of action foreshadows the deadly force that will be used to eliminate Jesus. Herod probes the wise men for more information, asking them when they first saw the star before sending them on their way to Bethlehem. From Herod's subsequent massacre of all children ages two and under, we can presume that they had been following the star for more than a year. Rather than seeking Jesus for himself, Herod seeks to link his own deadly intentions to the magi's search, requesting that they send word so that he, too, might pay homage to the child. Of course, we know that Herod has no intention of honoring the child since he later commits mass murder out of fear that this child might threaten his throne.

The magi continue their journey no more than a couple of hours south of Jerusalem to the small town of Bethlehem, following the star to Jesus' precise location where they were "overwhelmed with joy." While Luke takes great pains to portray Mary and Joseph as visitors to Bethlehem, in Matthew they appear to have settled down and set up house. The magi enter the home where they find Jesus and Mary. They immediately acknowledge Jesus as a king, kneeling to pay homage and offering valuable gifts: gold, frankincense, and myrrh. This episode ends with the magi traveling home by another way after a dream warned them not to return to Herod.

Beyond today's texts, Matthew's narrative in chapter 2 picks up in excitement. A divinely inspired dream warns Joseph of Herod's violent intentions toward Jesus and commands him to relocate his family to Egypt, where they remain until Herod's death. In the meantime, when Herod discovers that the magi have not cooperated with his plans, he goes on a violent rampage, killing all children ages two and younger in and around Bethlehem. Commentator Dale Bruner notes an interesting symmetry in Matthew's account of Jesus' life: "For Jesus to live now, innocent children must die; for all to live hereafter, an innocent Jesus must die."[14]

The Text in Our World

God's gift of revelation causes upheaval; whether this upheaval is experienced as death throes or birth pangs is a matter of perspective. While the birth of an ordinary baby is bound to turn life upside down and forge new routines in a household, the birth of God incarnate promises to turn the whole world upside down and forge a new reality. As Christians, we are called to live boldly into this revelation, experiencing each season of the liturgical year in light of Christ's life, death, and resurrection even while we painfully long for the full realization of God's good intentions for the world. In the Gospel reading, we see the best and worst of human nature spring forth in response to God's gift of revelation. The magi's acceptance and openness to God's revelation lead to joy and worship as they are inspired to offer their best and most valuable gifts to Jesus. This same revelation hurls Herod into frightened tumult. Rather than accept the revelation, Herod's rejection leads to anger and the violent massacre of every infant in and around Bethlehem.

The biblical Herod is long dead, but Herod-like tendencies continue to live in us when fear and hostility turn us away from Christ.[15] It is a challenge to preach into an increasingly polarized political and cultural environment. As 2013 turns over and a presidential inauguration looms on the horizon, today's texts push us from the comfort of private religion to remind us of the challenges of responding to revelation and the costs of allegiance in the public sphere. While civil unrest is not a significant danger during government transition in the United States, many places in the world do not enjoy this safety. The magi likely came from present-day Iraq, a nation where government instability has been more norm than anomaly in recent years.

Receiving God's revelation with joy and self-giving rather than resistance is the work of our lives and is only possible through God's grace and power. We do not know what happened to the magi after their encounter with Christ, only that they returned home by another road. This new road may have led to other new directions in the lives of these "wise men." God's revelation is also at work in our lives, congregations, and world. It is unlimited in scope and means, but also completely out of our hands. God controls revelation. It is countercultural to surrender authority over our own lives to God—to recognize a higher allegiance that may come with personal and social costs. As congregations embark on this time after Epiphany, preachers should seek to highlight where God's revelation may be at work both in the text and in our communities and neighborhoods, challenging us to follow God's leading, offer our greatest gifts, and travel a new and different road.

Notes

1. Walter Brueggemann, *Isaiah 40–66*, Westminster Bible Companion (Louisville: Westminster John Knox, 1998), 3–4, 164–65.
2. Ibid., 203.
3. Paul D. Hanson, *Isaiah 40–66*, Interpretation: A Bible Commentary for Teaching and Preaching (Louisville: John Knox, 1995), 221; Brueggemann, *Isaiah 40–66*, 203.
4. Brueggemann, *Isaiah 40–66*, 203.
5. Sze-kat Wan, "Ephesians," in *Theological Bible Commentary,* ed. Gail R. O'Day and David L. Petersen (Louisville: Westminster John Knox, 2009), 408.
6. If Paul is no longer living and a follower of Paul has written Ephesians, the audience might be familiar with Paul's other letters but not directly with his work.
7. Thomas Yoder Neufeld, *Ephesians*, Believers Church Bible Commentary (Scottdale, Pa.: Herald, 2002), 140. Letty Russell refers to Paul as a "housekeeper" in God's household (idem, 141). See also Letty Russell, *Imitators of God: A Study Book on Ephesians* (New York: Mission Education and Cultivation Program Dept., General Board of Global Ministries, 1984), 57.
8. Letty Russell helpfully situates our role as assisting with divine "housekeeping chores"; Russell, *Imitators of God*, 59. See also Neufeld, *Ephesians*, 145.
9. Arguably, "astrologers," "astronomers," or "magicians" might be viewed as a less positive translation than "wise men." According to Dale Bruner, Jewish tradition would have viewed astronomy or astrology as competing with one's allegiance to God, a form of idolatry. In fact, every other New Testament reference to "magi" is negative. However, in this case God uses the

magi's fascination with and study of the stars to draw them to Christ—a further testimony to God's power. Dale Bruner, *Matthew, A Commentary,* vol. 1, *The Christbook: Matthew: 1–12* (Grand Rapids: Eerdmans, 2004), 58–60.

10. Ibid., 57.
11. Richard B. Gardner, *Matthew,* Believers Church Bible Commentary (Scottdale, Pa.: Herald, 1991), 44–45.
12. Matthew has already included Gentiles in God's plan in his genealogy—the magi continue this spirit of inclusion.
13. Bruner, *Matthew*, 65.
14. Ibid., 71.
15. Ibid.

January 13, 2013
Baptism of Our Lord / First Sunday after Epiphany / First Sunday in Ordinary Time

Revised Common Lectionary (RCL)	**Lectionary for Mass (LFM)**
Isaiah 43:1-7	Isaiah 40:1-5, 9-11
Psalm 29	Psalm 104:1b-2, 3-4, 24-25, 27-28, 29b-30
Acts 8:14-17	Titus 2:11-14; 3:4-7
Luke 3:15-17, 21-22	Luke 3:15-16, 21-22

Wouldn't it be great if every divine encounter could be as clear as Jesus' baptism recounted by Luke, when the Holy Spirit descends upon Christ in the bodily form of a dove accompanied by a heavenly voice proclaiming Jesus' identity as beloved Son of God? Of course, more often this side of eternity we join faithful believers from Scripture up to today who must make do with ambiguity, trusting God that what we see reflected dimly, we will one day know face to face. In the time after Epiphany we celebrate and bear witness to those occasions when God's revelation is made known to us with absolute clarity, when we cannot turn away from the brightness of God's glory. Today's texts bear witness to God's power and glory culminating in divine revelation following Jesus' baptism. For the RCL, the psalm and the first and second readings draw on water or baptismal imagery to highlight God's power and glory. The LFM texts highlight God's provision for God's people and the hope that God's promises are being fulfilled.

First Reading
Isaiah 43:1-7 (RCL)
Isaiah 40:1-5, 9-11 (LFM)

The RCL text from Isaiah 43 offers a powerful testimony to God's promise to act in the midst of history out of love on behalf of God's people. Read in the context of Epiphany and paired with Jesus' baptism, these verses show the connection between God's love, which drives God to act in human history, and God's glory. They are firmly rooted in the second section of Isaiah (also known as Second Isaiah), which was written during Israel's destruction and exile at the hands of the Babylonian Empire, on the cusp of Persia's divinely granted defeat of Babylon and promised freedom for scattered Jews to return home and begin to rebuild. God has preserved Israel during exile and will now intervene on Israel's behalf. Today's passage draws from the beginning of chapter 43, a long chapter that proclaims God's sovereign power which both created the world and takes charge of events unfolding in history. God's power is righteous and will not be mocked by idolatry, Israel's or Babylon's.

While chapter 42 ends by recounting Israel's sin and disobedient disregard for God, the first verses of 43 take on God's voice in a way that is both powerfully steadfast and profoundly tender. Despite Israel's inability to maintain proper relationship to God, God is relentlessly committed to Israel. Twice in these verses God's oracle tells the people not to fear (vv. 1, 5). The God who created and called Israel has also redeemed Israel and promises never to depart. While descriptions of God's presence accompanying them through water and fire likely referred to God staying with them through ordeals, Christians rightly draw connections to baptism where, upon our passing through water, God claims and names us as God's own. Here some may also hear echoes of sixteenth-century Anabaptist martyrdom where believers were drowned or burned at the stake for practices that threatened Christian orthodoxy and civil authorities.

Verse 3 marks a shift from personal metaphorical language to attend to geopolitical realities. The language speaks of prisoner exchanges and the cost of gathering Israel together again.[1] God loves Israel so much that God will trade peoples and nations to restore God's people. For Christians, we can see connections to God's actions here and God's ultimate offering of God's self as a ransom for others (Mark 10:45).[2] God gathers all of God's children, sons and daughters from every corner of the earth. God acts out of love. And this loving power ultimately brings glory to God alone.

The reading from the LFM comes from Isaiah 40, a passage that we usually associate with Advent. These verses serve as the source of John the Baptist's own prophecy, the background of Jesus' baptism. Chapter 40 poetically marks the transition from the first section of Isaiah written before exile to the second section that anticipates liberation and homecoming. The gap between chapters 39 and 40 is long, around 160 years, during which Israel is decimated by the Babylonian Empire— it is with this backdrop in mind that we receive the promises of Isaiah 40.[3] God's deliverance is not cheap or easy—Israel has suffered consequences. God's people have paid for their sin and shall be comforted; God is on the move in powerful ways— mountains will be made low and valleys lifted up. "Then the glory of the LORD shall be revealed, and all people shall see it together" (v. 5). The lectionary skips the protest of the prophet called to proclaim the message and picks up again at verse 9, which offers glorious testimony to the presence and power of God. After the experience of exile and loss, verses 10-11 speak of God's presence both in power and in intimate tenderness. The God who comes in "might" will also feed, gather, and gently carry God's "flock," Israel.

Cast into the context of Jesus' baptism, as Christians we can more fully enliven and expand God's character as portrayed by Isaiah with the character of Jesus Christ, God's beloved Son.

Psalmody
Psalm 29 (RCL)
Psalm 104:1b-2, 3-4, 24-25, 27-28, 29b-30 (LFM)

The psalms for the RCL and LFM both offer doxological praise for God's grandeur and majesty revealed to us in nature. Both draw on water imagery, offering a connecting point for Jesus' baptism in the Gospel reading. Psalm 29 is an ancient hymn, perhaps one of the earliest psalms; here we get a glimpse of the weightiness of God's glory.[4] God's glory is connected with a power and terrible dignity that rise as a storm in the metaphorical language of the psalmist. God's glory is manifested in the heavens and on earth, thundering over the waters and moving ashore where it pounds the land, toppling trees, flashing with fire, and rising with floodwaters. God makes the divine presence known in acts of nature, but God is envisioned as enthroned over nature—God is in charge here—indeed, even the wind and rain bend to the divine will and bring glory to God. The psalm reaches its climax in verse 9 when upon seeing the power of God manifested in the storm, the people in the temple cry out, "Glory." A sense of glory, weighty and heavy, rightly accompanies such language.

Those who have lived through a hurricane or terrible storm can understand firsthand the power of destruction that nature can bring upon us. Even those who have not experienced such a storm will remember vivid pictures of New Orleans after Hurricane Katrina. For those who have experienced disorientation and loss of control due to disasters of any kind, the psalmist reminds us that even in the most terrible moments, God is not absent from the storm. God's glory is revealed to us in natural events on earth. We cannot fully understand God's glory, but we can join the psalmist, who, marveling at the power and presence of God, cries out to this God of glory, "May the LORD give strength to his people! May the LORD bless his people with peace!" (29:11).

Psalm 104 is similar to Psalm 29 in bearing witness to God's regal power and strength with images that come from the world around us.[5] The first verses describe the power of God as a divine king, moving from radiant glory—"You are . . . robed in light as with a cloak" (vv. 1-2 NAB)—to God's actions as divine ruler riding in chariots of cloud and attended to by the winds and fire. The lectionary skips over the psalmist's continued metaphorical connections between God and nature and picks up again at verse 24, which marvels at God's care and provision for the creatures of the earth—their life and death and ours lie in God's hand. The rhythms of nature, life, and death are the work of God and reveal God's majesty and sovereignty to us.

Psalm 104's attention to creation as witness to God's power and glory offers abiding testimony to the importance of environmental preservation and caring for our planet.

Second Reading
Acts 8:14-17 (RCL)
Titus 2:11-14; 3:4-7 (LFM)

The RCL reading from Acts offers a brief episode of believers in Samaria accepting God's word and receiving the Holy Spirit after the apostles Peter and John laid hands upon them and prayed for them.[6] This pericope occurs amid a larger story about the spreading of the gospel in Samaria through the work and proclamation of Philip. Powerful preaching and works of power led to baptisms, and the gift of the Holy Spirit followed. Interestingly, one of the figures touched by Philip in the story is Simon, who practiced magic and is moved to baptism after seeing evidence of great power through the signs and miracles. Following the episode in today's text where the believers receive the Holy Spirit after the disciples lay hands on them, Simon offers to pay to have the disciples lay hands on him so that he, too, may receive the gift of the Spirit.[7] The disciples explain that he has not understood and fully received the life-changing nature of the gospel; his heart has not been fully changed. The balance between misunderstanding and belief reflected in this larger story within Acts 8 reflects our own experience with God's revelation in our lives. Conversion is a process of which baptism is only one step; initiation into what it means to follow Christ is a lifelong process that affects every part of our lives and grounds our future hope.

The LFM reading from Titus is also a text used for Christmas—linking Christ's birth to the beginning of Christ's earthly ministry. Jesus Christ is grace incarnate, indeed, offering salvation to all (2:11). Here, God's revelation is immediately followed by our response. It is impossible to remain untouched or unengaged in the midst of God's revelation—we are moved to renounce our former lives and broken patterns and to live upright and holy lives that bear witness to our status as Christ's own people (vv. 12-14). The verses from chapter 3 make it clear that our salvation is through Christ rather than our own actions, referencing the waters of baptism and outpouring of the Spirit, linking our own initiation into Christ with Jesus' own baptism.

Gospel
Luke 3:15-17, 21-22 (RCL)
Luke 3:15-16, 21-22 (LFM)

Today's Gospel reading from Luke picks up in the midst of John the Baptist's fiery sermon and then moves to the actual baptism of Jesus. John mentions fire three times in his sermon, twice in the RCL verses for today. The start of chapter 3 establishes John as a prophet—one who received a word from God for a particular time and people. The listing of specific rulers helps to situate Jesus' baptism and the start of his ministry around 25 to 30 CE.[8] While we heard the earlier verses from this chapter during the season of Advent, following our seasonal doctrinal emphasis on revelation, today's verses from John's sermon address confusion on the part of believers as to whether John might be the Messiah and then offer an account of Jesus' baptism that leaves no doubt as to who he is.

Luke situates John's witness concerning the coming Messiah as a direct response to the crowd's expectation and internal questioning. John offers a kind of revelation, contrasting himself sharply with the true Messiah. While John baptizes with water, the Messiah will baptize with the Holy Spirit and fire—this indeed will happen in Luke's second volume, the book of Acts. John also qualifies the righteousness of the Messiah—one who is so holy we dare not untie his sandals, and one who stands in judgment—who will ultimately separate wheat from chaff, gathering the wheat and burning the chaff away. John's preaching has a refreshing edge. Things will not continue as they are forever; actions have consequences. The chaff in our lives will not be around forever. Jesus Christ ultimately will burn away those things and behaviors that drag us down and come between us and God. The gospel can sometimes sound like bad news initially; it pulls us up short—God loves us too much to let us continue in behaviors that ultimately suck life from our souls. The lectionary skips verses 19-20, which conclude the section about John the Baptist, describing his imprisonment before turning to focus on Jesus as the central figure.

Mark and Matthew situate Jesus' baptism as a special separate case. Matthew goes so far as to have John acknowledge Jesus' power and protest his role as baptizer. Luke, however, situates Jesus' baptism in the midst of mass baptisms. While Mark and Matthew have the Spirit of God descend in the moment of baptism when Jesus comes out of the water, Luke describes the Spirit's descent as being in response to Jesus' praying. For Luke, divine revelation often follows prayer, as it did for Anna (2:37-38) and Zechariah (1:10-13).[9] The theophany that accompanies Jesus' baptism and prayer unfolds with three events: opening of the heavens, descent of the Spirit, and verbal declaration from heaven. While Mark and Matthew portray these events as visible to Jesus alone, Luke has them occur as a public event, although God's identifying statement, "You are my Son, the Beloved . . . ," is addressed directly to Jesus.[10]

The first sign of God's divine presence after Jesus' baptism is the "opening of heaven." In Luke's time people would have understood the heavens as more fixed and solid than people today, so having heaven break open is to have a barrier that separates divine and human momentarily ajar.[11] This sudden rupture between the realm of humans and the realm of God is echoed later at the moment of Jesus' death on the cross when the skies darken and the temple veil is torn in two (23:45). These brief encounters with God's power remind us of the relationship between creatures and Creator. They are the stuff of revelation, fleeting glimpses just beyond our reach and understanding. We can picture those who witnessed this rending of the heavens responding with terror or holy awe.[12]

After Jesus' baptism, the Holy Spirit descends upon Jesus "in bodily form like a dove."[13] Unlike Matthew and Mark, Luke specifically mentions the "bodily" nature of the Spirit. The Holy Spirit is a key actor and bearer of divine revelation throughout

Luke and Acts, already active to this point: resting upon John even before his birth (1:15), as the agent of divine conception for Jesus (1:35), present with Elizabeth during her pregnancy with John (1:41), guiding Simeon (2:25-27), and foretold by John as a sign of the baptism offered by the Christ earlier in today's texts (3:16).[14] The Spirit continues to be a significant force and presence from the moment of Jesus' conception all the way through Pentecost (Acts 2:1-4) and throughout the book of Acts. While Luke has already told us that Jesus was conceived by the Holy Spirit, Jesus is filled with the Spirit's power at this moment and empowered for his ministry.[15] In fact, in chapter 4 Jesus himself will announce his ministry with reference to the Spirit while teaching in the synagogue in Nazareth (4:18).

The final element is the voice from heaven: "You are my son, the Beloved, with you I am well pleased." Scholars note scriptural allusions to Psalm 2:7 and Isaiah 42:1, whereby the royal coronation tradition of Psalm 2 is blended with the "servant" focus of Isaiah 42.[16] However, any scriptural allusions are certainly in the background of the scene while the fantastic nature of the scene itself takes precedence; God has verbally affirmed a special relationship with Jesus and illustrated faith and certainty in the person of Jesus.[17] This deep affirmation, coupled with the gift of the Spirit, binds Jesus to God's will—Jesus' mission is God's mission. Although the devil will soon tempt Jesus with another calling, God's mission and the Spirit's anointing are the ones Jesus claims fully and completely. This is the mission about which Jesus speaks using Isaiah's words in chapter 4, "The Spirit of the Lord is upon me, because he has anointed me to bring good news to the poor. He has sent me to proclaim release to the captives and recovery of sight to the blind, to let the oppressed go free, to proclaim the year of the Lord's favor" (4:18-19). The scriptural allusions in God's declaration blend servant and royal traditions, offering a revelatory hint of the fullness of Jesus' identity. Nevertheless, Jesus' life will be primarily marked by the role of servant. The baptism and mission undertaken by Jesus will ultimately lead him to the cross. Only after his resurrection and ascension is Jesus fully enthroned at the right hand of God.

The Text in Our World

As we explore Jesus' baptism and entrance into God's divine mission, it is fitting to reflect on our own baptism and connection to God's mission in the world. The new birth offered to us in baptism is a kind of revelation—the gift of life that frees us from the bondage of death. Baptism changes us—we are claimed by God so that even in the midst of storms such as those described by the psalmist, we still experience God's presence and cry, "Glory." When we remember our baptism, we claim again the promises of God's future as envisioned by Isaiah. Despite these deep spiritual realities, many of us still struggle to connect our daily "nonstormy" lives with what we profess and believe as we remember our baptism. As with Christ, our primary calling is to serve others rather than reign over them. Our baptism and calling to discipleship offer us ongoing self-revelation. Through the power of God, we can direct our daily activities and lives through God's call to servanthood, bringing good news, liberation, healing, and hope to others. Not only ourselves but every aspect of our lives must pass through the waters of baptism and be claimed by God and repurposed for God's realm. It may seem easier for some listeners than others to envision their daily labors as service to God. However, any life can be claimed and used by God. While in seminary, I interned at St. James United Methodist Church where the pastor, Rev. Emmanuel Cleaver, also served as mayor of Kansas City and currently serves as a representative in the U.S. Congress. While news reports are frequently full of less than ethical behavior by officials in Washington, Rev. Cleaver continues to allow his baptismal identity and pastoral calling to affect his votes and actions as a representative. In 2010, Rev. Cleaver was barely reelected. For a congressional representative, it is a challenge to balance making ethical and Christian choices with representing and advocating for the people of one's district. Regardless of our vocation, following Christ is never easy. Whether we are retired and seeking to support extended family, providing care for young children at home, or serving as a bus driver or a high school teacher, as it did for Christ, our baptismal calling comes with a cost. Following Jesus this side of the eschaton means our lives are also marked by the cross. Because our baptism is truly a baptism into Christ, however, we are baptized not only into his death but into his resurrection. And like Christ, we, too, are gifted with the presence of the Spirit to guide and sustain us.

Notes

1. Walter Brueggemann, *Isaiah 40–66*, Westminster Bible Companion (Louisville: Westminster John Knox, 1998), 53.
2. Ibid., 54.
3. Ibid., 8.
4. Psalm 29 may show signs of appropriation of a Caananite hymn for Yahweh worship. James H. Waltner, *Psalms*, Believers Church Bible Commentary (Scottdale, Pa.: Herald, 2006), 155.
5. Selections from this psalm are also used during Pentecost.
6. Luke Timothy Johnson notes that the visit by disciples Peter and John in a sense also blesses and legitimizes the mission to Samaria from the standpoint of Jerusalem leadership. See Johnson, *The Acts of the Apostles*, Sacra Pagina, ed. Daniel J. Harrington, S.J. (Collegeville, Minn.: Liturgical, 1992), 4:148.
7. The Greek root of the word for magic is the same as the root for the magi or "wise men."
8. Sharon Ringe, *Luke*, Westminster Bible Companion (Louisville: Westminster John Knox, 1995), 49.
9. Ibid., 54.
10. Ibid.
11. Ibid.
12. Ibid.
13. Wind and fire are common images for the Holy Spirit as evidenced in the previous verses (3:16) and in the coming of the Spirit in Acts, but Ringe notes that the dove was likely already a common symbol of the Spirit for the church by the time of Luke's Gospel; ibid., 55.
14. Ibid.
15. Robert C. Tannehill, *Luke*, Abingdon New Testament Commentaries (Nashville: Abingdon, 1996), 84.
16. Ringe, *Luke*, 55; Tannehill, *Luke*, 85.
17. Tannehill, *Luke*, 85.

January 20, 2013
Second Sunday after Epiphany / Second Sunday in Ordinary Time

Jesus is on the move; God incarnate is among us! This season of revelation and manifestations of God's glory continues with images of God's glory and justice for restored Israel in Isaiah, psalmists' tributes to God's absolute goodness and power, the Holy Spirit's showering of diverse gifts upon the church, and Jesus' gift of a joyful first miracle in the Gospel of John. The emphasis on incarnation, so crucial to John's theology, allows us to see revelation intimately. God can only be known through Jesus Christ, God-in-flesh, who lives among us full of grace and truth.[1] Thus Jesus himself, his words and actions, his life, death, and resurrection, is God's revelation among us. Jesus changes everything for the world, and through his first miracle in Cana we begin to see characteristics of God's eschatological vision for the world emerging incrementally in the midst of old creation.

First Reading
Isaiah 62:1-5 (RCL, LFM)

Drawn from the third block of material in Isaiah, during Israel's return to Jerusalem, these verses continue the sense that God's promises rendered earlier in the book of Isaiah are indeed coming true, despite present suffering and struggle. These verses connect powerfully as God's promises are communicated through Yahweh's direct address. The prophetic oracle begins by saying that Yahweh will no longer keep silent. For a people who have experienced exile and God's absence, followed by significant challenges as they seek to reestablish themselves and the temple after their return from Babylon, God's voice finally breaks forth and the glorious images of brightness and light shine forth again as God's glory is reflected on God's people.[2]

The promise of justice envisioned in these verses is timely for those struggling to rebuild Israel just as it is for the church today. For ancient Israel, the earlier vision of "God's new thing" (Isa. 43:19) has begun to feel like a dim memory—an unlikely dream drowned out by the realities of hard work, scarcity, the slow return of their scattered families and broader communities, and the failure to rebuild the temple.[3] The church today struggles with many of the same doubts and struggles. A couple of millennia into the age of the church, it is hard to imagine that God's vision for creation will ultimately prevail and that finally God's will shall be done on earth as it is in heaven. Church membership and attendance in North America are declining, but North American churches still control most of the wealth and resources for the broader church. Imbalanced resources coupled with theological and contextual differences have caused fissures in relationships with the majority of Christians who live in the global South. Like the returned exiles, we, too, wonder, "Where is God?" "Why is God keeping silent?" The verses immediately following our lection speak of sentinels on the walls of Jerusalem, of the prayers of insistent believers reminding God without pause or rest until they get an answer, until God acts (Isa. 62:6-7).

God's voice echoes through these verses with a promise for us, too: "I will not rest, I will not keep silent." God reveals God's self as engaged with human affairs and human concerns. "You will no longer be termed Forsaken, and your land shall no more be termed Desolate" (v. 4). Where toil has not yielded any gain and where people have experienced loss and separation, God promises fruitful harvest and deep connection—such as between a bride and groom. God's new creation is still dawning among us—such a powerful word offers hope for the church today.

Psalmody
Psalm 36:5-10 (RCL)
Psalm 96:1-2a, 2b-3, 7-8, 9-10 (LFM)

Today's verses from Psalm 36 praising God's steadfast love that shines forth provide sharp contrast to the portrayal of the "wicked" in verses 1-4. The narrow vision of the wicked turns inward, as they promote themselves and turn away from God. The wicked one follows a perilous downward path that leads toward evil. The hymn to God's goodness starting in verse 5 takes on a different tone—where the wicked one has a narrow vision and follows a downward path, God's steadfast goodness is expansive; the imagery of the psalm draws our eyes upward and beyond the limits of human engagement. God's love extends to the heavens. God's righteousness is like mighty mountains. God takes charge of all of creation and people are invited to take refuge beneath the "wings" of God. God provides for the needs of God's people, offering them abundant feasts and life-giving drink. Such an image echoes John's account of Jesus' miracle at the wedding feast when water is turned to wine in Cana. Verse 10 begins a prayerful petition for God's continued presence and care. The psalmist desires to live in dependence upon God—not to turn toward the destructive path of total self-sufficiency. A life fueled completely on our own energies does not match God's vision for full life. When we rely only on ourselves, the wine tends to "run out" and we are left with empty jars, disappointment, and thirst for something miraculous and trustworthy. The steadfastness of God in this psalm is the same steadfastness exemplified in the person of Jesus Christ, who not only was content to rule in the heavens and from the depths and heights of mighty mountains, but also desired to draw near to people and to take the fullness of human existence, suffering, and death into the life of God so that it, too, might be fully redeemed and bear the signs of God's everlasting steadfast love.

Psalm 96 offers glorious praise to God's sovereignty and glory and sets humanity's calling firmly within the realm of witness. Numbered among what scholars call "enthronement psalms," Psalm 96 was likely a hymn used in corporate worship celebrating God's reign.[4] Praise hymns follow a specific format where invitations to praise God are accompanied by reasons why we offer this praise.[5] Today's lection focuses on the invitation parts of the hymn, each verse beginning with an imperative verb inviting "all the earth" to sing, declare, ascribe glory, worship, and say. Not only is the whole earth called to bear witness to God's glory and power, but they are called to do so amid the nations. While the direct context for this psalm might be worship in the temple, the witness is clearly directed outward—this is public worship among the nations. Too often we limit the scope of our own worship; we forget its public nature. Worship is an act of public witness performed "before a watching world."[6] In worship we perform a "counterliturgy," which often feels out of step with other liturgies that guide our lives—liturgies of consumerism, nationalism, productivity, and self-centeredness. In worship, we join ancient Israel in declaring before the nations that "the LORD is king." In time after Epiphany when we celebrate God's glorious revelation in Jesus Christ, we are invited to respond to God with outward witness, both in corporate worship and in our day-to-day lives.

Second Reading
1 Corinthians 12:1-11 (RCL)
1 Corinthians 12:4-11 (LFM)

In the context of conflict at Corinth, amid discussion of specific controversies, Paul attends to matters of community worship and anchors spiritual revelation firmly in the work of God through the Holy Spirit. Some in the congregation have viewed themselves as having special wisdom, and Paul's repeated use of the cross earlier in the letter serves to anchor wisdom in the physical life and death of Jesus Christ. The focus on physicality continues through the letter, appearing here in discussions of the physical manifestations of gifts of the Spirit—moving eventually to the metaphor likening members of the church to members of a physical body.

In chapter 12, Paul speaks into a situation where some members of the community are focused on the spiritual gift of speaking in tongues and have elevated their own gifts to such a stature that they no longer feel dependent on other members of the community, on Paul's leadership, and perhaps even on God. Verses 1-4, which are included in the RCL reading, serve as a preface where Paul writes about discerning among the spirits and spiritual gifts, recognizing that proclamation of Christ's lordship is inspired only by God through the power of the Holy Spirit—but the simplicity and frequency of such a basic proclamation also illustrate how the Spirit has gifted every professing Christian in the congregation. Indeed, revelation is a gift from God, but it is a gift given freely; God's revelation is not limited to those with status and specialized knowledge. God's revelation is also not limited to Israel. Verse 2 highlights the "pagan" or non-Jewish background of some members.[7] As chapter 12 proceeds, Paul carefully ties a variety of gifts to God—spiritual gifts are as diverse as the members of the church, and all the gifts work together for the common good. The diversity of gifts mentioned in verses 4-11 serves as a helpful reminder for congregations today that still struggle to affirm a variety of ways of being within the body of Christ. As these wonderful and diverse gifts are all given by the same Holy Spirit, diversity must be part of God's intention for the church. The fact that these gifts fall evenly on the church—without favoring only wealthy or powerful members—continues to confound the wisdom of the world. As denominations today fracture over a variety of social and political issues, it is tempting to feel as though life would be easier and congregations might be better able to serve faithfully if like could group with like, that is, without those who oppose our views.

Allowing God's Spirit to call us beyond our differences is a profoundly countercultural move in a politically polarized nation. Bill Bishop and Robert Cushing's 2008 book, *The Big Sort,* continues to portray accurately a nation where like clusters with like, where children are seldom exposed to ideas not supported by their parents, and where neighbors all support the same political figures.[8] The result of this sorting is that people struggle to understand those who hold different beliefs because they have not met them or had a chance to engage in conversation with them. The church has long illustrated this sorting principle along socioeconomic, political, cultural, and racial lines, yet the apostle Paul reminds us that God does not sort spiritual gifts by placing like with like. As impossible as it seems, God's gifts are meant to work together, unfolding through diverse means. In the midst of schism and disagreement, we are still called to work together to discern God's movement among us.

Gospel
John 2:1-11 (RCL, LFM)

The Gospel of John does not have its own year in the lectionary; instead, texts from John are interspersed within all the years of the lectionary cycle. The Second Sunday after Epiphany in Year C is the only time this story of Jesus' first miracle, during a wedding celebration at Cana, appears in the lectionary. Similarly, unlike other miracles that are repeated in different Gospel accounts, this miracle only occurs in John. Scholarship has illuminated that John may have been written during a period of intense conflict within Judaism following the destruction of the temple in 70 CE.[9] John's language and images are deeply Jewish, echoing language and imagery from the Hebrew Scriptures.[10] John's audience was likely Christian Jews who were immersed in conflict with other Jewish traditions.[11] In John every story is heavy with theological significance. During this season of revelation, when God's glory appears among us, John's shaping of Jesus' first miracle has much to teach us about who Jesus is and the nature of his ministry.

Today's text falls in the first major section of John, when Jesus' hour "has not yet come," which largely focuses on Jesus' life, travels, and teaching. Just prior to our verses for today, Jesus' self-revelation has inspired exclamations of witness from John the Baptist and disciples Andrew, Philip, and Nathanael, who are moved to profess Jesus' identity as Lamb of God, Messiah, Promised One, Son of God, and King of Israel. Jesus has called them to "come and see" even greater and more miraculous things. These first seeds of faith will take root and flower as life with Jesus unfolds. As we join the disciples and others, Jesus begins to reveal his glory—incrementally showing us a fuller picture of who he is and thus who God is. This revelation is unveiled most completely when his "hour" arrives, in his death, resurrection, and ascension. The calling of the disciples has just happened in the days before the wedding; now on the "third day" Jesus and his disciples have been invited to attend a wedding in Cana where Jesus' mother is also in attendance.

It may be helpful for the preacher to sketch or draw the basic plot of the miracle event before delving into specific details. The miracle in Cana unfolds according to a recognized pattern for miracle stories: verses 1-2 set up the context, verses 3-5 set up the complications that ask for Jesus' action, verses 6-8 describe the actions that prepare for the miracle, and in verses 9-11, we have the miracle itself.[12] Significant word clues heighten the sense of importance and tension in this event; Jesus' own reference that his "hour has not yet come" (v. 4) lets us know that this event is part of something much larger that is yet to come. However, the writer's summary in verse 11 names this event as a significant beginning, "the first of his signs" where Jesus "revealed his glory," inspiring belief in his disciples.

The problem that provides an occasion for Jesus' first miracle seems rather commonplace. In the midst of the wedding celebration, the wine has run out. Certainly this is an unfortunate turn of events for the bridegroom and his family, but this is not a dire situation of life and death. Nevertheless, Jesus' mother approaches him, hopefully expectant that Jesus can do something to remedy this situation. Jesus' cool response to his mother, coupled with the reference to "his hour" not yet having arrived, indicates that Jesus is not bound by social convention or human relationships. Jesus is about God's work and will reveal his glory on God's time rather than ours. Moments when Jesus reveals his glory prior to the hour of his death and resurrection are still linked to those events. Jesus' glory, like the Christ event itself, is of a unified whole.[13] And so, despite the indication that Jesus couldn't care less about the wine, his mother continues to trust that Jesus can and will do something. The writer goes to great lengths to describe the water jars, telling us the type of jars, the number of jars, the purpose of the jars, and their size—six huge stone jars for the Jewish rites of purification, each holding twenty or thirty gallons. Jesus instructs the servants to fill the jars with water and give some of the contents to the chief steward. Not only has Jesus created a huge amount of wine; according to the steward it is superb wine—the best wine of the evening. While the steward does not know the true origin of this delicious wine, the servants and disciples are "in" on the truth.

The Text in Our World

Like Jesus' other signs, words, and actions, this miracle offers us a window into who Jesus is and the nature of God's intentions for the world. Will we follow the steward and embrace a mundane explanation of the miracle, or will we join the servants and disciples who reveled in the power and glory of God? The unexpected abundance and delight of this miracle reveal God's generosity and direct us toward the eschatological feast of the Lamb when all will sit at table with the crucified and risen Lord. The complication in this text of the wine giving out is a compelling one for preachers to relate to the lives of listeners and the life of the church in general. Many today no longer see the church as an important instrument for good in the world, and who among us has not had that experience of the wine giving out in life? One minute everything is great, but in an instant everything changes. Mere words can drain the wine completely out of life: "You're fired"; "It's cancer"; "There's been an accident"; "I've met someone else."

The surprising nature of this miracle keeps us on our toes. Like Jesus' mother, we cannot predict or control when, where, and how God will make God's glory known among us. Yet we can depend on Jesus to make his glory known and to inspire faith, joy, and new life. Even the guests, with no knowledge of the wine's miraculous origins, enjoyed the delicious gift of good wine late into the evening against all expectations. As a foreshadowing of Jesus' glory present in his resurrection and ascension, his first sign, too, is full of joy and unmerited grace. We continue to experience Jesus' life-giving presence among us. When the wine runs out in life, Jesus turns water into wine. We experience new life through words of hope: "I care"; "I'm listening"; "You're welcome"; "There's still hope"; "I love you."

Besides the obvious overtones of God's glory and revelation, preachers may decide to thematically link today's Gospel passage explicitly with the church's celebration of Eucharist, whether or not the congregation actually receives the sacrament during worship. Just as the presence of new wine in these verses reveals the power and glory of Christ, so, too, does our sharing of wine together around the Lord's table. The Gospel of John is full of sacramental images; Jesus not only provides the wine—Jesus is the true vine that bears much fruit (15:1-5), as well as the bread of life (6:53).

Notes

1. Eugene Peterson's translation of John 1:14 is especially evocative: "The Word became flesh and blood, and moved into the neighborhood." Peterson, *The Message* (Colorado Springs: NavPress, 2002).
2. Paul D. Hanson, *Isaiah 40–66*, Interpretation: A Bible Commentary for Teaching and Preaching (Louisville: John Knox, 1995), 185–88.
3. Ibid., 219.
4. J. Clinton McCann Jr., "The Book of Psalms," in *The New Interpreter's Bible: 1 and 2 Maccabees, Job, Psalms,* ed. Leander Keck et al. (Nashville: Abingdon, 1996), 4:1064–65.
5. Ibid., 1064.
6. This phrase is borrowed from the subtitle of John Howard Yoder's *Body Politics: Five Practices of the Christian Community before the Watching World* (Nashville: Discipleship Resources, 1991).
7. Richard B. Hays, *First Corinthians*, Interpretation: A Bible Commentary for Teaching and Preaching (Louisville: John Knox, 1989), 209.
8. Bill Bishop and Robert Cushing, *The Big Sort: Why the Clustering of Like-Minded America Is Tearing Us Apart* (New York: Houghton Mifflin, 2008).
9. Gail O'Day, "The Gospel of John," in *The New Interpreter's Bible: Luke–John,* ed. Leander Keck et al. (Nashville: Abingdon, 1995), 9:504–505.
10. Ibid., 505.
11. Ibid., 506.
12. Ibid., 536.
13. Ibid., 537.

January 27, 2013
Third Sunday after Epiphany /
Third Sunday in Ordinary Time

Revised Common Lectionary (RCL)
Nehemiah 8:1-3, 5-6, 8-10
Psalm 19
1 Corinthians 12:12-31a
Luke 4:14-21

Lectionary for Mass (LFM)
Nehemiah 8:2-4a, 5-6, 8-10
Psalm 19:8, 9, 10, 15
1 Corinthians 12:12-30 or 12:12-14, 27
Luke 1:1-4; 4:14-21

A colleague recently described the discipline required to sit at her desk with the computer cursor blinking away waiting for inspiration to strike—for the right language to emerge from that creative mix of human and divine that accompanies the pastoral vocation. She had to fight the urge to turn to work that felt more controllable or resolvable, like answering e-mails or even doing the laundry. There are moments in life when it seems that we will muddle around in darkness forever. But then, the Spirit moves. Disparate or isolated elements suddenly make sense, like a puzzle that suddenly comes together when missing pieces are found or when siblings separated at birth and adopted by different families meet as adults. Our texts today speak to the dawn of revelation, those moments when life suddenly and perfectly makes sense and we know who we are and where we belong. Nehemiah shows us the effects of Israel receiving God's law anew, recovering identity and purpose, while the psalmist writes passionately of how God's goodness is made manifest in the glory of creation and the perfection of God's law. In the epistle, Paul seeks to unify the fractious Corinthians by comparing the relationship between parts of the body to the relationship of those who are members of the body of Christ. And in our Gospel reading from Luke, Jesus interprets Isaiah's scroll, revealing himself as the fulfillment of God's promises.

First Reading
Nehemiah 8:1-3, 5-6, 8-10 (RCL)
Nehemiah 8:2-4a, 5-6, 8-10 (LFM)

Today's reading from Nehemiah is an inspiring one for preachers. The word is read and interpreted so that listeners—in this case the assembly of Israel—deeply understand God's law and are moved to the point of weeping. The reaction of the people in Nehemiah's context is understandable. The books of Nehemiah and Ezra are some of the latest books in Hebrew Scripture. They tell of Israel's return to their land from exile in Babylon and the relearning and rebuilding of the people of God. They were written during a challenging time for the people of Israel, but are infused with hope. God is present with them, revealing who God is and thus who Israel is in relationship to God.

Cupbearer to the king and eventual governor of Judah, Nehemiah is moved by the plight of scattered Jews returning to Jerusalem to find the city's walls and gates in ruins. He calls upon God to be faithful to God's promises of restoration, confessing Israel's past failure to keep God's commands and his present desire to return to God. With the king's permission, Nehemiah begins to rebuild the walls of Jerusalem so that the returned inhabitants might not feel constant shame. The rebuilding is both internal and external, and the journey is difficult. Those who would rebuild the walls face external challenges and mockery from Israel's enemies and challenge from within. Times are difficult and some Jews are engaged in exploitative business practices against each other. Some are charging extreme interest and others are selling members of their own families into slavery to pay debt. Yet God is present to the people in the midst of these difficulties, offering protection and guidance through the law and the leadership of Nehemiah.

Today's text picks up after the walls of Jerusalem are rebuilt and the people want to claim fully their identity as God's people and followers of God's law. By situating these events during the seventh month, the author shows that this newly reconstituted people is within the tradition of Israel and is gathered to observe the festivals of the seventh month.[1] The people gather for worship together, and the text offers many interesting details: men and women were gathered together; they heard the Torah read in the public square for several hours; the people paid attention; and Ezra the scribe read from a kind of pulpit or wooden platform that helped to project his reading. Leaders and Levite interpreters were present and the whole congregation participated in acts of worship, standing up for the reading, replying "Amen," and lifting their hands. Nehemiah, Ezra, and the Levite interpreters encouraged the people to respond with rejoicing because the people were deeply moved to the point of weeping when they heard the reading. Some scholars hold that the people wept because they remembered their sin and the sin of their ancestors when they came face to face with God's law. Others interpret the people's emotion as evidence that the reading of the Torah opened up new revelation for Israel that helped to give meaning and direction for their lives, revelation so powerful that they responded with both weeping and rejoicing to express their love of and delight in the law.[2] We can imagine the power of hearing the Torah read in this context; the first five books of our Bible bear witness to the foundational experiences of God and people. They tell of God's acts of creation and the calling of the ancestors, God's forging an everlasting covenant, and God's bringing slaves out of Egypt and into the promised land. They encompass story, genealogy, poems, songs, and laws to establish and guide the fabric of Israel's life. Just as the reading of Scripture in public worship continues to be a source of revelation for us today, the reading of this Scripture was not merely the reading of a historical document. This reading is a witness to God's activity among them and their identity as God's people—this revelation has profound implications not only for recovering their past identity but also for shaping their present actions and their future destiny in God.

Psalmody
Psalm 19 (RCL)
Psalm 19:8, 9, 10, 15 (LFM)

We can imagine worshipers in the square with Nehemiah and Ezra perhaps singing Psalm 19 as they engage in intentional formation to learn to live as God's people.[3] In its entirety Psalm 19 covers three main arenas of prayer: the glory of God as revealed by the heavens, the perfection of the law that surpasses nature, and a prayer calling for God's forgiveness and persevering strength in living according to God's law. The whole psalm attests to God's sovereignty and God's glory, and this revelation is made known through repetition with poetic power. Readers with a literary eye may desire to track the many parallel phrases. For preachers, the first third of the psalm is evocative. Without using actual speech, the created order bears witness to God—none can escape it. The heavens "tell" God's glory. Day and night "pour forth speech" and "declare knowledge." Yet this revelation is not enough; God's explicit revelation in Scripture surpasses natural revelation. Yahweh's name appears six times in verses 7-9. Through the gift of Torah, God makes God's self known intimately to God's people. And the positive effects of the law for humanity are attested to by the psalmist: reviving the soul, imparting wisdom, bringing joy to our hearts, providing enlightenment and new vision, and engendering an enduring sense of holy awe. Yet God does not stand in distant and holy isolation from people; the final section of the psalm points to a God who meets us in our weakness, offering forgiveness and strength to join all creation in bearing witness to God. Verse 14 picks up on the speech image from the first verses of the psalm. Just as creation "speaks" to God's glory, as preachers we regularly pray that the words of our mouths and meditations of our hearts be acceptable offerings to God, who meets us with the strength of a rock and the mercy of our redeemer.

Second Reading
1 Corinthians 12:12-31a (RCL)
1 Corinthians 12:12-30 or 12:12-14, 27 (LFM)

In last week's reading from 1 Corinthians, Paul emphasized the same Spirit as the source of varied gifts. This week he details the diverse workings of the Spirit's gifts with the understanding that these gifts all work together as members of the body of Christ. The fractious Corinthian congregation is struggling to see all members as equal contributors to the church body. According to historical scholarship, in Paul's day the metaphor of the body was a common one for describing the working of societies or organizations.[4] This metaphor of different body parts with different jobs was specifically used to keep people in lower classes "in their place," as organic proof that some parts of the body were more significant than others.[5] In contrast, Paul uses this familiar metaphor to show how all parts of the body are necessary and dependent on one another. Every part of the body is needed for the body to function. The body of Christ functions differently from other "bodies" or institutions in that every member is significant and each member should be cared for.

The Spirit continues to open God's revelation for us through this passage. Our world and even our churches still suffer from a sharp divide between the "haves" and the "have-nots." It is so easy to think of ourselves as indispensable members of Christ's body and to discount the contributions of others. During a summer in Kansas City, Missouri, I had the opportunity to worship with an unusual congregation. Seventy percent of Grand Avenue Temple's membership was comprised of urban sojourners, people without addresses who lived in the urban core. The rest of the congregation included young professionals living downtown, elderly members from a retirement community who had a long history with the church, and families driving in from the suburbs. This congregation stressed everyone's importance and provided ways for each person present to contribute to the life of the congregation. Worshipers were invited to tithe 10 percent of the money they had in their pockets that day and were also invited to share other gifts during the offering time in worship, such as singing a song, playing a harmonica, or telling a story or a joke. The congregation provided hot meals on the weekend and everyone was invited for lunch after worship. Each participant or member of the community was invited to help with the meal and the upkeep of the building. Even in contexts where diversity is flattened out and socioeconomic divisions are hidden, congregations should strive to make sure that all participants are welcomed and invited to play their part in helping the whole body of Christ to function as a witness to God's presence in the world.

Gospel
Luke 4:14-21 (RCL)
Luke 1:1-4; 4:14-21 (LFM)

The preface to Luke's Gospel offers us a window into Luke's motivations for writing. Luke joins others who have sought to testify with a written account of the Christ event and the birth of the church. Scholars are divided concerning the identity of "Theophilus," whose name means "Lover of God." Theophilus may represent a community, readers in general, or a particular individual—perhaps even a Roman official turned convert![6] Our reading from chapter 4 follows Jesus' baptism and successful turning from temptation in the wilderness. We are told in 3:22 that the Spirit descended upon Jesus and again at the beginning of chapter 4 that Jesus is full of the Holy Spirit. Luke repeats this descriptor here in verse 14. At the beginning of his ministry, Jesus is described again as "filled with the power of the Spirit." Inspired and empowered, Jesus is traveling around the region of Galilee, teaching in synagogues with great acclamation. Since he is receiving such positive press in the area, it is only natural that he should also return to his hometown of Nazareth to teach in the synagogue there. This is the "boy wonder" who once amazed the teachers at the synagogue in Jerusalem (Luke 2:45-47), all grown up!

If the folk in the Nazareth synagogue were expecting something powerful from Jesus that Sabbath day, he did not disappoint. Despite their high expectations, he still manages to surprise them. Just as he had done at synagogues throughout the region, Jesus stands, accepts the scroll of Isaiah, and unrolls to read. Scholars have evidence of a fixed cycle of readings by the first century, not unlike our modern lectionary.[7] Yet Luke tells us that Jesus finds particular verses, implying that Jesus has specifically chosen this text from Isaiah 58:6 and 61:1-2 announcing good news for the poor, release to captives, restored sight for the blind, and freedom for the oppressed.[8] He sits and, with everyone's eyes intently focused upon him, reveals himself as the fulfillment of these historic and foundational promises: "Today this scripture has been fulfilled in your hearing."

Through Scripture and immediate revelation in the teaching of Jesus, we are given a foretaste at the beginning of Jesus' ministry of what Jesus' activity on earth will look like, what God's plan for life among us looks like, and insight into the very character of Jesus that will mark his life, death, resurrection, and ascension. These are God's eschatological promises brought into the immediate present. Jesus has been anointed by the Holy Spirit in baptism, and his work will be marked by care and provision for those on the bottom rungs of the social ladder. Jesus will embody a countercultural pattern that is also our calling as members of Christ's body, the church.

The Text in Our World

Modern-day migrants and refugees would likely relate to the loss of identity and dissolution of family and peoplehood expressed in Nehemiah and the hopeful promises fulfilled in the person of Jesus Christ in Luke's Gospel. A couple I knew in a congregation in Ontario came to Canada as asylum seekers from Columbia. They had arrived with only limited English, unable even to order coffee. After having worked as prominent journalists before, they took new jobs on a janitorial staff at a local university. Because it was unsafe to return to their home country, they were unable to say good-bye when the man's father grew ill or to attend his funeral. Our congregation could not eliminate the terrible circumstances that forced their migration or erase the challenges and losses they faced, but we could listen to their story and offer support where possible. As brothers and sisters in Christ, a small group from the congregation became a second family for this couple and eventually served as sponsors for citizenship. It was a significant day when the members of this family became Canadian citizens, were finally freed from the fear of being sent back to Columbia, and were able to seize more fully new opportunities and healing. This family and other displaced persons in our midst offer us revelation in the form of new insights into contexts outside our own where citizens cannot freely express their views and where choices to defy unjust systems of power have horrific consequences. Closer to home, they also reveal how cultural and political patterns in North America are too often held captive to racism and how a lack of hospitality can deepen the grief and challenges already faced by those fleeing situations of war and threat. The preface to Luke's Gospel stresses Luke's desire to be a careful steward of the story of salvation. We, too, are called to be careful stewards of God's story and carefully to find ways to invite those who may be quite different from us to find their place within God's sweeping action in history so that their own stories, no matter how horrific, might be redeemed by God.

In the Gospel reading from chapter 4, Jesus offers good news to those who have been on the losing side of society: the poor, the captives, those suffering from physical challenges, and those caught in oppression. As future readings will bear out, that which sounds like good news to some may sound like bad news to others. For those of us who enjoy power and privilege, Jesus promises to shake things up—no more business as usual!

Jesus' words were controversial in his time and they continue to be controversial today. Many congregations struggle to engage in prophetic ministry with integrity. Sex offenders are one of the most hated groups in prison and they continue to experience suffering and marginalization even after they complete prison terms. Conditions of release, parole, chemical castration, and public registries rightly seek to protect the public from victimization, but these ex-offenders are people, too, and are embraced by Isaiah's vision. As Christ's body, some congregations have reached out to ex–sexual offenders with the goal of reducing recidivism and the hope that one day there will be no more victims. One successful program, Circles of Support and Accountability, is administered through restorative justice programs of Mennonite Central Committee (MCC) and surrounds newly released sex offenders (called "core members") with a small group of trained volunteers and MCC staff. The group checks in with each other daily and meets frequently over coffee or in a volunteer's home. The volunteers serve as a sounding board for ideas and help the core members find suitable housing and employment.

Besides these basic needs and general help adjusting to life outside of prison, Circles of Support also provides meaningful relationships and accountability to each member involved. The program is highly successful: compared to released offenders who are not in the program, core members with a circle are 70 percent less likely to reoffend. In some settings, core members and volunteers gather monthly for alternative worship services, since release conditions prevent most core members from attending traditional worship services. Despite the proven success of the program, it is a challenge for Circles of Support to find churches that are willing to open their doors for worship gatherings. Congregations frequently have members who have survived sexual abuse and it is deeply upsetting for churches to reach out to people who have abused children and other vulnerable persons. Some congregations have also formed support circles for survivors of abuse. These courageous congregations and volunteers are bearing witness to God's vision for creation—for release to those held captive by forces of all kinds, from abuse, to broken sexuality, to stigmatization. We join these congregations in prayer as we look ahead to the ultimate eschatological fulfillment of God's promises embodied by Jesus Christ.

Notes

1. The Day of Atonement and the Feast of Booths both fall in the seventh month.
2. Frederick Carlson Holmgren, *Ezra and Nehemiah: Israel Alive Again*, International Theological Commentary (Grand Rapids: Eerdmans, 1987), 125.
3. Some scholars hold that during the time of Ezra and Nehemiah this psalm may have been expanded to also sing praises for the perfection of the Law. James H. Waltner, *Psalms*, Believers Church Bible Commentary (Scottdale, Pa.: Herald, 2006), 107.
4. Richard B. Hays, *First Corinthians*, Interpretation: A Bible Commentary for Teaching and Preaching (Louisville: John Knox, 1997), 213.
5. Ibid.
6. Fred Craddock, *Luke*, Interpretation: A Bible Commentary for Teaching and Preaching (Louisville: John Knox, 1990), 15–16.
7. R. Alan Culpepper, "The Gospel of Luke," in *The New Interpreter's Bible: Luke–John*, ed. Leander Keck et al. (Nashville: Abingdon, 1995), 9:105.
8. Interestingly, Jesus does not read the next clause of Isa. 61:2, which proclaims "the day of vengeance of our God."

February 3, 2013
Fourth Sunday after Epiphany /
Fourth Sunday in Ordinary Time

Revised Common Lectionary (RCL)	**Lectionary for Mass (LFM)**
Jeremiah 1:4-10	Jeremiah 1:4-5, 17-19
Psalm 71:1-6	Psalm 71:1-2, 3-4, 5-6, 15, 17
1 Corinthians 13:1-13	1 Corinthians 12:31—13:13 or 13:4-13
Luke 4:21-30	Luke 4:21-30

As finite human beings, we can only experience the unveiling or revelation of God's glory—a hallmark of the season of Epiphany—within a dynamic of the many times in which God's ultimate plan is not revealed or actively veiled from us. Our vision is rightly limited by God. At times we are called to play a role in God's unfolding drama of salvation without understanding the full implication of that role. At times we are called to seize a prophetic vision that stands at the periphery of our view—a vision that the world cannot see or chooses to ignore. Today's texts bear witness to those who are called to participate in God's unfolding plan for creation. From Jeremiah's call to prophesy, to the cry of the psalmist seeking refuge in God, Jesus' unwelcome interpretation that causes his neighbors to turn on him in Nazareth, and Paul's reminder that as we mature in faith, we are called to love, God often calls us beyond the seen. In faith we are called to trust God's full and complete vision that surpasses what we can see only in a mirror dimly. Stepping into God's call is a tremendous risk and often puts the faithful at odds with the world, yet accepting the costs of faithfulness is part of maturing in faith.

First Reading
Jeremiah 1:4-10 (RCL)
Jeremiah 1:4-5, 17-19 (LFM)

When God calls, God does not take "no" for an answer. Jeremiah's call begins with divine revelation: "The word of the LORD came to me saying . . ." Jeremiah resists God's call, but he is in good company. We recall Moses offering many excuses, Gideon blaming his weak family, and Jonah flat-out running away and landing in the belly of a big fish. Today's verses from the book of Jeremiah detail the prophet's call to speak God's words in the midst of an excruciating period in Judah's history. Jeremiah's call can be interpreted as narrating what actually happened to Jeremiah or as representing a pattern or construct used by the editor to help readers move past the humanness of God's prophetic oracle and to claim fully the message as God's own words for God's people.[1] Either interpretation ultimately moves us to look beyond Jeremiah's own limitations as God's prophet and to catch hold of God's power and God's vision and will for Israel and the nations. The repeated use of the revelatory phrase "the word of the LORD . . ." in verses 2, 4, 11, 13, and at least fifty times in the whole book, reminds us again and again that God is the main actor here. Yet in the midst of the inevitability of God's call upon Jeremiah, we find hope for God's call among us. Jeremiah was born with a God-given destiny. God chose Jeremiah. God took the initiative to call Jeremiah to play a particular role as a prophet among the nations.[2] So it is in our lives: God has called and claimed each one. The truth of our identity—borne out in our baptisms—is that we belong to God. It follows that Jeremiah's youth was no obstacle to God. This serves as a reminder to those of us in church leadership that God may speak through the voices of teenagers and young adults. Jeremiah's resistance is understandable—the life of a prophet is extremely difficult. The word of the Lord spoken by Jeremiah was not the kind of word to win him friends! But Jeremiah's own objection is also no obstacle for God. In fact, God promises to be with Jeremiah and protect him so that he can live out God's call fully.

In verses 9-10, 17, and 19, God's call to Jeremiah gets specific. God empowers Jeremiah with God-given political authority. God calls him with a set of verbs that seem suited more to a garden than the geopolitical arena. Jeremiah is called to be destructive and creative: plucking up, pulling down, destroying and overthrowing, but also building and planting. These verbs offer us a foretaste of God's own actions later in the text.[3] Jeremiah was called to herald significant change for God's people and the nations, and significant change often has both a destructive and a constructive element. While much of Jeremiah's prophecy will fall on the destructive side of this equation, God's creative and constructive impulses have the final say. Jeremiah also promises restoration and return of the exiles; God will forge a new covenant with Israel—God's law will be written on their hearts and God will forgive their sin (31:31-34).

The LFM reading includes verses 17-19, which reiterate and emphasize God's call to Jeremiah as well as God's presence and empowerment amid the deep challenges of following that call. Jeremiah is told to "gird up"—in a sense, to prepare as for battle. The work before Jeremiah will be difficult, but he must not "break down" or abandon his work, as the consequences would be deadly. But just as we, along with Jeremiah, begin to think that this task may truly be impossible, verses 18-19 offer an extended promise of God's protection and ultimately God's deliverance. Indeed, the one who calls is the one who animates life in pursuit of the call and brings God's promises to fulfillment.

Psalmody
Psalm 71:1-6 (RCL)
Psalm 71:1-2, 3-4, 5-6, 15, 17 (LFM)

One can almost imagine Jeremiah later in life, uttering the prayer of the psalmist in Psalm 71. This psalm is a lament, but is deeply infused with hope. It follows the typical pattern for a lament psalm, moving from petition to praise, but unusually this psalm in its entirety follows this cycle three times rather than only once.[4] The RCL reading draws from the first cycle of petition and praise, while the LFM adds verses 15 and 17, which come from the second cycle of praise. In verses 1-4 the psalmist cries out to God for deliverance, protection, saving, and refuge. God is referred to as a "rock" and "fortress." While some suggest that the psalmist is suffering from physical ailments due to old age (vv. 9, 18), this need not be the only interpretation.[5] Regardless of life stage, the psalmist is clearly in a place of absolute dependence on God. The psalmist has relied on God from birth, has been deeply formed in a pattern of dependence on God, and knows that God can ultimately be trusted (vv. 5-6). God is stronger than the wicked, unjust, and cruel. The cycle of petition in verses 9-13 is followed by a second cycle of praise. Verse 15 echoes verse 8 in referring to the psalmist's mouth bearing witness to God. Verse 15 alludes to human limitations in knowing the scope of God's salvific plans, but despite these limitations and the present experience of suffering, the psalmist cannot stop talking about God and praising God. Verse 17 again refers to the psalmist's youth, telling us that this relationship with God is a lifelong affair.

Second Reading
1 Corinthians 13:1-13 (RCL)
1 Corinthians 12:31—13:13 or 13:4-13 (LFM)

Perhaps the biggest challenge facing us in addressing Paul's writing to the Corinthian congregation in chapter 13 is the tendency to allow modern sensibilities concerning romantic love and the popularity of this text as a reading for weddings to so color our interpretation that we cannot hear anything fresh. The LFM reading rightly links chapter 13 to the themes of chapter 12 that we addressed in previous weeks: the concern that all gifts come from the same Spirit and that all members of the community are necessary—no gift can be jettisoned and no member sent away without hurting the functioning of the whole. The love Paul writes about in chapter 13 is what makes the claims of the previous chapter possible; it is what gives hope that a fractured congregation with disordered practices might yet bear witness to God in the world as the whole body of Christ, God's love.[6]

In chapter 13, Paul is at his best as a preacher, employing an almost poetic tone that reveals both the error of Corinthian practices and the promise of redemption and hope. This chapter is "bad news" in that it lays bare the loveless nature of Corinthian behavior, but read in light of God's love for humanity—so deep that God in Jesus Christ is willing to die for humanity—it is powerful good news for the Corinthians and for us. Verses 1-3 unfold as a set of conditional statements where amazing gifts and acts—gifts and acts of which the Corinthians are especially proud—are deemed ineffective without love. Speaking in tongues, prophetic powers, faith, and self-sacrifice *without love* must be used *with love* in order to be effective tools of the Spirit. Love is the means through which this fractious body of Christ in Corinth can actually come together and serve God's purposes. Verses 4-7 illustrate what love looks like and, unfortunately, it does not look like the behavior of the Corinthians. In describing love both positively and negatively, Paul uses the exact same language that he used earlier to describe the Corinthians. The descriptors "envious," "boastful," "arrogant," "rude," and "insisting on one's own way" would have surely found their mark in the hearts of the first community of listeners to this letter.[7] After all the negatives, Paul offers us four positives: "Love bears all things, believes all things, hopes all things, and endures all things." Without God's love, neither the Corinthians nor Christians today could stand as witnesses amid a world that is too often the very antithesis of Paul's description of love.

The eschatological flavor of this passage is heightened in verses 8-13. Part of coming to spiritual maturity is the call to display love in the midst of an unloving world as a foretaste of God's perfect love that has ultimately conquered sin and death. All of our human gifts are effective tools of the Spirit in the world in a provisional way, while God's love is the final destination of creation. We hold this promise in trust and despite our own limited view of the future. Our encounter with God's revelation is incomplete—"we see in a mirror, dimly"—but one day "we will see face to face," we "will know fully." Until that time, we imperfectly use our gifts of the Spirit together in love for the glory of God.

Preachers who focus on this passage will do well to remember that the text does not address a generic love but love in the midst of hardship and challenge within a very specific context. For us, too, love cannot be practiced apart from the challenges and joys of flesh-and-blood relationships, romantic and nonromantic. I once met with a spiritual director who suggested that I use 1 Corinthians 13:4-7 as a way of examining my own life each day, substituting my own name for "love." Unsurprisingly, each day I fell miserably short. So often we are not patient or kind. Like those Corinthians long ago, we continue to be envious, arrogant, rude, irritable, and resentful. Nevertheless, God has chosen to work through us! Counter to all worldly logic, God continues to work through flesh and blood, through the incarnate Christ and through his church. It is God's love alone that can animate and empower faithful witness.

Gospel
Luke 4:21-30 (RCL, LFM)

Today's Gospel reading picks up where last week's reading left off. Jesus is teaching in his hometown synagogue and has just finished reading from the scroll of Isaiah, "The Spirit of the Lord is upon me, because he has anointed me to bring good news to the poor. He has sent me to proclaim release to the captives and recovery of sight to the blind, to let the oppressed go free, to proclaim the year of the Lord's favor." Then Jesus tells them that today the Scripture is fulfilled in their hearing. The people were impressed; we can imagine them exchanging approving looks and murmuring with pleasure. They can hardly believe that this is Joseph's son, one of "their own"![8] They bask in God's grace, joyful at the proclamation of God's favor and liberating intentions for them. If only Jesus stopped there. But Jesus does not stop with the approval of his former neighbors and friends; Jesus is called to preach a message that cuts through to the heart of things. Indeed, in the person of Jesus Christ, God's eschatological realm breaks into the present time. The hopes and vision of the scroll of Isaiah find their end in Jesus Christ. But God's good news is not easy, and sometimes it comes as a "hard word," an unpopular message. Much like Jeremiah and other reluctant prophets earlier in Israel's history, here at the outset of his ministry, Jesus, too, will live into the fullness of the message he is called to proclaim in word and deed—a challenging message of judgment and grace that will eventually cost him his life.

In today's part of the narrative, Jesus seems to glide straight from hopeful proclamation to words that challenge the status quo. In the first part of this narrative, Jesus has begun to reveal his identity as fulfillment of God's promises. In verses 23-29 he continues his self-revelation with proclamation that puts him at odds with those in the Nazareth synagogue.[9] Jesus is aware of the disconnect between what he will say and the expectations of the crowd: "You will say, 'Do here also in your hometown the things that we have heard you did at Capernaum.' . . . Truly I tell you no prophet is accepted in the prophet's hometown." Before launching into his unpopular teaching, Jesus offers a kind of warning: "You will probably not like where this conversation is going." Jesus proceeds to share instances from the lives of the prophets Elijah and Elisha drawn from 1 Kings 17:8-24 and 2 Kings 5:1-19, illustrating that this good news proclaimed in the scroll of Isaiah is not limited to the Jewish people alone. These particular examples were especially freighted because they highlight God's provision for non-Jews with particularly low socioreligious status.[10] When Elijah comes to the widow at Zarephath, he offers care and miraculous provision for a non-Jew *and a woman*.[11] Elisha reaches out to Naaman, a non-Jew *with the disease of leprosy*.[12] We as readers already have a sense of this impulse of Jesus' identity and ministry from earlier in Luke's Gospel. In his blessing in 2:32, Simeon foresees that Jesus will be "a light for revelation to the Gentiles and for glory to your people Israel," and John the Baptist's interpretation of Isaiah in 3:6 proclaims that "*all flesh* shall see the salvation of God." However, this is fresh news to the Jews gathered in the synagogue that day. The controversial nature of Jesus' mission is encountered as unexpected and unwelcome revelation. The listeners are filled with a rage so strong that formerly friendly neighbors become an ugly mob intent on killing Jesus then and there. Jesus' escape from the crowd is maddeningly underplayed in Luke's account. We are left to imagine how he managed to pass through the crowd and go on his way. Jesus' mission has only begun, but he has boldly revealed himself as one at odds with his religious community. The way forward will not be easy.

The Text in Our World

The hard edge of revelation still poses a steep challenge for modern-day prophets, as it did in the days of Jeremiah and Jesus. Two potential outcomes of courageous acts of faith are set in stark relief by two alumni commended this year during homecoming celebrations at Eastern Mennonite University, where I teach. Glen Lapp and Leymah Gbowee both followed their Christian faith in the midst of serious challenge in their local contexts. Lapp chose to follow God's call to engage in medical relief work in Afghanistan, while Gbowee was born into a situation of hardship and suffering in war-torn Liberia. The outcome of their faithful acts could not be more different. Gbowee is a joint recipient of the 2011 Nobel Peace Prize, while Lapp lost his life at the hands of the Taliban in August 2010. Their courageous words and nonviolent actions stand as a witness to God's revelation of good news among us that continues to be both costly and world changing.

Glen Lapp was born in Honduras but grew up in a Mennonite congregation in Lancaster, Pennsylvania. He was committed to Christian nonviolence, gifted with the ability to learn languages easily, and felt called to cross-cultural service at different times in his life. He taught English in Nepal and served as a nurse with Havasupai Nation Native Americans at the Indian Health Center in the isolated village of Supai, in Arizona's Grand Canyon. He returned to Pennsylvania to work at the Lancaster Regional Medical Center in 2003. A trip to Afghanistan in 2004 to visit a friend opened his heart to the Afghani culture and people, and he returned to Afghanistan as a medical relief worker through International Assistance Mission (IAM), a Mennonite Central Committee partner organization, working as an executive assistant and the manager of a provincial program working specifically with vision and eye care.[13] On August 5, 2010, Lapp and nine other Christian aid workers were returning to Kabul from a service trip to a barely accessible region of northern Afghanistan, having traveled by Jeep, horseback, and on foot, when they were ambushed by Taliban, robbed, and shot in a secluded area in Badakshan Province. While the workers were only providing medical care, seeking to live out their Christian calling without explicitly trying to convert others, the Taliban accused them of spying and spreading Christianity. Lapp is remembered by friends as "compassionate and humble."[14] In a report he filed with Mennonite Central Committee, Lapp described his work as "treating people with respect and with love and trying to be a little bit of Christ in this part of the world."[15]

In the midst of civil war in Liberia which lasted from 1989 to 2003, Liberian peace activist Leymah Gbowee moved from trauma victim to empowered survivor and used networks in the Lutheran Church to organize women to end the war in Liberia and bring about political change.[16] The Women of Liberia Mass Action for Peace was an interfaith movement that involved public prayer and nonviolent actions, including sit-ins demonstrating with signs, dance, and singing near a road traveled by then-president Charles Taylor, and a well-publicized "sex strike." The women continued to protest during peace talks among tribal warlords held in Ghana, blocking their exits so they had to stay and talk to one another and threatening to strip naked (bringing great shame upon the men) if they did not reach a peace agreement. God's Spirit empowered Gbowee and the women of Liberia to pray and act to bring about peace and change for themselves and their children, including successful peace talks and the fair election of the first female president of Liberia.

Activists and Christian leaders such as Lapp and Gbowee serve as examples and witnesses to the transformative potential of the gospel, but they also remind us that God often calls us beyond the edges of what is comfortable or acceptable. Not every act of discipleship is as costly as Glen Lapp's or as widely recognized as Leymah Gbowee's, but God's revelation consistently calls us to stand with Christ at the leading edge of God's transformation of creation. When we accept God's call, we cannot know the exact pathway our lives will follow. Like Paul we see in a mirror dimly, but we fully claim and fully trust the resurrection reality of God's ultimate vision for creation that exists just beyond our own limited point of view.

Notes

1. Walter Brueggemann, *To Pluck Up, To Tear Down: Jeremiah 1–25*, International Theological Commentary (Grand Rapids: Eerdmans, 1988), 23.
2. While God calls Jeremiah to prophesy to the nations, much of his prophecy is actually directed to Judah, although at the end of the book in chapters 46–51 he does direct judgment to other nations and peoples.
3. God "plucks up" twice in 12:14 and once in 18:7; 24:6; 31:26; 42:10; and 45:4. God explicitly does not "pull down" in 42:10. God or an appointed instrument "destroys" twenty-six times in 5:6, 10, 17; 6:5; 11:19; 12:17; 13:14; 15:3; 17:18; 18:7; 23:1, 25:9; 31:28; 36:29; 46:8; 47:4; 49:28, 38; 50:21, 26; 51:3, 11, 20, 25, 62. The same root is used thirty-five times in other variations. "Overthrowing" occurs again in 31:28. God or God's agents actively "build" in 18:9; 24:6; 29:5, 28; 31:4, 28; 35:7, 9; and 42:10. "Plant" occurs in 2:21; 11:17; 12:2; 17:8; 18:9; 24:6; 29:5, 28; 31:5, 28; 32:41; 35:7; 42:10; and 45:4.
4. J. Clinton McCann Jr., "The Book of Psalms," *The New Interpreter's Bible: 1 and 2 Maccabees, Job, Psalms*, ed. Leander Keck et al. (Nashville: Abingdon, 1996), 4:958.
5. James H. Waltner, *Psalms*, Believers Church Bible Commentary (Scottdale, Pa.: Herald, 2006), 344.
6. There is no doubt that love is a significant theme in 1 Corinthians 13; Paul uses the word *agape* ten times. Anthony Thiselton, *The First Epistle to the Corinthians*, The New International Greek Testament Commentary (Grand Rapids: Eerdmans, 2000), 1027.

7. For "envious/jealousy," see 3:3; for "boastful," see 1:29-31; 3:21; 4:7; 5:6; for "arrogant/puffed up," see 4:6, 18-19; 5:2; for "rude/shameful behavior," see 7:36 and discussion of sexual misconduct in 5:1-2; women prophesying without covered heads in 11:2-16; and mistreatment of the poor during the Lord's Supper in 11:20-22. Full discussion in Richard B. Hays, *First Corinthians*, Interpretation: A Bible Commentary for Teaching and Preaching (Louisville: John Knox, 1997), 226–27.

8. Joel Green points out that this comment becomes a kind of ironic joke shared between the readers and narrator who know Jesus' identity as Son of God, not son of Joseph. It follows that Jesus will not behave as an "insider" here. *The Gospel of Luke*, The New International Commentary on the New Testament (Grand Rapids: Eerdmans, 1997), 215.

9. This is the beginning of the fulfillment of Simeon's prophecy in 2:34, that Jesus was destined to be "a sign that will be opposed."

10. Green, *Gospel of Luke*, 218.

11. Ibid.

12. Ibid.

13. Mennonite Central Committee News, "Obituary, Glen Lapp," Mennonite Central Committee, http://www.mcc.org/stories/news/obituary-glen-d-lapp.

14. Eastern Mennonite University Communications, "Distinguished Service Award, Glen Lapp '91: He Offered Up His Life," Eastern Mennonite University, http://www.emu.edu/alumni/homecoming/2011/distinguished-service-award/.

15. Ibid.

16. Learn more about Gbowee's story from her memoir *Mighty Be Our Powers: How Sisterhood, Prayer, and Sex Changed a Nation* (New York: Beast, 2011).

February 10, 2013
Fifth Sunday in Ordinary Time (LFM)

Lectionary for Mass (LFM)

Isaiah 6:1-2a, 3-8
Psalm 138:1-2a, 2b-3, 4-5, 7-8
1 Corinthians 15:1-11
Luke 5:1-11

When we encounter the presence of God in our lives, the ordinary is transformed into the holy, the extraordinary. Suddenly, in the presence of God we experience not only divine revelation about who God is but also revelation about who we are. Today's texts speak of divine encounter and honest self-assessment in the light of God's presence. While last week's texts told of the difficulty of bearing witness to revelation beyond the world's grasp, this week's texts speak of the dramatic encounter between divine and human. We cannot dare to stand before the living God, but again and again God reaches out to invite people to step into God's call, to play a role in God's unfolding vision for creation. Isaiah's dramatic vision reveals the glory of God and the fragile humanity of the prophet: "Woe is me, I am doomed! For I am a man of unclean lips, living among a people of unclean lips, and my eyes have seen the King, the LORD of hosts!" (Isa. 6:5 NAB). In our epistolary reading from 1 Corinthians, Paul's encounter with the risen Christ inspires his assessment, "I am the least of the apostles, not fit to be called an apostle, because I persecuted the church of God" (1 Cor. 15:9 NAB). In the Gospel reading from Luke, Jesus miraculously fills the fishermen's nets with fish after a night of fruitless fishing, inspiring Simon Peter to confess, "Go away from me, Lord, for I am a sinful man!" Yet in each of these cases, God chooses to engage with people no matter how sinful or fragile. Psalm 138 bears testimony to God's love and faithfulness to creation. A live coal cleanses Isaiah's lips and he responds to God's call, "Here am I; send me!" God empowers the apostle Paul as a powerful witness to the wonders of the gospel and power of God's grace. In the Gospel reading, the fishermen leave everything and follow Jesus when he calls them to be his disciples and "catch people" instead of fish.

First Reading
Isaiah 6:1-2a, 3-8

Today's reading from Isaiah recounts the prophet's call in the midst of an intense experience of theophany. This passage has long been instructive in the life of the church. In verses 1-8, we find a pattern to be emulated in Christian worship: praising God, confessing, receiving pardon, and sending forth, but this was not its initial purpose. Isaiah's encounter with God infuses the whole book with a sense of divine authority.[1] Interestingly, the account of Isaiah's fantastic vision, which clearly occurs beyond ordinary time and space, begins by situating the experience within temporal time—the year that King Uzziah died, 742.[2] But immediately we are swept into the context of the vision. Isaiah describes a grand scene unfolding in the very throne room of God: The Lord is seated on a high throne, the hem of the holy robe so broad that it fills the entire temple; six-winged seraphs attend God, flying near but also demonstrating proper awe by covering their faces and feet. The space is filled with a sonic witness to the glory of God as the seraphim chant, "Holy, holy, holy is the LORD of hosts! All the earth is filled with his glory!" (v. 3 NAB). The entire space reverberates and shakes as the air is thick with smoke. This is the scene of heavenly worship—of unabashed and unending praise to God.

This encounter with the Holy is too much for Isaiah; mere mortals cannot stand in the presence of God and live. Isaiah cries out, "Woe is me!" Isaiah is completely aware of his own sinfulness. The book of Isaiah is deeply aware of human shortcomings. In the chapters prior to this account, Isaiah has already spoken strong words of judgment on Judah for its failings in relationship to God and toward one another. In chapter 5, these failings will lead to Judah's destruction at the hands of foreign invaders. Yet God does not condemn Isaiah, but offers a means of cleansing and forgiveness. While it is nearly impossible to imagine a human surviving an encounter between mouth and hot ember in the natural world, in Isaiah's vision, a seraph turns from attending to the Lord to attend to Isaiah. The seraph takes a hot coal from the altar of the temple and applies it to the prophet's lips, saying, "Now that this has touched your lips, your wickedness is removed, your sin purged" (v. 7 NAB). With this one ritual action, Isaiah can stand in the presence of God Almighty. After his own paralyzing fear and guilt have been removed, Isaiah is present to the events of the throne room. God is at work here, calling forth servants and sending forth messengers. Aware of the question in the air, "Whom shall I send? Who will go for us?" Isaiah answers, "Here am I, send me!" (v. 8 NAB).

In contrast to last week's encounter with the prophet Jeremiah, Isaiah does not resist God's call, complain, or apparently regret his hasty response in the heavenly throne room. Isaiah's bold response stands as an encouragement and challenge for us as we seek to proclaim God's word in our congregations and communities.

Psalmody
Psalm 138:1-2a, 2b-3, 4-5, 7-8

Psalm 138 offers deep, "whole-hearted" thanksgiving to God. God's power and glory have exalted God's name and word beyond the earthly powers of kings and the spiritual powers of "the gods." The presence of God is so significant to the psalmist, the singer of this psalm bows down toward the temple—the place where God's presence draws near. The root of the psalmist's personal thanksgiving is expressed simply in verse 3: "On the day I cried out, you answered, you strengthened my spirit" (NAB). As the psalm progresses, the psalmist envisions all the kings of the earth joining the song of praise to God, for God has preserved the singer who is filled with hope, even in the midst of trouble, that God's purposes will be fulfilled, that God's enduring love will never forsake God's people. The joyous and thankful tone of Psalm 138, sung in the midst of trouble, is especially striking in its placement in the psalter following the unresolved anguish of Psalm 137, which tells of the agony of exile and anger toward Babylon: "How could we sing a song of the Lord in a foreign land?" (137:4 NAB). "Blessed the one who pays you back what you have done us!" (137:8b NAB). Following Psalm 137 with 138 allows for human thankfulness for God's faithfulness to stand alongside cries of lament and bears witness to the complexities of the human situation and the unsearchable depths of our God, who is large enough to receive and bless the gamut of human emotional expression.

Second Reading
1 Corinthians 15:1-11

After writing about spiritual gifts and "orderly" worship that builds up the church in chapter 14, in today's verses Paul addresses the last of the divisive issues causing strife within the Corinthian congregation: the resurrection of the body. Verse 12 makes clear that some in the congregation do not believe in the resurrection of the body. The overly spiritualized Corinthians are uncomfortable with bodily death and resurrection—this helps explain Paul's use of the cross and all its ugly reality at the outset of the letter and his use of the body of Christ as a metaphor for the church. In the midst of this context, Paul speaks a powerful witness to the core of the gospel, the good news that has saving power. Jesus died and was raised from the dead and Jesus appeared in bodily form to the disciples and even Paul himself. The resurrection of the body is good news for embodied humans!

Paul's language in verse 3 of "handing on what he had received" (NRSV) is the same language he used to talk about the Lord's Supper. This language anchors Paul's claims beyond Paul himself in the authority of the budding tradition of the new Christian church and in accordance with Hebrew Scripture—the belief in resurrection of the body is one of the foundational beliefs for the church. Without this foundational belief, the Corinthians "believe in vain." In verses 3-5, scholars understand Paul as likely quoting from a widely held confession of faith—something like the creeds we recite in worship today.[3] Paul adds weight to this belief with other witnesses, not only Cephas and the other disciples, but more than five hundred brothers and sisters, many who are still alive, and finally Paul himself. Jesus' resurrection is not ancient history—it lies in the reachable past. The church has a direct link to these witnesses.

Paul's discussion of his own encounter with the risen Christ has added weight given the tension around his own authority in the Corinthian congregation. In keeping with his earlier pattern of minimizing himself, he proclaims his own unworthiness in order to bring glory to God. Paul himself is not worthy, but through the grace of God he is able to live into God's calling. "For I am the least of the apostles, not fit to be called an apostle, because I persecuted the church of God. But by the grace of God I am what I am, and his grace to me has not been ineffective" (vv. 9-10). Paul then sets aside the question of who has authority among the congregation by claiming the gospel itself as authoritative, so that it does not matter who proclaims it, but the gospel proclaimed among the Corinthians has grasped them.

Paul's body-centered message to Corinth is a timely one for us today. Many today are also uncomfortable with the resurrection of the body—this is echoed in our funeral practices, many of which focus on remembering or celebrating the life of the deceased rather than proclaiming that death is not the final verdict on the deceased one's life. In chapter 15, Paul gives us confessional anchors that allow us to stand firm in the face of death: "For just as all die in Adam, so too in Christ shall all be brought to life" (15:22 NAB). Indeed, "death is swallowed up in victory" (15:54 NAB). The resurrection of the body is a necessary step in the fulfillment of God's promises.

Gospel
Luke 5:1-11

Luke's version of Jesus calling his disciples comes later in the narrative and with more details than Mark and Matthew, coming after Jesus has already established himself as a powerful teacher and healer. After he is nearly run off a cliff in Nazareth, Jesus travels around Galilee, teaching, healing, and casting out demons. The people recognized his authority and the demons proclaimed his identity as Son of God. The end of chapter 4 has Jesus teaching and proclaiming the good news in Judea, but the beginning of our passage today places us back in Galilee. Luke fleshes out his call story in ways that differ from Mark and Matthew's versions. He calls the "Sea of Galilee" the "Lake of Gennesaret" and includes more description, a profession by Simon Peter, and a miraculous catch of fish that foreshadows great success in the disciples' calling to catch people.

After all his teaching and displays of power in chapter 4, Jesus has attracted quite a crowd. His outdoor setting for teaching here is much less formal than the synagogue context of our readings the past two Sundays. In 5:1 the crowd is pressing in on him so much that it is necessary for him to teach them from a boat a short distance out from the shore. The boats on the shore belong to Simon and his partners, James and John; they were washing their nets after a long night of fruitless fishing.[4] After Jesus finishes teaching the crowds, his focus turns to the fishermen cleaning their nets. He asks Simon to head out into deeper water and let down his nets just one more time for a catch. Simon protests that they have been fishing all night with no luck, but he is willing to humor this teacher.[5] Shortly after they let out their nets, they haul in a staggering catch—enough to break their nets![6] They signal their partners to join them with the other boat, but the catch is so large that their lives are in danger; the boats are full to the point of sinking. The miracle of this catch is overwhelming to Simon Peter; he recognizes that he is in the presence of divine power and expresses his own fragility and imperfection. Jesus tells him, "Do not be afraid; from now on you will be catching people" (v. 10 NRSV). Jesus' use of the phrase "from now on . . ." clues us in that this experience will be life changing for the fishermen.[7] After they bring their boats to shore, they leave everything and follow Jesus.

This calling story, like the call of Isaiah, has many interesting physical details. It may be helpful for the preacher to imagine what it would feel like to be a figure in this story: the weariness and bleary eyes of the fishermen after a long night of casting out and hauling in empty nets; the breeze gently rocking the boat as Jesus teaches; what Jesus may have taught or said from the boat to the crowd; Peter and his partners peering down into the cool depths of the deeper water as they let down their nets one more time; the nets disappearing into the inky darkness of the water; the unbearable weight of the catch; slippery, writhing fish bulging through the nets; the sound of straining fibers as the nets threaten to give way; the men's muscles screaming in agony as they release the catch into their boats; the boats riding low in the water, water spilling over the side of the boats as they begin to sink. Including these physical details in the sermon will help the listeners imagine the physicality of this story.

The revelatory experience of being called in this instance bears similarity with other biblical call stories, including our first reading from Isaiah. Like Isaiah, Simon Peter's encounter with a divine miracle, the overwhelming catch, makes his own inadequacy and sinfulness plain. Like Isaiah, Peter, too, expresses fear to be in the presence of holiness—but Jesus calms his fear. Earlier readings from Luke in chapter 4 have already made clear that God's good news will stretch outside the boundaries expected by the religious establishment of the synagogue in Nazareth. Jesus has come to bring good news to those on the margins of society: the poor, the imprisoned, those with physical limitations, and the oppressed. With Simon Peter's self-description, we can add "sinners" to this group who will experience good news.[8] Not only is Jesus' call extended to Simon Peter and the others, but they respond so completely, leaving everything behind to follow Jesus, that they also serve as an example of the right response to Jesus' call. Like Isaiah, they leap headlong into what will prove to be a consuming and challenging mission—the divine miracle that spurred their response was so generous that they almost drowned in their sinking boats! This calling to follow Jesus will be their lifework. The amazing catch foreshadows the amazing growth of the church that Luke will also chronicle in the book of Acts.

The Text in Our World

Most of us can relate to the experience of fruitless fishing regardless of profession or life stage. We think of the student up all night struggling to understand material before an exam or working on a paper and struggling to find the right words to bring concepts alive. We think of the man laid off fourteen months ago and searching for work, having gone months without even a nibble at his résumé. We think of a woman experiencing depression, seeking help and trying medication but experiencing no relief. The work of pastoral ministry calls us to engage with those in the midst of long nights and empty nets but can often feel more like the experience of the disciples in boats overloaded with fish: we struggle with nets and lives that are full to the point of breaking. A *New York Times* article discusses the dangers of clergy burn-out, citing infrequent or inadequate vacation time and the ability to be reached at all times through cell phones and social media.[9] A deeper understanding of Sabbath in congregations can help pastors and others be refreshed and renewed by God. At its core, the practice of Sabbath communicates dependency on God rather than on self or material possessions for one's well-being. In the moment of responding to God's call, Isaiah and the disciples were completely dependent on God—a posture of radical dependency is also necessary to continue to follow God. Like those first disciples, Jesus calls us to head out for deeper waters. We cannot dabble on the edge of our calling to discipleship. We cannot allow fear to hold us back. We can engage our calling with hope and faith, because the one who calls us is our traveling companion and invites us to leave our heavy baggage behind. Life with Jesus promises a generous haul of fish even in waters deemed desolate by prior experience. The power of God makes following God possible, and the promise of a life of "catching people" lies ahead for those who dare to leave their former lives on the beach and follow Jesus.

Notes

1. Walter Brueggemann, *Isaiah 1–39*, Westminster Bible Companion (Louisville: Westminster John Knox, 1998), 58.
2. Ibid. The first twelve chapters of Isaiah are generally associated with the work of the eighth-century prophet.
3. Richard B. Hays, *First Corinthians*, Interpretation: A Bible Commentary for Teaching and Preaching (Louisville: John Knox, 1997), 255.
4. It is interesting to note that Jesus sits down to teach the crowd; this was also the posture for preaching in the early church. The preacher sat while the congregation stood until the medieval period.
5. Fishermen worked at night because during the day the fish could see the nets and could avoid them. Joel Green, *The Gospel of Luke*, The New International Commentary on the New Testament (Grand Rapids: Eerdmans, 1997), 232.
6. Luke Timothy Johnson notes the similarity here to Jesus' mother Mary's protestation that conception was not possible since she was a virgin and to barren Elizabeth's suddenly fertile womb.

With Jesus, the impossible is possible! Johnson, *The Gospel of Luke,* Sacra Pagina (Collegeville, Minn.: Liturgical, 1991), 3:90.

7. See also Green, *Gospel of Luke,* 235.

8. Fishermen were not particularly despised or dishonest, and the text gives us no specific evidence of "sins" at this point, but this is Luke's first use of the term *sinner* and its use here may provide evidence of Luke's understanding of "sinners" as those who recognize an expansive gap between themselves and the divine, those who, in Joel Green's words, "recognize themselves in need of divine redemption" (Green, *Gospel of Luke,* 233–34). Interestingly, while Peter calls himself a "sinner," in this passage he has shown faith as he follows Jesus' command to put down his nets again and a sense of holy awe after the miraculous catch.

9. Paul Vitello, "Taking a Break from the Lord's Work," *New York Times,* August 1, 2010, http://www .nytimes.com/2010/08/02/nyregion/02burnout.html.

February 10, 2013
Transfiguration of Our Lord /
Last Sunday after Epiphany (RCL)

Revised Common Lectionary (RCL)

Exodus 34:29-35
Psalm 99
2 Corinthians 3:12—4:2
Luke 9:28-36 (37-43)

Transfiguration Sunday marks the final Sunday in the time after Epiphany and the last Sunday before the season of Lent begins. Epiphany and the time that follows is a season of God's revelation among us, of God's glory made manifest. It is fitting that before the season of Lent, before the journey to the cross, we have a foretaste of Jesus' ultimate eschatological glory—we join the disciples and are reminded for a shining instant that Jesus is indeed God's own Son and Chosen One. All of today's texts shine with God's glory—weighty revelation—illustrating that unbearable instant when divine and human meet. Such glory is too much for us, and these texts maintain some tension between God's transcendent "otherness" and intimate and personal immanence. We cannot bear the full glory of God; God must guard or protect us. But even with this protection, no one can emerge from an encounter with direct revelation unchanged. In Exodus 34, Moses returns from an encounter with God on the mountain with a shining face and must use a veil because the people are afraid of him. In our text from Luke, Peter and the disciples are terrified when God's presence comes upon them in a cloud. In a desperate attempt to contain that which was clearly beyond them, Peter suggests that they build three dwellings on the mountain, one each for Moses, Elijah, and Jesus. Paul's letter calls the Corinthians and us to claim our freedom in Christ to live transformed lives—lives that are touched by and reflect God's own glory.

First Reading
Exodus 34:29-35

Today's reading from Exodus comes after God delivered Israel from slavery (chaps. 12–15), God's provision of manna and water (chaps. 16–17), God's gift of the Law (chaps. 19–24), extended instructions to Moses concerning the building of the ark and the tabernacle (chaps. 25–31), and Israel's violation of the commandment against idolatry with the golden calf (chap. 32). Moses breaks the stone tablets containing God's commandments, the people experience punishment for their sin, and God threatens to abandon Israel after fulfilling the promise to bring them to the promised land, but Moses intercedes for the people and God finally relents and promises again to dwell with Israel. This dynamic is only possible because of God's gracious and unending love for Israel, but it is facilitated in part through the unique relationship between God and Moses. Exodus 33:11 tells us that God would speak with Moses as a "friend." It is out of this frank and deep relationship that Moses is able to call upon God truly to be the God of Israel—marking God's people as distinct from every other people by God's very presence with them. To seal this promise, Moses asks to see the fullness of God's glory and goodness. God agrees to engage with Moses, but direct encounter with God is dangerous; God must shield Moses from seeing the face of God, revealing the "backside" of God's glory. Thus God renews the covenant with Israel through Moses and Moses returns from the mountain carrying new stone tablets. While God has protected Moses from the most severe consequence of encountering God's glory, death, Moses has still been physically changed. Moses' face is shining.[1]

The Israelites rightly sense that Moses has been with God—indeed, he is radiating with the vestiges of God's glory. Moses has to reassure Aaron and the leaders so that he can give the people the commandments from God. After Moses finishes speaking with the people in this intermediary role, he veils his face. This becomes a pattern and a sign that Moses is bringing God's word to the people: when he meets with God he unveils his face, and when he reports to the people he does so with his face shining. When he isn't serving in this intermediary role between God and the people, Moses veils his face. Moses' shining face serves as a visible sign that he has been in God's presence—the people not only hear God's word but see evidence that their leader has been in the presence of God.[2]

As preachers we might find it interesting to imagine the credibility or terror we could gain if we stood in our pulpits with shining faces to proclaim God's word. Each week we labor over the Scriptures, seeking God's word for us and the communities we serve, and through the power of the Holy Spirit we do encounter God and are transformed by this encounter. Encountering God enlivens and illumines our lives with a brightness that is visible to everyone around us. Our faces may or may not be shining, but listeners should see evidence of encounter with God shining forth from our lives. The character and behavior, or *ethos*, of the preacher play a significant role in how listeners receive the sermon. We come to the congregation as ones who have witnessed God's presence and power. The preacher's encounter with God is like a flickering flame that can help to set listener's hearts and lives on fire so that listeners also experience the presence of the living God in the midst of worship. Terence Fretheim describes Moses' shining face as "the vision of the face of God which is available to the community of faith."[3]

Psalmody
Psalm 99

Psalm 99 is an enthronement psalm that emphasizes the holiness and awesome power of God. Yet this psalm specifically mentions Moses and Aaron by name, and scholars note several links between the praise of this psalm and the song of praise offered by Moses and the Israelites in Exodus 15.[4] The tensive dynamic of God's transcendent otherness, which must rightly be veiled from us, and God's desire to be in relationship with people and actively engage with human history, is evident throughout this psalm. Calls for the people to worship and the liturgical refrain, "Holy is he," are interspersed amid evidence of God's engagement with them in the sometimes dirty, day-to-day business of life. The psalmist alternates images of God's power and glory with specific links to the particularity of Israel's own history. God is envisioned as enthroned above the cherubim but also as specifically great in Zion. God cares enough about creation to establish equity and execute justice. The psalmist names specific leaders—Moses, Aaron, and Samuel—and recalls that the Lord was responsive to their cries and present to them in a pillar of cloud. The psalmist notes acts of faith and unfaith in verses 7 and 8. Israel both kept and violated God's decrees and desires; the psalmist describes God as forgiving but unwilling to put up with injustice and wrongdoing. Relationship with God is marked by this entangled, complex dynamic driven by God's complete love. To understand this dynamic, preachers may think metaphorically of God behaving like a parent to a rebellious teenager. God's love means that God suffers when Israel sins and violates covenant. God's love also means that God must set limits—even if those limits are painful to Israel. Ultimately, God's love is the foundation of God's forgiveness. This dynamic, visible in the psalm, reflects something deep about how God relates to people—a dynamic that we see again in the life, death, and resurrection of God incarnate, Jesus Christ. God's holy love also calls us to live holy lives; like the shining face of Moses, our lives cannot remain unaffected by our encounter with the tough and forgiving love of God.

Second Reading
2 Corinthians 3:12—4:2

Paul's relationship with the congregation in Corinth was complex and painful at times. Second Corinthians offers us further evidence of their conversation both in person and through correspondence following Paul's letter written in response to reports from "Chloe's people" (1 Cor. 1:11). Today's reading from 2 Corinthians picks up Paul's epistolary response to the Corinthian congregation midstream. In chapter 3, Paul has been defending his ministry and then interprets Israel's tradition, comparing the first covenant that God made with Israel with the covenant inaugurated through Christ, referencing Exodus 34:29-35.

Paul begins our reading today by citing the hope that fuels his and the Corinthians' bold ministry and faith. Paul's interpretation of Exodus and Israel's relationship to Christ is challenging for us to claim as Christians who firmly hold a "whole" Bible, made of our "First" or "Old" Testament of Hebrew Scriptures and our "Second" or "New" Testament, especially given the complexities and importance of interfaith relationships. Most biblical scholars and preachers today would not follow Paul's line of interpretation with Exodus 34. Paul's interpretation of Moses' veiling suggests that he may have veiled his face after speaking to the people not to reserve or shield them from God's awesome presence in reflected glory *shining on his face*, but because Moses wanted to protect them or prevent them from seeing the glory *fading from his own face*. Paul then writes of the Jewish people themselves as having hardened or veiled minds that keep them from seeing the truth that the first covenant is being changed and fulfilled in the new covenant. Positively, Paul now turns to the freedom offered by the power of the Spirit. Like Moses, we who know Christ encounter God with unveiled faces—and we are being transformed so that our lives might reflect Christ's glory.

Paul's claim that we are able to encounter God with unveiled faces and experience real transformation is an expression of his bold and hopeful faith—faith that God is actively engaged in our world, turning suffering into glory. Just as Paul's claim is challenging to fathom in the midst of Paul's own suffering and the suffering of the early church, it is extremely difficult to grasp in the midst of suffering in our lives, in the lives of those we love, and in the world at large. Yet this is the paradox of the cross, the stumbling block that Paul writes about in 1 Corinthians, which also lies at the heart of the gospel, that God is in the business of miraculous transformation, making a way where there is no way and bringing new life out of death. Because this is the nature of who God is and how God works in our world, we, like Paul and the early Christians, also do not lose heart. At the end of our reading for today, Paul returns to his defense; some in the Corinthian congregation apparently do not agree with Paul's message. But by the power and mercy of God, Paul stands by the gospel. That some believe and others do not is also troubling to us; the mystery of that which is veiled and unveiled challenges our desire to understand and to reach out to others with the gospel.

Gospel
Luke 9:28-36 (37-43)

The transfiguration continues the theme of revelation of Jesus Christ. The texts during the time after the Epiphany have offered us different windows into the nature and person of Jesus. Today's passage offers us a brief glimpse into the glorious and divine identity of Jesus, but the fantastic nature of the experience on the mountain can make it challenging to preach. We do not regularly experience divine revelation through encounters that are so overwhelming and unambiguous. The behavior of the disciples is also challenging—we would like to imagine ourselves behaving differently in the presence of divine glory! The addition of verses 37-43 offers an additional perspective following the miraculous events on the mountain.

The transfiguration appears in each of the Synoptic Gospels, but Luke offers his own version with unique nuances.[5] As in Matthew and Mark, the transfiguration in Luke follows Jesus' foretelling of his suffering, death, and resurrection. But Luke places the events on the mountain eight days later rather than six, and groups John's name with Peter when listing the three disciples accompanying Jesus. Luke also specifically mentions prayer as the purpose for going up to the mountain, which links this experience of divine revelation and the heavenly voice from the cloud with God's spoken revelation that accompanied prayer at Jesus' baptism.[6] It is in the midst of prayer that Jesus' appearance is changed, his clothes become white, and Moses and Elijah join him. In 9:31, Luke specifically mentions that Moses and Elijah appeared with Jesus in "glory," and that they were discussing Jesus' departure that he would accomplish in Jerusalem.[7] Luke also tells us that the disciples were tired; they likely missed the conversation among Jesus, Moses, and Elijah, but managed to stay awake to experience the vision of glory. We have not seen the last of the sleepy disciples; in Luke 22, when Jesus prays on the Mount of Olives before he is arrested, the disciples also sleep. We can imagine a somewhat groggy Peter suggesting that they build three tents or dwellings for the transfigured Jesus, Moses, and Elijah. Before the words are even fully out of his mouth, a cloud overshadows them, filling them with awe and fear. God's voice comes from the cloud—unambiguous revelation: "This is my Son, my Chosen; listen to him!" With the last of these powerful words still ringing in their ears, they look around and notice that they are alone with Jesus. Luke ends his version more simply than Mark and Matthew, where the disciples question the resurrection and ask about Elijah's coming. As Luke tells it, the disciples keep quiet and tell no one what they had seen.

Theologically, we might interpret the transfiguration as a sense of Christ's Alpha-and-Omega glory—the glory he shared eternally with the Father prior to the incarnation and the glory to which he returned in his ascension. The divine identity of Jesus is made clear in God's pronouncement from the cloud: as Son of God, Jesus is a member of the Trinity; further, Jesus is also God's elect, the one chosen to accomplish God's saving purposes. While orthodox Christology holds the divine and human completely together in the person of Jesus Christ, it is tempting for us to focus on the more relatable and human-centered actions of Jesus, such as feeding, healing, and teaching, practices that are more recognizable to us. The transfiguration reminds us of the limits of our human perspective: there is so much more to God, there are aspects of God that are completely beyond our reach, what Luther refers to as "God unpreached." Part of human brokenness is not only the drive to contain the divine, voiced by Peter's suggestion that they build booths to house the transfigured Christ, Moses, and Elijah, but also the tendency to forget that there is much that is veiled from us. Nevertheless, we can take solace from the experience of the disciples on the mountain with Jesus. After the voice has finished, the disciples find themselves alone with Jesus. The person of Jesus Christ is God's most complete revelation to us—a revelation intentionally relatable, as relatable as our own flesh and bone. While theologically balanced preaching must address God's immanence and transcendence, God's command to "listen to [Jesus]!" rings out from that mountaintop theophany and in our ears today. We cannot begin to know the depths of the divine, but we can and must continue to listen to Jesus.

In terms of scriptural interpretation and continuity between our two testaments, the account of the transfiguration offers positive balance to Paul's interpretation of Hebrew Scriptures in 2 Corinthians. The appearance of Moses and Elijah positively links God's revelation to Israel with God's revelation in Jesus Christ.[8] The images associated with this divine encounter read almost like a recipe for a classic experience of theophany in the Hebrew Scriptures: the mountain, the cloud that engulfs them, Jesus' "changed" and dazzling appearance, and fearful humans who stand in the presence of divine glory, even the reference to Jesus' "exodus" or departure. These images hold power and familiarity for us, and they reinterpret the Hebrew Scriptures in light of God's revelation in Jesus Christ. In Luke 4, Jesus identifies himself in the role of one who will proclaim release and liberation, reinterpreting the prophetic tradition.[9] Here in the transfiguration, the identity of Jesus as liberator is deepened and we see continuity between the mission of Jesus thus far and the destiny of Jesus' mission to liberate the world from the power of sin and death for all time.[10] The transfiguration was also important to the early church; in 2 Peter, the witnessing of the transfiguration is viewed as a kind of marker for the disciples' divine authority over false prophets—a sense of God's power and seal set upon Christ and their own ministry in Christ's name (2 Peter 1:16—2:1).

The story of Jesus healing a boy with a demon the day following his glorious transfiguration on the mountain is included as an optional addition to today's reading. Encountering this addition, we may be reminded of the Zen proverb, "After enlightenment, the laundry." Luke has omitted conversations between Jesus and the disciples as they descend from the mountain in Mark and Matthew, and shortens this incident. Jesus and his disciples return from the mountain and a large crowd is waiting for them. Life doesn't look so bright and glorious below. From the midst of the crowd, a man cries out on behalf of his son, his only child who is suffering from convulsions and foaming at the mouth, symptoms of seizures common to those with epilepsy. The disciples were unable to cure the boy and this father is desperate.

Following other pronouncements against "this generation," Jesus cries out judgment directed toward those present: "You faithless and perverse generation, how much longer must I be with you and bear with you?"[11] Commentator Alan Culpepper links Jesus' references to Moses' song of lament in Deuteronomy 32:4-6.[12] We may also find poignancy in the repeated references to "this generation," in that "this generation" actually lived and walked with God incarnate, yet they join every generation in their inability to grasp fully and live up to God's intentions among them. But it is precisely for "this generation" and all generations that Jesus will suffer and die, granting "this generation" and every generation new life and the joyful calling to bear witness to Jesus' resurrection from the dead. While some from "this generation" will ultimately come to understand Jesus more fully, in the verses before and after this story, Jesus' followers clearly do not comprehend the revelation that they have been given. In the midst of the miraculous theophany on the mountain, Peter makes his imperceptive suggestion that they build dwellings for Jesus, Moses, and Elijah. Further, although Jesus does not command it in Luke's version, the disciples keep silent about Jesus' transfiguration and the divine pronouncement on the mountain. The disciples are unable to cure the boy, so Jesus himself steps in and rebukes the spirit, healing the child. After the spirit is cast out of the boy and the crowd is still basking in amazement, Jesus again foretells his coming death, but they do not understand and do not ask him to explain (9:43-45).

The Text in Our World

The complete Gospel reading for today spans the heights of a heavenly mountaintop encounter and the frustration and brokenness found among the crowds below. The spectrum here highlights the tension inherent in God's revelation to us. Because of our humanity and essential difference from God, God's revelatory call to us is only unlocked through the power and movement of the Holy Spirit in us. Like the disciples who were earlier granted the power of healing, we find ourselves unable to control the Spirit's movement. As preachers, we cannot ensure the efficacy of our words; only the Spirit's spark in our words and within our listeners can complete the circuit and allow revelation to unfold. Yet despite the challenges illustrated in the text, Jesus emerges as the key. Jesus stands as the sole recipient of God's pronouncement and Jesus steps in, offering healing and hope to a suffering child and his father when the disciples fail. Like the disciples long ago, so often we fail to perceive what Jesus is doing among us. In preparing sermons, we find it easy to name places of brokenness in our lives and world where we need God's healing presence and touch, while it is immensely challenging to name concrete instances where God is at work among us, allowing us fragmentary glimpses of God's ultimate redemptive purposes. Yet, paradoxically, this is our calling: to bear witness to what God has done, is doing, and will do for the world. God's revelation continues to unfold among us. It is present when a group from a retirement community visits a local school each week to tutor students who need a little extra learning support. It is present when a congregation in a Memphis, Tennessee, suburb opens its doors to a congregation from a mosque in the midst of renovations during Ramadan. It is present when a grieving father who has lost a child receives a call to serve as an interim pastor to a congregation dealing with conflict and turmoil, and both experience healing. As we move into the season of Lent and again experience Jesus' journey to the cross, the finality of the tomb in the darkness of Good Friday, and the unexpected new life of Jesus' resurrection, the light of divine revelation continues to be present with us and God's mountaintop call continues to echo in our ears and through the ages: "This is my Son, my Chosen; listen to him!" (For more information on today's text from 2 Corinthians, see Michael P. Knowles, *We Preach Not Ourselves: Paul on Proclamation* [Grand Rapids: Brazos, 2008].)

Notes

1. Discussion in commentaries offers more background on the history of the translation of the word *shining*, which has also been translated as "horned." Artists as diverse as Michelangelo and Marc Chagall have visually depicted Moses with horns as a result of this translation choice. Terence E. Fretheim, *Exodus*, Interpretation: A Bible Commentary for Teaching and Preaching (Louisville: John Knox, 1991), 310.
2. This visible sign may be helpful in guarding the people from the temptation to create another golden calf. As embodied people we need visible signs; this is why the sacraments are such an important gift in the life of the church.
3. Fretheim, *Exodus*, 311.
4. J. Clinton McCann Jr., "The Book of Psalms," in *The New Interpreter's Bible: 1 and 2 Maccabees, Job, Psalms*, ed. Leander Keck et al. (Nashville: Abingdon, 1996), 4:1074–75. McCann suggests that these verbal links may be an intentional way of recalling God's mighty acts during a later time in Israel's history when such an affirmation is needed.
5. Compare Luke's version with Matthew 17:1-8 and Mark 9:2-8.
6. One should also note the public nature of God's declaration here, "This is my Son . . . ," compared to "You are my son . . . ," directed to Jesus at his baptism in 3:22.
7. In Luke 2 the glory of the Lord appeared to shepherds to herald Jesus' birth (2:9), and Simeon praised God and blessed Jesus, saying that he would bring "a light for revelation to the Gentiles and for glory to your people Israel" (v. 32). Luke Timothy Johnson, *The Gospel of Luke*, Sacra Pagina (Collegeville, Minn.: Liturgical, 1991), 3:153.
8. See also Frederick Dale Brunner's discussion of the transfiguration in Matthew in *Matthew: A Commentary*, vol. 2, *The Churchbook: Matthew 13–28* (Grand Rapids: Eerdmans, 2004), 168–69.
9. Joel Green, *The Gospel of Luke*, The New International Commentary on the New Testament (Grand Rapids: Eerdmans, 1997), 379.
10. See also ibid.
11. See other "this generation" pronouncements in Luke: 7:31; 11:29-32, 50-51; 16:8; 17:25; 21:32.
12. Alan Culpepper, "The Gospel of Luke," in *The New Interpreter's Bible: Luke–John*, ed. Leander Keck et al. (Nashville: Abingdon, 1995), 9:209.

Lent

L. Susan Bond

Memento mori is a Latin phrase that means "Remember your mortality." The phrase has also been used in reference to a genre of artistic work designed with symbols and images to remind viewers of their mortality, including skulls, skeletons, coffins, and tombs. The genre began in ancient Rome, but during the Middle Ages it became a central artistic theme in paintings and tapestries and it grew to include Christian images of heaven, hell, and divine judgment. The language finds expression in Christian liturgies of Lent: "Remember your mortality. Ashes to ashes, dust to dust."

Ash Wednesday launches us into the penitential season of Lent that traditionally calls believers into disciplines like prayer, fasting, and reflection. Lent, also called *Quadragesima*, is a forty-day period of penitence and was probably added to the church's calendar as late as the fourth century (post-Nicene) as a period of preparation for catechumenates.[1] It's a movable observance, one of many fast days that is unfixed, functioning as the prologue to Easter's annually shifting lunar dating.

Ash Wednesday is a solemn day of repentance, and the marking with ashes takes symbolic cues from the Jewish antecedents of ritual mourning and repentance. Bodily marking shows up all over the Hebrew Bible: Cain is marked with a sign of warning and divine protection on his forehead (Gen. 4:15); slaves are marked with signs of ownership (Exod. 21:6). The imagery of dust/dirt/humus associated with the creation narrative of Genesis also informs Christian claims about our human need for divine breath, our humility, and our mortality. Ashes to ashes, dust to dust.

Notions of purging and purification associated with Ash Wednesday and the Lenten season are also related to the Jewish practices of ritual bathing, the imposition of ashes, and repentance. Themes of liberation from slavery (the exodus), the symbolism of forty days and forty years, and the need for reconciliation are Jewish concepts that carried over into the Lenten cycle. The confession liturgies of the early church grasped this concept, the need for us to be reconciled to each other and to God, and to demonstrate the recognition of this in public corporate worship.

Within contemporary American Christianity, the Lenten cycle is most familiar among Catholics, Lutherans, Presbyterians, and Episcopalians. However, some of the traditional "low-church" denominations are increasingly adding Lenten observations to their practice. What is consistent about these practices is their uniformity in considering Lent a time for individual reflection and sacrifice, eclipsing the possibilities for Lent to be a time of reflection on the embedded practices of a whole community in their interactions with the broader world. When Pope Benedict XVI called for the Catholic Church to repent for its complicity in and blindness to clergy sex abuse, it was a communal summons, not merely an individual summons: "The church has a profound need to relearn penance, to accept purification, to learn on the one hand forgiveness but also the necessity of justice. And forgiveness does not substitute justice. . . . We have to relearn these essentials: conversion, prayer, penance."[2]

Notes

1. The development of the Lenten penitential season is fairly complex. One dimension of the development is the extension and integration of Pascha into Easter celebrations. As the church became more institutionalized, the pre-Paschal period of instruction and preparation was extended. Thomas J. Talley indicates that a fairly established Lenten period may have been operative as early as the second or third century. In Thomas J. Talley, *Origins of the Liturgical Year* (New York: Pueblo, 1986), 31–33.
2. John Thavis, "Pope Says Sex Abuse Crisis Is 'Terrifying' Example of Church Failings," May 11, 2010, http://www.catholicnews.com/data/stories/cns/1001965.htm.

February 13, 2013
Ash Wednesday

The images for these Ash Wednesday readings are vivid and, in many ways, conflicting. The prophetic readings from Joel and Isaiah are crowded and noisy, full of trumpets and gathering assemblies set against a backdrop of ominous skies and danger. The other three readings turn in the opposite direction, moving inward and using the language of intimacy, secrecy, and solitude. These contrasts provide us with different ways of thinking about faithful living, the context of ethical life, and the theological dimensions of repentance and forgiveness. While we are certainly more familiar with a traditional Christian piety of personal reflection and privacy, we'll want to keep both approaches in mind and in conversation with each other. Instead of the typical language of head and heart, these texts present us with the polarities of individual and community, inner change and outward behavior. What are we to make of Joel's call to "blow the trumpet in Zion" in light of Matthew's call, "Do not sound a trumpet before you"? "The readings for Ash Wednesday leave us with conflicting admonitions: to put on sackcloth and ashes, and to wash our faces and comb our hair. They remind us how essential it is that entire communities repent with one voice."[1]

Another theological theme presented by these readings is that of God's character and divine *modus operandi*. Joel's vision presents us with a God who visits destruction upon the faithful, only to offer a reprieve that's conditional upon our human actions. While God's faithfulness and righteousness and mercy (God's *hesed*) are proclaimed throughout the texts, there are echoes of works righteousness as well. Preachers will have to reflect carefully on their claims to avoid contradictions between conditional and unconditional forgiveness.

What all of today's lections have in common, though, is the claim that faithful living will require changes and adjustments and a constant attentiveness to what God desires of us. Ash Wednesday marks a time for the faithful to take stock of themselves, from the individual heart of the solo believer to the broadest social justice activities of feeding the hungry and caring for laborers. Taken together, the combination of texts reminds us that there is no matter too small or too large for God's divine justice. From the privacy of Matthew's prayer closet to the streets of Zion, God's desire is for us to turn away from distortions of our faith and to return to God's holy vision of a just world.

First Reading
Joel 2:1-2, 12-17 (RCL)
Joel 2:12-18 (LFM)

Apocalyptic warnings, while not always respected, are certainly not unusual for either testament. Preachers may initially be reluctant to dabble in apocalyptic, especially given a recent worldwide phenomenon initiated by Harold Camping of the Family Radio broadcasts, where some phase of apocalyptic scenario was predicted for May 21, 2011. According to Camping's calculations, Jesus would return on May 21, the righteous would be raptured into heaven, and there would be an additional five months of fire, plagues, and other disasters for those who missed the rapture. According to Camping, the end of the world would be on October 21, 2011. Camping's followers had one clear message for the world: "Repent!"

The main exhortation in the book of Joel is indeed to "return to the LORD," but without knowing more about the full context, we preachers will be tempted either to tame this exhortation into private confession and personal piety or to literalize it into global Armageddon. Preachers should spend a few minutes reading the entire book. Not only is it short; it's also the home of a widely quoted bit of Scripture: "I will pour out my spirit on all flesh; your sons and your daughters shall prophesy, your old men shall dream dreams, and your young men shall see visions. Even on the male and female slaves, in those days, I will pour out my spirit" (2:28-29).

The whole narrative of Joel is divided into two parts. The first part opens with a summons to the elders, the priests, the old, the young, and those yet to come. It describes a scourge of locusts and a drought, but scholars are divided on whether "locusts" and "drought" are literal references to the natural world or if they're metaphors for military aggressors. Due to this devastation, the people are not only hungry and unable to make the appropriate ritual sacrifices, but they are ashamed of their inability to honor God. Honor and shame are key components of the book; at the beginning, the people are ashamed of their poverty and poor ritual life; but by the end of chapter 2 God promises that "my people will never again be put to shame" (2:27).

It's unclear that the children of Israel have sinned or transgressed in any particular way, so their "return" or "repentance" should be handled carefully. As Ronald Simkins suggests, it's the fact of the devastation itself that causes Israel to feel abandoned, ashamed, and desolate. If the writing is dated to the Babylonian exile or immediately after, we could understand that Israel questioned God's providence *in toto*: "If we are chosen, why has God abandoned us?"

But, as Simkins also suggests, if Israel's sins are not enumerated, maybe the covenant model of reciprocation is insufficient. Maybe God has never abandoned Israel, or has already forgiven Israel for sins that have been discounted.[2] In that case, Israel should not be ashamed of its inability to provide the cultic sacrifices. Israel should return to the Lord "with all your heart, with fasting, with weeping, and with mourning; rend your hearts and not your clothing. Return to the LORD, your God, for he is gracious and merciful, slow to anger, and abounding in steadfast love, and relents from punishing" (2:12-13). In other words, Israel is misguided in considering the current devastation as a punishment from God, so they should stop being ashamed, for their shame is a poor witness among the nations. As Simkins writes, "The locust plague had been interpreted as a sign of Yahweh's absence, bringing shame on his people. But Yahweh's destruction of the locusts and restoration of the land will demonstrate Yahweh's presence among his people. Their mourning will be turned into joy, and they will no longer be ashamed before the nations."[3]

So this is good news for us as well. Rather than spend our Lenten season cataloguing our sins and hoping to get back in God's good graces, we should accept it as a given that our troubles are not caused by a wrathful God who requires sacrificial behavior in some sort of *quid pro quo* transaction. Completely consistent with the gospel claims, we already belong to God, and we simply have to be reminded of that fact so that we can rejoice and celebrate God's never-ending presence in our midst. We don't have to tear our garments or don sackcloth, or (dare we say it?) even mark ourselves with ashes.

Since most of us *will* be involved in worship communities that practice Ash Wednesday and Lent, we can shift the focus from our unworthiness and the slow boil of penitential piety to the still-stunning breadth of God's mercy that allows us to avoid the funereal tone of the season and raise our voices in praise and thanksgiving.

Isaiah 58:1-12 (RCL alt.)

The first thing to notice about the Isaiah reading is that it's another noisy episode dealing with issues of cultic practices. In our corporate worship life, we don't encounter these kinds of shouting matches during the worship service itself, but many of us in free-church traditions have encountered heated exchanges during worship committee meetings or in other smaller venues. We argue about what kinds of bread to use in communion, debating the relative merits of whole loaves, wafers, and little sanitized bread pellets. We may have arguments over what kinds of music to offer, what to do with the children, or even whether folks should be exuberant or solemn during the service.

In those faith communities where worship practices are not subject to democratic discussion, we know that occasions arise where folks criticize the practices of other communities of believers. We pass judgment on the way other groups engage in ritual behavior, dismissing certain forms of baptism as misguided or even faulty. So even if we initially consider this textual portion alien, a quick reality check will inform us otherwise. We know what it's like to have heated disagreements and holier-than-thou certitudes about how to worship.

Part of the irony if we compare this Isaiah passage with the Joel passage is that Joel's community is worried about not having enough food to sacrifice, while Isaiah's group is obsessed with how to fast. Both groups have a food obsession that distracts them from God's purposes. We remember too the Pauline exhortation about food offered to idols or Peter's dream about unclean animals, so we know this obsession with cultic practices didn't end with the prophetic tradition.

The passage contrasts obsession with cultic details to the issues of social justice and what "true" worship looks like. The structure of the passage assumes a back-and-forth exchange between God and the people, with the prophetic figure acting as interpreter/translator. The opening verses (vv. 1-2) are between God and the prophet, calling for the prophet to be loud and clear: "Shout out, do not hold back! Lift up your voice like a trumpet! Announce to my people their rebellion." For contemporary preachers, the charge is the same: "Don't hold back." If we're going to put ashes on foreheads, we should make it significant and not just ritual cultic behavior.

The second section quotes the words of the people, "'Why do we fast, but you do not see? Why humble ourselves, but you do not notice?" (v. 3). Scholars point out that the form and language may be associated with rituals of mourning and lamentation. I like to think of it as singing the Exile Blues.

In the third and final section, the tongue-lashing begins. The prophet assumes the divine voice and clarifies the problem. "You're only interested in yourselves when you come here to fast and pray. The whole time you're here paying lip service to me, you're oppressing and neglecting other folks." Or, as some preachers would say, "You can talk the talk, but you can't walk the walk." If we were hoping we could make a painless contrast between "legalistic" Jewish ritual and "heartfelt" Christian worship, we'll be disappointed. The contrast is between ritual behaviors and ethical practices of community justice. Like the prophet Micah, Isaiah calls his community to be merciful and just: "If you remove the yoke from among you, the pointing of the finger, the speaking of evil, if you offer your food to the hungry and satisfy the needs of the afflicted, then your light shall rise in the darkness and your gloom be like the noonday. . . . You shall be called the *repairer of the breach*, the restorer of streets to live in" (58:9b-10, 12b, emphasis added).

Noting that this portion of Isaiah is probably postexilic, Shauna Hannan urges preachers to avoid the metaphorical strategy that psychologizes "exile" into a discussion of our inner wastelands: "For this Sunday, I encourage preachers not to hide behind the metaphorical exiles of our lives. If you are like me and have not been in forced exile, go out into your community and find those refugees."[4] While some preachers will argue that Christians are "in exile" or "resident aliens" in American culture, this is yet another example of the metaphorical psychologizing of exile and probably won't do full justice to the prophetic call.

Rather than identify ourselves as the exile community, we will do better to identify ourselves as those who "step into the breach." As Christoph Schroeder argues, standing in the breach involves becoming an intercessor on behalf of the disenfranchised and dispossessed, those who are in some form of exile precisely because of social injustice. To intercede conjures all the other images and metaphors we use about Jesus, who stepped into danger on our behalf. A classical hermeneutical approach will be to use substitutionary sacrifice models where an individual or group takes the punishment as a kind of divine scapegoat to absorb divine wrath. But rather than imagine the breach is between God and humanity (to prevent God from inflicting divine wrath upon us or unsuspecting others), we must imagine that God is on the side of those who stand in the breach and that God is an agent, not of sacrifice and substitution, but of eliminating wrath and its consequences altogether.

The phrase "standing in the breach," in its biblical use, plays with the imagery of a walled city, whose protection against violence has been compromised; the wall has been breached. We don't have to imagine that God is the agent or author of the violence; we can as faithfully assign that task to the social forces that threaten social stability and cohesion. In this particular text, the prophet speaks on God's behalf about what has happened and what has been breached. By naming specific groups of people (the poor, the hungry, the oppressed), it's clear that the danger comes not from God, but from human social agents that impoverish and oppress others. Schroeder writes:

> What does this practice of justice entail? According to this metaphor, it involves acting on behalf of others. . . . To stand in the breach is risky. It would require putting one's own life in danger, exposing it in order to save the life of the community, thereby ensuring the social cohesion and solidarity of the society. Whoever does this, whoever looses the bonds of injustice, lets the oppressed go free, shares bread with the hungry, rescues the homeless, and covers the naked (vv. 6-7), shall be called "the repairer of the breach."[5]

This interpretation is supported by the claims of the text that don't fit in with more traditional approaches. When we stop worrying about our own fasting (while others starve!), and when we step into that breach on their behalf, then our light will shine and God will be in front of us and behind us. God is in the business of repairing breaches and loosening the bonds of injustice, so we will find the divine presence when we engage in that work. The prophetic task is not to get God on the side of the believers; it's to get the believers to join God's justice-making project and to point to God's future of a just world.

So, back to the Ash Wednesday symbols and practices. Preachers have an opportunity on this night to reframe the approaching weeks of repentance as weeks of turning toward God. "Ashes to ashes, dust to dust, remember to whom you belong." We can reinterpret the sign of the cross on the forehead as an anointing in God's justice-making project, not as a sign of our individual intentions, but as a symbol of the group to whom we belong. What could be more powerful an image than a group of repentant believers, all marked with the sign of an ashy cross, going into the world to feed the hungry and free the oppressed? Let's mark ourselves with ashes, pick up the cross, step into the breach, and follow Jesus on the Way.

Psalmody
Psalm 51:1-17 (RCL)
Psalm 51:3-4, 5-6, 12-13, 14, 17 (LFM)

The backdrop of this psalm is 2 Samuel 12, where King David repents of his sin of adultery with Bathsheba. According to the Samuel texts, David not only committed adultery with Bathsheba, but he sent her husband, Uriah, off to the frontline of the battlefields so he'd be killed by the enemy. David's in-house prophet, Nathan, tricks David into a confession by using a parable about stealing sheep, unfortunately comparing a woman to a farm animal and reducing the complex sins of adultery and murder-by-proxy to the one simple sin of "stealing" somebody else's woman. Preachers need to attend to the background of the psalm and to the entire sweep of sinfulness behind the Davidic heritage for one primary reason: the attempts to minimize and personalize the sins of David were already at play with the earliest interpretations of the disaster.

We live in an era where the sins of simple infidelity are considered more important than the sins of objectifying women or of sending men into battle. In the last thirty years we've seen televangelists, political leaders, and even an American president take to the airwaves to repent publicly of sexual indiscretions. Some have lost careers without even committing sexual acts, but for simply sending text messages on sexual topics. The point of this reflection is to clarify the peculiar religious heritage behind American understandings of sin and repentance. Sins are generally understood to be personal in nature; sins are generally understood to be sexual infractions. No one in the United States is required to repent of phony reasons to send men to die on foreign battlefields; no one is expected to repent of capital punishment.

Regardless of the dating and authorship of either the Samuel narratives or the psalms, traditional hermeneutics has linked Psalm 51 to the David/Bathsheba/Nathan stories. Within Christian tradition, Psalm 51 is the *Miserere mei* ("Have mercy on me"), or simply the *Miserere* ("Have mercy"), and is one of the penitential psalms associated with Ash Wednesday and the Lenten season.

The connection between this Hebrew Bible text and traditional individualistic (and moralistic) Christian piety is easy to see. The primary metaphors of the psalm are also primary images of the Christian purity/pollution paradigm, a binary system that refers to sin as dirtiness or stain and that refers to redemption in the metaphors of cleansing or washing. The references to Christian baptism are almost irresistible. The references to a "clean heart" are likewise catnip to contemporary Americans because they resonate with evangelical emphases on a religion "of the heart." Most contemporary Christians are unaware that the Hebrew Bible uses the term *heart* to refer to matters of intention and will. In Hebrew Scriptures, matters of "the heart" are not solely related to episodes of inner emotion, but primarily to matters of ethical intention. Walther Eichrodt explains, "The great majority of instances of the word refer to intellectual and volitional processes . . . when Hosea wishes to characterize the senseless political behavior of the Northern Kingdom, he says that Ephraim has no heart, that is to say, no understanding; when Jeremiah wishes to stigmatize Israel's child sacrifices as utterly contrary to the will of Yahweh, he says that Yahweh never commanded it, and that such a thing never came into his heart."[6]

What David is calling for is a complete life intervention, including an emotional reaction, an intellectual reorganization, and a complete change of will and intention. No wonder the language is so overwhelming. David is not just apologizing for a particular sin, but begging for a purging of his entire being and his way of understanding himself in his world. Patrick D. Miller writes, "Look at the verbs: have mercy, blot out, wash me, cleanse me, purge me, wash me, let me hear joy, hide your face, blot out, create, put a new spirit, do not cast away, do not take, restore, sustain, deliver. The depth of the psalmist's awareness of his sin is matched only by the sense of need it has created."[7] Miller goes on to argue that David would not have realized the personal and social devastation created by his acts without the prophet Nathan calling him out on his sins.

It's probably best to understand David's sin as an abuse of political power embedded within systemic abuses of power.[8] In our day and age, we'd consider his bedding of Bathsheba to be sexual harassment. Who can say no to the king? When she becomes pregnant, David panics and has to attempt a cover-up; he sends Uriah to the battlefield.

But he cannot ultimately escape. Nathan's prophetic truth telling becomes the literary and theological foil to David's web of lies and deceptions. If we move the narrative out of the traditional piety of individualism and into the model of social justice, we have to explore our own complicity, as Americans and as Christians, in the systemic abuse of power.

There is no cheap grace in this passage, no easy reconciliation. According to the theology of the psalm, calling for mercy requires that we recognize the full contamination that occurs with our sinful acts. And, most painfully for preachers, it means that we must become truth tellers like Nathan for this moment of radical realization to occur.

No wonder our liturgy uses the language of mortality, death, and ashes. Only if the sin is profound will we need such a wide, wide mercy. No wonder that the *Miserere mei* has become a classic! And no wonder Augustine raged against the Pelagians with their theology of works righteousness! We cannot do it ourselves—our sin is too massive and complex; we need the kind of reconciliation offered through the one we know as Christ.

Second Reading
2 Corinthians 5:20b—6:10 (RCL)
2 Corinthians 5:20—6:2 (LFM)

This Pauline text occurs twice in the lectionaries: as a reading during the time after Pentecost (Year B) and as an Ash Wednesday lection for all three years. Even though the larger pericope begins with the compelling charge to be "ambassadors for Christ," that phrase isn't part of today's reading. Nevertheless, it should be the assumed background for Paul's comments. Paul changes the metaphorical understanding of the preacher from "herald" to "ambassador." The change is both theological and practical. Glenn Miller notes, "To deal with the emperor's ambassador is to negotiate with the emperor himself. The ambassador is entrusted with a mission and given much flexibility in how that mission is carried out. Indeed, an ambassador may come with threats or with more gentle persuasions in order to persuade people of the importance of the emperor's offer of peace or trade."[9]

As a theological change, it means that preachers are not primarily voices for God, but are reconciling ministers on behalf of Jesus the Christ. This isn't a top-down ministry, but one that operates on the ground. The theological change indicates the practical difference. Who you are dictates how you act. As he does in so many other epistles, Paul finds himself once again defending his apostolic credentials and what we assume was an unconventional method of church planting.

Today's text begins with Paul's entreaty to Corinth and to us, "Be reconciled to God" (5:20), with the additional warning "not to accept the grace of God in vain" (6:1). This is no casual warning; Paul insists that the time for reconciliation and salvation is "Now!" (6:2). There is a Markan immediacy to Paul's urging, a sense of eschatological (if not apocalyptic) urgency. As I wrote elsewhere,

> "The basic structure of Paul's apocalyptic thought is grounded in the idea that the world is constantly in danger of temptation and corruption by the powers and principalities. While Paul (and the other early writers) may have had images of some spiritual demons flapping around, the notion of powers and principalities can't be reduced to the presence of simple supernatural beings or agents. The powers function to hold communities together in corrupt systems of relationship, abuse of power, and domination strategies."[10]

If the powers function to deceive communities in corrupt systems of relationship, no wonder Paul considers our active reconciliation to be so critical. No wonder he warns us not to accept God's grace in vain. If we have received God's grace, then we belong to a new order of humanity, an order that's recognizable by transformed human relationships. Anything short of reconciled/reconciling communities is a fundamental betrayal of the gospel and of the grace we've received.

But beyond that betrayal, there is, for Paul, always the concern about our ability to discern the reign of God as it breaks into human history. If we cannot tell the difference between the old order dominated by power schemes and the new order of God's *basileia tou theou*, how will we bear witness to God's *basileia* as it emerges? Paul Minear's work on New Testament apocalyptic claims that such prophetic discernment was a key component of the Pauline corpus. One of the marks of prophetic address was the ability of the interpreter to be "alive to the conflicts which that vocation and those tasks cause—conflicts within the prophets themselves, within the covenant community, and between that community and its neighbors."[11]

For Paul, if the Corinthians were not reconciled to one another and were not engaging in reconciling ministries, it signaled to him that they just didn't get it. They didn't understand the nature of their own salvation, the nature of their changed selves, the nature of their communal new creation, or the future reconciliation toward which God lures the kingdom mired in death.

Paul's plea to the church is simple: "If you don't know how to be new creatures, how can you be the advance guard, the ambassadors for Christ?" And this brings us back, full circle, to Paul's defense of his apostolic credentials. Paul urges us to take him seriously because of the way he acts. He lists three categories of "validation," starting by enumerating the hardships he's endured in his missionary work, then moving to his claims of character or "virtues," then enumerating the sets of oppositions or paradoxes. In every section, ending with the final series of antitheses, Paul is establishing a contrast between the community that is reconciled and the one that is not. I disagree with the conventional interpretations that Paul is elucidating something like a Buddhist Middle Way. The form of the final list ("as . . . and yet") is not so much marking a territory between extremes as it is an identification of the *kata sarka* contrast of 5:16b ("in the flesh") he's already established. As Miller asserts, "They should reconcile with him for the sake of Christ who died for all; they should reconcile with Paul because the apostle is a new creature whose sins have been removed. Above all, they should reconcile because Paul is God's ambassador, and no matter what people may say about his ministry, the Corinthians know that he has been faithful to his commission."[12] He is making a bold contrast between the way he's been perceived and the way he sees himself as reconciled to God in Christ. Paul gives us a sense of urgency in seeing ourselves and all the world as being reconciled. "When we look to Christ, to our reconciliation with God, to our ministry from God, we have no time for enmity or hostility. The message itself demands that we treat everyone as though they were already what they are 'in Christ'—new creatures."[13]

When we consider the fragmented reality of Christianity within our own nation and around the world, we realize that in order to bear witness to God's reconciling future, we cannot engage in polemic or hostility toward those with whom we disagree, no matter how fierce that disagreement may be. This is not to counsel easy capitulation or simply "making nice," since we also know that the powers and principalities operate within faith communities; the powers function to hold communities together in corrupt systems of relationship, abuse of power, and domination strategies.

Paul is calling for a kind of nonviolent rhetorical resistance to the powers and principalities, wherever we encounter them. Our posture toward others *is* our witness to God's in-breaking reign. It's too easy for Christians on the right or the left to bash each other as inauthentic, as "non-Christian," as corrupt. When we do that, we don't understand the nature of our own salvation, the nature of our shared inheritance, or the future reconciliation toward which God lures our broken world. When we engage in rhetorical bad-mouthing, we're bad ambassadors; we betray the gospel and the grace we've received.

Not long ago I delivered a lecture about public theology and a path toward reconciliation between the discourses of the Christian Right and the Christian Left. My mistake was in taking it for granted that others within the context of theological education would agree with me that ecumenicity and reconciliation within the body of Christ are desirable or necessary to our witness. So I was caught off-guard during the Q&A when one theologian slammed my comments as naïve: "I don't care about the Christian Right!" he bellowed. "I think we should cut ourselves off from them and stop trying to find common ground." The temptation to agree with him was powerful, and I wish I could report that I countered with bold Pauline words about being reconciled and being ambassadors. I don't remember exactly what I responded, but I wish that the spirit of Paul had risen from the gathering and cried out, "Be reconciled to God and do not accept the grace of God in vain."

Gospel
Matthew 6:1-6, 16-21 (RCL)
Matthew 6:1-6, 16-18 (LFM)

If we've been reading Matthew front to back, this passage about praying in private should create enough confusion to make us flip back to Matthew 5:14-16 and the beginning of the Sermon on the Mount: "You are the light of the world. A city built on a hill cannot be hid. No one after lighting a lamp puts it under the bushel basket, but on the lampstand, and it gives light to all in the house. In the same way, let your light shine before others, so that they may see your good works and give glory to your Father in heaven."

Which line of thought are we supposed to follow? Are we supposed to be public Christians and let our lights shine, or are we supposed to be private Christians hiding in a prayer closet? Matt Skinner notes that it's too bad nobody observed Ash Wednesday during the first century: "Jesus would have had a ball with it, given his penchant for directing special criticism toward religious people and their overt expressions of piety. Smudged foreheads are public expressions. . . ."[14]

And there's no doubt that Jesus is alerting us to a critical issue in the way we practice our faith and our piety, whether we're doing it for the glory of God or for our own benefit and the favorable opinions of others. The sixth chapter of Matthew's Gospel is in the middle of the narrative block (chapters 5–7) during which Jesus elaborates his teaching ministry. Jesus inaugurates his ministry in a public setting that includes his newly recruited disciples as well as ordinary crowds: faithful Jews and uninitiated Gentiles. Matthew makes sure we understand the parallels between Moses' Ten Commandments and Jesus' Beatitudes by having Jesus deliver the sermon "on the mount." We should be cautious, however, of assigning the status of rules to the Beatitudes; Warren Carter argues that we should see the entire Sermon on the Mount as a set of examples or signs by which to discern the in-breaking reign of God: "In offering a vision of life based on God's empire, the sermon informs and forms disciples further about this existence to which they've committed themselves. For the crowd, the sermon provides the 'rest of the story.' Having experienced God's gracious presence in healing, they now hear God's vision of life based on God's reign."[15]

Like Paul's words in the Corinthian text, this passage (and the whole Sermon on the Mount) alerts listeners to the difference between the ways of God and the ways of the world. We miss the point if we reduce the instruction to prayer location (public versus private) or to prayer motivation (showy versus sincere). We certainly don't want to engage in the tired old anti-Judaisms or the hackneyed false dichotomies that creep into our interpretations, and subsequently into our sermons. Matthew's words and worldview are fully continuous with intertestamental Judaism, even though the Matthean community uses Jesus and the Jesus story as its central interpretive symbols. Both communities call for prophetic reform; both call for penitential practices like almsgiving, fasting, and prayer; and both call for the rejection of improper motivations. Our entire set of lectionary readings for Ash Wednesday witnesses to the reality that true worship and false worship were taken seriously by both communities. Jesus' instructions do not reject cultic practices; they simply reiterate them. Matthew's Jesus stands on the shoulders of Joel and Nathan and Isaiah and cries out the same warnings.

"Beware!" Jesus cries from the mountaintop. "Don't practice your piety, your righteousness, or your faithful acts for the purpose of impressing others." Then, just getting warmed up, Jesus engages in what Skinner has called a kind of "burlesque overkill." Jesus refers to the blowing of trumpets while giving alms, to the hypocrites wailing on the street corners to pray, to the maskers who disfigure their faces while fasting. Skinner is probably referring to the imagery of the Greco-Roman theater that some New Testament scholars see lurking in the words of Matthew's Jesus. "The term *hypocrites* derives from the theater, the actor who plays a part. . . . Here the term suggests playing a public role of aiding another in accord with God's will, whereas the real inner interest is in one's own honor and reputation. In pursuing one's own honor, the synagogue practice imitates the dominant cultural patterns of reciprocal and conspicuous giving."[16]

We don't identify much with the conventions of public theater these days, unless we consider sporting events or giant prayer rallies held in sports stadiums, where the notions of role playing and religious *quid pro quo* go hand in hand. Imagine the athlete-gladiator, with blackened cheeks, kneeling to ask God to help Team A beat the spandex off Team B. Don't forget the John 3:16 guy in the bleachers with a rainbow clown wig. And don't forget the giant political prayer rallies, where the politicians charge entrance fees, hire gospel singers, and garner media attention for their events.

Now imagine Jesus saying, "When you pray, don't put black streaks on your cheeks or wear a rainbow wig. Don't invite CNN to your rallies and don't allow flip cameras or cell phones." This contemporary update sounds silly. Why would Jesus talk about rainbow wigs and cell phones? What's up with that, Jesus?

> But the humor intensifies very serious warnings. Charity is not charity when an intent to garner attention and influence lies behind it. Prayer is not prayer when the one praying is more interested in calling attention to one's own efforts, eloquence, or importance than in conducting honest communication with God. Fasting, which enacts humanity's utter dependence upon God (fasting in scripture has connections to repentance, petition, lament, and the yearning for God's justice), instead mocks that dependence when the fast is poisoned by attempts to impress others with the depths of the faster's devotion.[17]

Notes

1. Susan B. W. Johnson, "Living by the Word: Remorse and Hope," *Christian Century* 114, no. 4 (January 29, 1997): 95.
2. Ronald L. Simkins, "Honor and Shame in Joel," *Semeia* 68 (1994): 48.
3. Ibid., 49.
4. Shauna Hannan, Preaching This Week: Lectionary for August 22, 2010, Thirteenth Sunday after Pentecost, Isaiah 58:9b-14, Commentary on First Reading, http://www.workingpreacher.org/preaching.aspx?lect_date=8/22/2010&tab=1.
5. Christoph Schroeder, "'Standing in the Breach': Turning Away the Wrath of God," *Interpretation* 2, no. 1 (January 1998): 19–20.
6. Walther Eichrodt, *Theology of the Old Testament* (Philadelphia: Westminster, 1967), 2:143.
7. Patrick D. Miller, "Preaching in a Narcissistic Age, Psalm 51," *Journal for Preachers* 21, no. 2 (Lent 1998): 7.
8. Larry W. Spielman, "David's Abuse of Power," *Word & World* 19, no. 3 (Summer 1999): 251–59.
9. Glenn T. Miller, "2 Corinthians 5:11—6:13," *Interpretation* 54, no. 2 (April 2000): 187.
10. L. Susan Bond, "Preaching Paul," *Quarterly Review* 24, no. 3 (Fall 2004): 239–40.
11. Paul S. Minear, *New Testament Apocalyptic* (Nashville: Abingdon, 1981), 31.
12. Miller, "2 Corinthians 5:11—6:13," 188.
13. Ibid.

14. Matt Skinner, Preaching This Week: Lectionary for Wednesday, February 25, 2009, Ash Wednesday, Matthew 6:1-6, 16-21, Commentary on Gospel, http://www.workingpreacher.org/preaching_print .aspx?commentary_id=252.

15. Warren Carter, *Matthew and the Margins: A Socio-political and Religious Reading* (Sheffield, UK: Sheffield Academic, 2001), 129.

16. Ibid., 160.

17. Skinner, op. cit.

February 17, 2013
First Sunday in Lent

Revised Common Lectionary (RCL)	**Lectionary for Mass (LFM)**
Deuteronomy 26:1-11	Deuteronomy 26:4-10
Psalm 91:1-2, 9-16	Psalm 91:1-2, 10-11, 12-13, 14-15
Romans 10:8b-13	Romans 10:8-13
Luke 4:1-13	Luke 4:1-13

The Mardi Gras celebrations are over, the smudged foreheads are gone, and the five Sabbaths of Lent lie ahead. For the church this is a busy time, full of anticipation that tilts toward Palm Sunday, Maundy Thursday, Good Friday, Holy Saturday, and Easter week. Lent is one of those seasons when preachers look for as much help as possible for their sermon preparation. I think this is partly because of the busyness of the season, but also because of what lies ahead. How do we prepare believers for the announcement of the resurrection, which is at once new and "déjà vu all over again"? Do our Lenten sermons prepare congregations to suspend disbelief in the miraculous, or do they hint at some alternative, demythologized interpretation? If we favor the latter, we'll be pleased with Luke's social-justice agenda and will use these Sundays to establish that foundation.

There's a novel I recommend, Martin Gardner's *The Flight of Peter Fromm*, about a young preacher preparing for his first Easter sermon. Peter Fromm is wracked with anxiety all during Lent, wondering how on earth he'll do justice to Easter without selling out his intellect. His mentor says, "On Easter Sunday in particular he must be careful not to offend either side. Give the impression of taking the Easter myth too literally . . . and you alienate your liberals. Fail to treat it with sufficient reverence, and you antagonize your conservatives. I always looked forward to Easter tightrope-walking with such trepidation."[1] The tightrope walking begins in Lent.

First Reading
Deuteronomy 26:1-11 (RCL)
Deuteronomy 26:4-10 (LFM)

The narrative in Deuteronomy comes after a long discussion of legal matters and serves to remind Israel that God is about to lead them into the promised land. Walter Brueggemann has claimed that the theme of land shows up in the Hebrew Bible more often than the theme of covenant itself. Land is important, signifying God's providence, Israel's security in God, and the promise of future prosperity and future generations. The wilderness, out of which they come, is a geography that is contrasted with the land, a place of redemption and belonging. The people have suffered between the exodus and their entry into the land, and they've managed to persevere only because God has provided sustenance for them; manna and water ratify their hope and trust. God has acted on their behalf in the past; they assume God will continue to keep divine promises. So they live in hope, grounded in the words of God's covenant and by the providence of God's hand, and they manage to survive the wilderness without falling completely captive to the temptations along the way.

Moses is the speaker, addressing the people on behalf of God, fulfilling the basic role of the prophet. He reminds them of what God has given them. In the span of eleven verses, Moses uses forms of the verb *give* seven times, three times in the first three verses (God has given the land) and three times in the last three verses (God has given additional gifts of bounty). The seventh instance comes in the sixth verse, distinct because it refers to the hardship given by the Egyptians. The celebration that Moses directs the people to make is a cultic remembrance, offering the first fruits as a direct commemoration of the gifts of liberation and homeland to the Israelites.

Brueggemann also argues for an analogy between exile/land and death/resurrection. The fact that Paul and the Johannine author use land imagery specifically to understand resurrection as a restoration to the land of the living allows Brueggemann to see that the theme of land in the Hebrew Bible functions similarly to the themes of resurrection, new earth, and divine realm in the New Testament.[2]

What we need to take from Moses' sermon is the claim that God is with the community of believers even in the wilderness, even when basic resources are scarce, even when we cannot fully grasp the inheritance. Forty years in the wilderness for the Israelites, forty days in the wilderness for Jesus, and forty days in Lent. The church year and the lectionary locate this sermon from Moses as part of the Lenten discipline by design, so that we'll use these weeks to reimagine our identity and purpose as children of God.

The sermon calls us together as a community formed by the memories of God's providence for us collectively, and not as a community fragmented by personal memories of what God has done in private lives. The communal worship of God, the communal recitation of God's providence, is specifically for the whole community and not just a recollection of fragmented individualized mercies. We should also recognize that the sermon and the "thanksgiving" festival it establishes are not focused on thanking God for material or natural bounty. This isn't "Thanks for the harvest, God," but gratitude for God's presence in history rather than in nature. The "wandering" Israelites were surrounded by nature religions, so it's critical to understand this distinction. The initial words of the sermon (in Hebrew, "When you enter") signal that the wanderers are coming to a new stage of their life together.

The community is even expanded to include the poorest and most disenfranchised, the aliens who reside among us. Notice, please, the overall expanse of the celebration, which is to give honor and resources to God and to give food to the excluded. Praising God and feeding people are two poles of the elliptical shape of proper celebration. The tithe and the charitable outreach are the same act.

And finally, we must note that all of this theological understanding is compacted into the form of a celebratory meal. Within Judaism this *Shavuot* or first-fruits celebration is variously called the Festival of Weeks or the Harvest Festival. Christianity will adopt "first fruits" metaphorical language to discuss the formation of the church and Pauline virtues. The early church will also pattern its early worship on the synagogue form in practicing agape-meal "tithes and offerings" as a collection for the poor.

We can hardly fail to recognize the eucharistic analogues of this reading and the Lukan reading ("Man does not live by bread alone"). The Sundays in Lent are still celebrations of the resurrection, exempted from penitential orientations, and they function both as reminders of God's activity on our collective behalf and as food-sharing practices. What a good way to establish our Lenten weeks, when we enter into an intentional reflection on God's activity in our life together and prepare to give ourselves and our bounty away to others.

Psalmody
Psalm 91:1-2, 9-16 (RCL)
Psalm 91:1-2, 10-11, 12-13, 14-15 (LFM)

Way back in 1857, the inimitable Charles Spurgeon preached a whole sermon on the third verse of Psalm 91, which speaks of God with the claim "For he will deliver you from the snare of the fowler and from the deadly pestilence." Spurgeon structured a three-point sermon, explaining the Satanic works and identity of "the fowler" and defending God's ability to protect Christians from temptation the same way the Holy Spirit protected the Lukan Jesus from temptation in the wilderness:

> If Moses wrote this Psalm he might represent the fowler as being in his case the king of Egypt, who sought to slay him, or the Amalekites, who pounced upon Israel in the plain, when they little expected it. If David penned it, he might have compared Saul to the fowler, for he himself says, he was hunted like a partridge upon the mountains. But we believe, if the verse be applicable to either of those cases, it was intended by the

Psalmist not to have a private interpretation, but to be applicable to all time; and we believe it is spoken concerning that arch-enemy of souls, the great deceiver, Satan.[3]

The next five verses of Psalm 91 expand the theme and the examples of God's protection from Satan's temptations. These verses might refer to Jewish beliefs about the particular kinds of demons that inhabit the deserts and the wilderness. Unfortunately, verses 3-8 are not included in today's reading portion. Scholars are quick to point out that the omitted verses might refer to anticipations of literal warfare and that the psalm itself has overtones of a king facing a battle. Today's reading emphasizes the confidence of the believer and the power of God, but it leaves out the details about how temptations manifest as fears and dangers and "things that go bump in the night."

It's helpful to keep the omissions (and the hints of battle metaphors) in mind as we attend to the remaining verses, which seem "ready-made for over-confidence and pious extravagances."[4] The remaining verses are the ones activated in the Lukan and Matthean versions of Jesus' temptation. We're left with a hymn of praise to the one who will protect Jesus and the church from threat and temptation. The psalm functions as a reminder that we should not put our trust in false powers, especially not in our own powers, but in the God who commands the angels and the powers of holiness. The remaining verses don't promise to protect us in battle or to protect us from disease, but have been used by the early church, recycled into the story of Jesus' temptation, to claim that God's primary protective device is actually one of discernment and the ability to avoid temptations. "From what is God able to protect us?" we ask. God protects us from the "troubling" of the mind, from misunderstanding, or, as Frederick Gaiser claims, from vocational confusion: "God's protection as announced in Psalm 91 might be misunderstood as a magical shield, keeping me from all harm—or it might be received as a gift that enables me to give myself in service of the neighbor."[5]

In fact, the psalm protects us from more than mere vocational confusion; it protects us from the temptations that challenge vocational understanding and identity. It stands as God's great "Be not afraid" of the psalmist. It reminds me of that old hymn by Robert Wadsworth Lowry, repopularized recently by the singer Enya, "How Can I Keep from Singing?":

> What tho' the darkness gather round?
> Songs in the night he giveth.
> No storm can shake my inmost calm
> While to that refuge clinging;
> Since Christ is Lord of heaven and earth,
> How can I keep from singing?

As Spurgeon ended his sermon on the psalm, he reminded his congregation that the psalm's divine promise continues to operate in Christian witness as a spiritual shield and armor that protect from spiritual dangers of despair, denial, capitulation, and complicity with evil. The psalm acknowledges that evil and real danger may surround us, but armed with the promise of divine presence, we'll be able to avoid the spiritual snares in the wilderness.

Second Reading
Romans 10:8b-13 (RCL)
Romans 10:8-13 (LFM)

All of today's readings have narrative structure, human action, great locations, and great props: Moses and food baskets; warriors in the demon-infested wilderness; Jesus arguing with Satan from rooftops. And then we get this tiny little abstract scrap from Paul's grand treatise on salvation. If the other texts are worthy of action films, this little reading from Romans is like a philosophical snippet from Louis Malle's film *My Dinner with Andre*: "Everyone who calls on the name of the Lord shall be saved" (v. 13).

For Paul, it didn't matter if you were Jew or Greek (Gentile). If you called on the name of the Lord, you could skip right over adherence to the law, skip right over circumcision, and be part of the saved community. If you read Romans all the way through, this is part of a long section where Paul discusses the difference between being bound by the law and being bound by Christ. The whole section echoes with references to the books of Moses.

Paul was such an exceptional speaker and writer that he could anticipate his crowd, even when he was writing from hundreds or thousands of miles away. He knows he's at the point in his argument where some heckler will shout out, "What about Deuteronomy 30? The part about obeying the commandments and the circumcision covenant, and keeping that word on your heart and lips?"

If Paul were standing in a twenty-first-century pulpit, he could expect questions about the inerrancy of the Bible, or questions about homosexuality, or questions about any number of other rules and requirements that believers impose upon themselves in order to secure salvation. In Paul's day the big question was about whether or not believers had to first become Jews in order to be Christians. No wonder Pauline epistles have to deal with issues like circumcision and food offered to idols! We want to tread carefully here or we'll follow the homiletical conventions projected by Martin Luther and continue the problematic method of contrasting legalistic Judaism with grace-filled Christianity.

But Paul was not contrasting Judaism and the law to Christianity and grace. He was making a completely different kind of argument. He was, in fact, arguing that the same way Judaism has the law and the covenant "near" the lips and the heart, so Christianity has the gospel near the lips and the heart. Paul is not arguing for difference; he's arguing for similarity and continuity. The same God is still working in the world to bring grace and inclusion. If we want to paraphrase Paul, we could imagine him saying, "Jews are redeemed by the law and the prophets; you're redeemed by Christ. The Jews are grandfathered in under requirements that don't apply to you; you are included under new protocols."

An analogy from the academic world may help. Every student entering an academic program enters under particular rules and requirements. When Abe entered seminary in 2008, he came in under a certain curriculum. Let's say that Abe had to take a course that had been in the curriculum for years: Intro to Ministry. But between 2008 and 2012 the school revises the curriculum and drops Intro to Ministry from the requirements. They've developed other courses over the last decade, courses that render that class redundant. When Mary enrolls in 2012, she's not required to take the class, even if Abe still has to complete it. Abe won't have to take any of the required courses for the new curriculum because he was not subject to those requirements.

Does this mean that Mary's seminary education disqualifies Abe's? By no means! Abe operated according to what was required for him and Mary will operate according to what's required for her. "Jews are redeemed by the law and the prophets; you're redeemed by Christ. The Jews are grandfathered in under requirements that don't apply to you; you are included under new protocols."

"Everyone who calls on the name of the Lord shall be saved," Paul teaches in Romans. We need not look any further than our own lips and hearts, for if we call on the name of the Lord, salvation is as close to us as our own hearts and mouths. "But what does it say? 'The word is near you, on your lips and in your heart' (that is, the word of faith that we proclaim); because if you confess with your lips that Jesus is Lord and believe in your heart that God raised him from the dead, you will be saved" (vv. 8-9).

Fitting in with the Lenten theme, the passage reminds us that our spiritual disciplines cannot save us but may, in fact, distract us. When taken together with the previous readings (and the upcoming Lukan reading), we realize that we don't need magic powers or good-luck charms to live fearlessly and confidently in God's protection. We simply proclaim that Jesus is Lord and we trust in that confession without condition.

Of course, during Paul's time, to confess Jesus as Lord or *Kyrios* was the same as saying that Caesar was *not* Lord and *Kyrios*. Claiming Jesus as Lord and Savior was an act of political transgression. This is not the direction that Luther's spiritualized theology would carry the Pauline trajectory, but it's what contemporary Pauline scholars pursue. Even if Paul was not leading a resistance group or calling for acts of civil disobedience, his theological worldview, grounded in radical grace and in the cross and resurrection, was inherently political and threatening.[6]

Scholarship on Pauline metaphors unintentionally lends support to a politicized or social-activist reading. Calling "on the name of the Lord," acting "in the name of the Lord," and being baptized "in the name of the Lord" (all phrases that are peculiar to Paul) are metaphors taken from the overlapping clusters of military and slavery metaphors. While we're familiar with some Pauline military metaphors (spiritual warfare, breastplates and helmets), we may not immediately recognize that Paul uses the language of Roman military conscription and loyalty to describe Christian confession. Those who joined the Roman military took their loyalty oath not only to Caesar (in the name of Caesar), but also to their superior officer on the ground (in his name). When they wore the Roman uniform, they did not belong to themselves, but to Caesar and their immediate superior officer. They fought "in the name of," and when they needed assistance, they called "on the name of."

There is certainly an Old Testament history about "calling on the Lord," but Paul's use of the phrase reinterprets those understandings. Paul gathers up all the midrash of the Old Testament and directs it at his Roman audience. As Richard Horsley notes:

> In the Letters to the Romans and Galatians as well . . . Paul opposes Christ and the gospel to Caesar and the Roman imperial order, not to the Law and Judaism. At the outset of his long main argument in Rom 1–11, Paul states that Christ has displaced Caesar, has been "declared to be the Son of God with power." His main point, when he reaches the climax of his argument in Rom 9–11, is that according to God's mystery/plan, Israel is to be included in the fulfillment of history along with other peoples.[7]

It's like playing "Hail to the Chief" whenever "the name of the Lord" enters the scene. The Gospel readings for Palm Sunday will include the same undertones of political theater and resistance. If we have taken the Lutheran option of spiritualizing the political subversion out of Romans, we'll face Palm Sunday with less support for social-activist readings.

Gospel
Luke 4:1-13 (RCL, LFM)

The story of Jesus' temptation in the wilderness occurs in all three Synoptic Gospels. The Synoptic versions share some details. In all three of the Synoptics, this episode occurs after Jesus' baptism by John the Baptist (Luke inserts his genealogy here), and the temptation occurs before the inauguration of Jesus' ministry and before the calling of the disciples. All three note the presence of the Holy Spirit, all three note the time frame of forty days in the wilderness (echoing forty years of wandering after the exodus), and all note that a devilish figure tempted him.

For early readers, the simple mention of forty days in the wilderness would have been tantamount to cuing the scary monster music. According to the superstitions and cosmologies of that time, you'd expect to find demons and evil spirits in the wilderness. Students of the sociology of religion or ritual studies will also note that the temptation story follows a classic mythic-ritual structure for a rite of passage. Rites of passage, like a vision quest for Native American youths, or baptism for the early church, have a predictable three-phase form. The hero/initiate departs a time and place of safety, enters a time and place of danger and testing, and emerges from the dangerous time/place with a new status and identity. In the language of ritual studies, the temptation story is a classic "liminal" phase where the hero/initiate is in between two worlds. Jesus is in between the worlds of his old vocation and his new vocation. Baptism has initiated this liminality. Will he emerge? Will he, like the Native American youth, have his guiding vision?

We still retain the notion of spiritual danger relative to baptism. The early church instructed that the time immediately surrounding baptism was a time when temptations were most likely to arise. The Anglican *Book of Common Prayer* still contains renunciations as part of a more ancient baptismal rite, asking adults or adult sponsors to renounce Satan. "Dost thou . . . renounce the devil and all his works, the vain pomp and glory of the world?" Third-century rites included exorcisms and fasting as part of the Lenten and Easter Vigil preparation for baptismal candidates.

So we can assume that the story of Jesus' temptation is not just a heroic narrative of mythic proportions; it's also a story for the church as it understands its baptism and vocation. Where Mark uses the Greek term for Satan (the adversary), Luke uses the Greek term for the devil (the slanderer). Luke's Gospel is intentionally concerned with the power of speech and the power of words. No wonder Jesus counters him with the word.

I suggest an artistic and imaginative approach to today's text. I suggest that we use the temptation story as an interpretive lens for what comes ahead in the Lukan year. As soon as Jesus resists the devil, he begins his ministry of solidarity with the poor and disenfranchised, and delivers his inaugural sermon, claiming, "The Spirit of the Lord is upon me" (4:18). I also suggest that we use the temptation story as a lens for understanding both the transfiguration (a high and lifted-up place) and the ascension (another high and lifting-up story). The transfiguration and the ascension also mark shifts in the nature of Jesus' ministry.

But, most critically, the temptation drama reveals the true nature of the temptations that individuals and communities must renounce in order to be with Jesus in his ministry to the poor and disenfranchised. Instead of getting distracted by questions of mythology and demythology, we should simply claim that the temptation drama is a lesson to the church about the ways that temptations will manifest themselves.

The "stones to bread" temptation can be interpreted a number of ways. The first and most obvious is that we will be tempted to do anything to provide for our daily sustenance or daily survival. On an individual level this could be preached as a warning about caring too much for food to eat. On a communal level this could be a critique of anything that we deem absolutely necessary for church life. What is the "daily bread" of churches? Is it something that we protect at the risk of actually sinning about it? The text doesn't say "daily bread," but a good preacher could associate this "need for bread" with the first reading for today, about bread sharing instead of bread hoarding. How does bread serve as a larger symbol for the eucharistic community? What kind of bread do we really need to survive as communities? Does bread signify our survival needs? Are churches so intent on ordinary survival, just staying alive, that we lose sight of our vocation? I tell my preaching students that "bread" is never just "food" in the New Testament.

The next temptation is that the devil takes Jesus "up" (which seems to be a time and not a place) and shows him, in an instant, all of the kingdoms of the world. Then he offers him glory and authority over everything he sees. Kingdoms, glory, and authority should signal to us that this is a reference to some kind of secular or political power. If the first temptation was for survival, this temptation is for gaining some kind of worldly mastery and "glory" over others. Jesus will be surrounded by "glory" again in the transfiguration, but it will not be political or secular glory. How are our communities of faith seduced and tempted by the exercise of power over others? We don't have to look far and it doesn't even have to be during an election year before we recognize the way political figures brag about their faith in order to secure political advantage or use their faith to "slander" and gain advantage over others. Jesus reminds us that we serve God alone, and don't owe political or secular allegiances, whether they're national or military or political.

Finally, the devil invites us to test God's faithfulness. The last part of this Gospel reading brings us back to the language of Psalm 91, with its grandiose claims of divine protection. This part of a sermon must be handled carefully, because we do not want to reinscribe the religious platitude that God will protect us from physical harm or from other kinds of harm. As we noticed during the discussion of Psalm 91, God's primary protective device is actually one of discernment and the ability to avoid temptations. "From what is God able to protect us?" we ask. God protects us from the "troubling" of the mind, from misunderstanding, or from vocational confusion.

Some final comments are in order. The Holy Spirit is with Jesus during this whole episode. Jesus has left his family behind, he has yet to call his disciples, he's hungry, but he is not alone. The Holy Spirit cannot eliminate temptation encounters, but is God's active and immediate presence during the liminal times, between making a commitment and making good on that commitment. These are the moments of hesitation, of second thoughts, of cold feet. These are the times when we seek rationalization for taking an easier or more rewarding path. Fred Craddock points out:

All this is to say that a real temptation is an offer not to fall but to rise. The tempter in Eden did not ask, "Do you wish to be as the devil?" but "Do you wish to be as God?" There is nothing here of debauchery; no self-respecting devil would approach a person with offers of personal, domestic, or social ruin. That is in the small print at the bottom of the temptation.[8]

Notice clearly what kind of discernment the Holy Spirit provides. We have tended to mystify the Holy Spirit to the point that we can say very little that's substantive. We couldn't pick the Holy Spirit out of a lineup. Luke's Holy Spirit helps Jesus rebuke the temptations for ordinary survival, the temptations to wield authority and political power, and the temptations to expect magical protections. One of the primary gifts of the Holy Spirit is the gift of discernment. If there's some benefit to us, some social, domestic, or personal gain, we should call on the words of Scripture, preached by Jesus in front of the slanderer, and prevail over temptation.

Notes

1. Martin Gardner, *The Flight of Peter Fromm* (Amherst, N.Y.: Prometheus, 1994), 225–26.
2. Walter Brueggemann, *The Land: Place as Gift, Promise, and Challenge in Biblical Faith,* 2nd ed., Overtures to Biblical Theology (Minneapolis: Fortress Press, 2002), 165.
3. C. H. Spurgeon, "The Snare of the Fowler," A Sermon (no. 124), March 29, 1857, http://www .spurgeon.org/sermons/0124.htm.
4. "First Sunday in Lent," in Fred B. Craddock, John H. Hayes, Carl R. Holladay, and Gene M. Tucker, *Preaching Through the Christian Year C* (Valley Forge, Pa.: Trinity Press, 1994), 137.
5. Frederick J. Gaiser, "'It Shall Not Reach You': Talisman or Vocation? Reading Psalm 91 in Time of War," *Word & World* 25, no. 2 (2005): 198.
6. For more insight into the variety of social and political groups operative in early Christian contexts, see Richard A. Horsley's works: *Sociology and the Jesus Movement* (New York: Continuum, 1989); *Jesus and the Spiral of Violence: Popular Jewish Resistance in Roman Palestine* (Minneapolis: Fortress Press, 1992); *Paul and Empire: Religion and Power in Roman Imperial Society* (ed.) (Harrisburg, Pa.: Trinity Press, 1997); *Bandits, Prophets, and Messiahs: Popular Movements in the Time of Jesus* (with John S. Hanson) (Harrisburg, Pa.: Trinity Press, 1999); *The Message and the Kingdom: How Jesus and Paul Ignited a Revolution and Transformed the Ancient World* (with Neil Asher Silberman) (Minneapolis: Fortress Press, 2002); and *Jesus and Empire: The Kingdom of God and the New World Disorder* (Minneapolis: Fortress Press, 2002).
7. Richard A. Horsley, ed., *Paul and the Imperial Roman Order* (Harrisburg, Pa.: Trinity Press, 2004), 4.
8. Fred B. Craddock, *Luke*, Interpretation: A Bible Commentary for Teaching and Preaching (Louisville: John Knox Press, 1990), 56.

February 24, 2013
Second Sunday in Lent

Revised Common Lectionary (RCL)	Lectionary for Mass (LFM)
Genesis 15:1-12, 17-18	Genesis 15:5-12, 17-18
Psalm 27	Psalm 27:1, 7-8a, 8b-9, 13-14
Philippians 3:17—4:1	Philippians 3:17—4:1 or 3:20—4:1
Luke 13:31-35 or Luke 9:28-36 (37-43)	Luke 9:28b-36

We've now firmly established that Lenten disciplines are less about the individualized sacrificial rituals we set before ourselves and more about our commitments to come together to discern the temptations before us as communities of faith. On the First Sunday of Lent we noted the language of the Deuteronomistic text about "when we enter." We overlay that with an image from Ash Wednesday, the artistic image of the *Memento Mori*, calling us to remember our mortality. We have now fully entered into the discussion of our mortality, our "being unto death," as Martin Heidegger phrased it. We have entered into our own death, our own inevitable hurtling toward our finitude, our finality. Ashes to ashes, dust to dust.

With the early church, we enter into a liminal, in-between time, a time for temptations, a time between making a promise and keeping that promise, a time between old life and new creation. With the early believers, we leave our earthly clothes behind and strip down naked to prepare ourselves for baptism into a new way of being-in-the-world. We await rebirth. We meet Abram in a fiery dream, the psalmist crying out for salvation, a terrified and tearful Paul, and Jesus on a mountain.

First Reading
Genesis 15:1-12, 17-18 (RCL)
Genesis 15:5-12, 17-18 (LFM)

Ash Wednesday started with claims from the Hebrew Bible's prophetic book of Joel. The First Sunday of Lent took us backward a few books into Deuteronomy and the sermons of Moses. The lectionary takes us farther back into the Hebrew Bible and closer to the original covenant even as it moves us closer to the end of the Jesus story and resurrection. The lectionary readings are working in two directions, pressing ever forward into the New Testament at the same time they work us backward into the Hebrew Bible, almost as if Easter and creation were two sides of the same coin, or two book pages stapled together at the manger scene. The Lenten readings remind us not only of the prophetic voices of the Hebrew Bible, but of God's covenantal relationship with the people of God.

The Genesis reading takes us all the way back to Abram, before he became Abraham. God and Abram are having a conversation about the covenant they are about to enter into. Not only does God speak in this narrative; God also "appears" as a character. This is a divine double-header, including both divine speech (theophany) and divine manifestation (epiphany). God promises to make Abram the father of many nations and to deliver him into the land that stretches from the river in Egypt (probably the Nile) to the river Euphrates, near Babylon.

The conversations include a back-and-forth pattern where God makes a promise and Abram expresses either fear or concern. Without responding directly to Abram's final concerns (he still lacks an heir from Sarai), God instructs him to bring specific covenant animals and to cut them up for a covenant ceremony. These are not sacrifices proper, but symbolic ritual elements that would have been familiar to Abram as such. God initiates the covenant, and Abram's obedience (even without verbal assent) confirms it. Abram's cooperation *is* his response. We're assured by verse 6 that Abram believes and that God reckons it to him as righteousness.

The animals were cut in half and each half placed apart from the other half so as to form a pathway that the two covenant parties would walk between from opposite directions, passing each other in the middle. The split animals symbolized what would happen to the party who didn't keep his or her end of the promise. The practice gave rise to the expression "cutting a covenant." God's promise is generativity and property. Abram has not yet agreed to circumcision.

Now, instead of the typical walk between the split animals, Abram falls into a deep sleep full of "terrifying darkness" while "a smoking fire pot and a flaming torch," representing the presence of God, pass between the animal parts. God walks the covenant path alone.

The text is included in our Lenten readings for its powerful symbolism of divine presence, the symbols of smoke and torch, and the theme of a God who acts in history to make specific promises to those whom God has chosen. No doubt the early church would have reinterpreted the patriarchs, the prophets, and the covenant makers as prototypes for understanding the person and the role of Jesus.

The story was recorded as part of the books of Moses, and Abram/Abraham becomes a model of faithfulness for future generations of Israelites, not only for understanding the exodus, but also for understanding the Babylonian exile. Abram became an archetype of the kind of enduring faithfulness required for being in relationship with God. The memory of God's faithfulness becomes a beacon of hope for Israel during times of crisis.

And of course, we keep telling ourselves the story of Abram, a bizarre story of animal carcasses, smoke, and fire. David Buttrick notes, "We should not drop the ritual from our sermons as some messy account of oath-taking that is fortunately passé in our wised-up modern world. No, here is God condescending to reveal the divine nature to somewhat uncertain Abram. 'You want to know who I am? I am God who keeps promises and whose promises are guaranteed!'"[1]

The key verse, of course, is the one-liner about Abram's righteousness. We've probably all heard sermons preached from a Reformation-theology perspective that use verse 6 as a Hebrew Bible example of justification by grace through faith alone. We shouldn't overlook the fact that Abram's faith wasn't blind; he'd already been delivered by God and had reason to count on God's promises. We should also keep in mind that, as Buttrick points out, Abram's faith wasn't just an assent to a proposition; it was active trust: "Abraham actively trusts the promises of God, which is the only way to respond to God's free, covenant relationship with us. Active trust is a credit to us in God's sight."[2]

In keeping with our Lenten themes of liminal times and spaces, a preacher might want to focus not on speculating about the incredible acts of God, but rather on active trust during the "terrifying darkness" of not being able to see God's actions. Abram is a model of faithfulness primarily because he is an active promise truster. As Walter Brueggemann tells us, "The future of God's goodness is open to those who trust in that future, neither holding on to the present nor conjuring an alternative future of their own. Faith is reliance on God's promise of overcoming the present for a new life."[3]

Psalmody
Psalm 27 (RCL)
Psalm 27:1, 7-8a, 8b-9, 13-14 (LFM)

The raw honesty and terror of Psalm 27 should bring us to our knees. Despite centuries of repetition and liturgical editing, the psalm stands as an expression of the struggle between unconditional trust and a collapse into despair.

The psalm is structured in two main sections and a coda. The first six verses are full of praise; the next six verses anticipate a variety of worst-case scenarios. The final two verses provide a summary of hope. In some ways the psalm is like traditional wedding vows, which start with a generic promise then shift to specific obstacles (better/worse, sickness/health, wealth/poverty).

James Luther Mays argues that this psalm demonstrates the direct connection between trust and need. The excess of praise is matched by an excess of supplication. The fact that we trust in God and can count the ways God has protected us doesn't diminish the fact that disasters still lie ahead and that we seek constant reminders of the presence of God. For the psalmist, nothing could be better than to be in the sanctuary all the time, safe from enemies and disaster, beholding the beauty of the Lord's face, but life doesn't allow that kind of escape.

Some preaching considerations are in order. The psalm certainly lends itself to the assumption that God protects us from real enemies and real disasters; it can easily fall prey to magical thinking and the pitfalls of presenting an omnipotent God. If God can prevent disasters, how do we interpret them when they happen?

But notice that the psalmist isn't asking God to prevent disasters. The psalmist is asking God to assist him with the problems of fear and loss of faith. In a brief reflection called "Fear Factor," Peter Steinke discusses how fear threatens faith: "Fear takes over, overwhelming the imaginative capacities and advanced reasoning. The fearful one becomes locked into the present and loses the ability to envision something other than what is now threatening."[4] Fear disables our ability to trust because it becomes the center of reality. No wonder the angels in Luke's Gospel are always shouting, "Fear not!"

Preachers need to keep in mind that the role of disasters and real threats is not interpreted by the psalmist as something that God doles out to test us. They are presented here precisely as temptations belonging to the human condition. God's role is to remain steadfast and righteous; the believer's role is to trust God.

Rabbi Abraham Heschel claims that the role of the prophet is to cast out fear. The psalmist is not only praying to God, but also talking to himself. This is a constant theme in both testaments, that God's promises for an abundant future are to be trusted no matter what. "For surely I know the plans I have for you, says the Lord, plans for your welfare and not for harm, to give you a future with hope" (Jer. 29:11). A seminary professor used to remind students that prayer was not a matter of getting God on our side, but of getting us on God's side.

One thematic connection between this reading and the other readings for today is the theological problem of fear and distrust in the face of failure or impending disaster. Another theo-symbolic connection is the claim of God's presence and God's face (most dramatically in Genesis and in the transfiguration). The hints of the temple and sanctuary situate the theological conversation in the context of congregational life and worship. The prophetic role of the church is to cast out fear and to name God's activity and presence in the midst of the human world.

Second Reading
Philippians 3:17—4:1 (RCL)
Philippians 3:17—4:1 or 3:20—4:1 (LFM)

There's a standard gag in old Marx Brothers movies where someone with a distinctive gait would say, "Walk this way," to which Groucho would respond with a one-liner beginning, "If I could walk *that* way . . ." If I could walk that way, I wouldn't need a cane, or talcum powder, or a doctor, or new shoes. The gag became such a comic staple that it reappeared in Mel Brooks's film *Young Frankenstein*. The humor in the gag resides in the ambiguity of what it means to "walk this way." Does it mean to copy the behaviors of another? Or does it mean to follow another to a destination?

"Brothers and sisters, join in imitating me, and observe those who live according to the example you have in us" (3:17). Today's epistle reading opens with Paul instructing the believers at Philippi to imitate him.

The notion of imitation as part of educational or ethical formation wasn't new for Pauline listeners. Imitation was standard pedagogical practice within the Hellenistic world, where young students would learn their letters by literally tracing over what the master had previously written. Paul uses the metaphorical world of the teacher/student when he refers to the law as a pedagogue in Galatians 3:23-25, or when he speaks of "pedagogues in Christ" in 1 Corinthians 4:15 (NRSV: "guardians"). Many of his family-life metaphors operate the same way, making claims about "babes in Christ" or those who have not "matured" (1 Cor. 3:1-4).

Later Christian tradition pursued the notion of copying or tracing the behaviors of another. Thomas à Kempis's *The Imitation of Christ*, from the fifteenth century, is one of the best-selling Christian books of all time, promoting Jesus as a moral exemplar who provided ethical guidelines for Christian life. Charles Sheldon's 1896 book, *In His Steps*, was subtitled "What Would Jesus Do?" About a hundred years later Sheldon's question would be resurrected in the WWJD phenomenon.

Elisabeth Castelli has written extensively on the theological problems with imitation (mimesis) as an ethical mandate, suggesting that it fuels a hierarchical drive against freedom, against diversity, and for Christian uniformity.[5] Besides the ethical problem, there's also a serious practical problem that many preachers simply ignore: How do we imitate someone from two thousand years ago? What do we imitate? Do we live off the grid? What about abortion debates? Do men shave? Do we walk everywhere? Do we choose celibacy.

But what if the ambiguity in the old Marx Brothers gag helps us? What if Paul is not promoting a rule-bound deontological ethic, but a teleological ethic that takes its cues from a future goal? Maybe Paul is not instructing the church to do what he does, but to follow him where he's going.

The cues for a different interpretation are within the lection itself. Paul rejects the behaviors of "enemies of the cross" not by offering a new set of ethical rules, but by positing a different eschatological goal. "Our citizenship is in heaven," he says (5:20). While new Christians might be as immature as kids getting out of school, released from the "pedagogy" of the law, they are discouraged from behaving as if they can do whatever they please. Questions of Christian freedom, Christian identity, and transformation are the subtext of this lection. Paul is always arguing against two misunderstandings of Christian ethics: the Judaizing trajectory that wants to require the law and circumcision, and the hedonistic trajectory that thinks anything goes. While we live *in* the world, we don't take our cues *from* the world. We are being transformed into the body of Christ's glory, into the resurrection, into the body of Christ, into the church.

Barbara Brown Taylor discusses our dual citizenship and our dual parentage this way: "We are God's own children, through our blood kinship with Christ. We are also the children of Adam and Eve, with a hereditary craving for forbidden fruit salad. Frisk us and you will find two passports on our persons—one says we are citizens of heaven, the other insists we are taxpayers on earth."[6]

For Taylor and for Paul, Christian faith is always and everywhere a liminal existence. We live in between the resurrection and the second coming with a foot in each kingdom, but God in Christ will not fail us. We live in the great possibility that God has a future for us greater than we imagine (don't settle for less!), which is nothing less than the reconciliation of the world. We're already being transformed.

Walk this way.

Gospel
Luke 13:31-35 (RCL)

The Revised Common Lectionary offers two Lukan readings for today. Only one of them, Luke 13, is listed for Lutherans, since they celebrated Jesus' transfiguration two weeks ago. The alternative RCL reading (the transfiguration) coincides with the Gospel reading from the Lectionary for Mass and it will receive a longer reflection.

Luke 13:31-35 could be titled "A Warning and a Lament." In the span of five brief verses, Luke supports his narrative turn toward Jerusalem, where Jesus faces certain death. In the first part of the reading a Pharisee warns Jesus that Herod is after him. The verses about Herod are found in Luke alone, an oddity since Matthew's Gospel takes pains to chronicle Herod's slaughter of the innocents, which Luke doesn't mention. Luke's other mentions of Herod are brief and function primarily as historical markers or as devices to maintain narrative tension. Right before the transfiguration, Herod is mentioned three times. In Luke 8:3 we discover that some women in Herod's household were funding John the Baptist. In 9:7 we discover that Herod is perplexed that some say John the Baptist has risen from the dead. In 9:9 we discover that Herod is curious about Jesus. The transfiguration is recounted in 9:28-36, then Jesus "sets his face toward Jerusalem" and starts the journey within which the Herod/Jerusalem story occurs. The journey motif is a favorite of Luke, characterizing the theological perspective that Christian faith is like a journey "on the Way."

While he's on the way to Jerusalem, some Pharisees come to warn Jesus that Herod has issued a death warrant on him. In Luke's Gospel, Pharisees are ambivalent characters. They're not the black-hat villains of Matthew's Gospel, but they're not entirely benevolent. As Amy-Jill Levine notes, "When 'some Pharisees' warn Jesus that Herod seeks to kill him (13:35) they can be seen as attempting to thwart Jesus from his mission."[7]

Jesus retorts, "Go and tell that fox for me, 'Listen, I am casting out demons and performing cures today and tomorrow, and on the third day I finish my work. Yet today, tomorrow, and the next day I must be on my way, because it is impossible for a prophet to be killed outside of Jerusalem'" (vv. 32-33). In other words, Jesus identifies Herod as an enemy, tells the Pharisees that nothing will stop him, and claims prophetic status. This isn't new; Jesus started his ministry by reading Isaiah scrolls in the synagogue. He's always claimed prophetic status in Luke.

Maybe this is why Jesus turns his attention to Jerusalem. In the second part of the reading, Jesus cries out over Jerusalem as the city that rejects its prophets. The text suggests that Jesus has been there before, but it hasn't happened in Luke's telling of it. For many scholars this part of Luke is awkward and serves more as a transition than as a significant part of the story. It allows for a reference to "the third day" and it allows Jesus to restate his prophetic status. Some scholars and preachers will claim it as a liminal moment between the transfiguration and the entry into Jerusalem, but it's an odd passage that requires us to displace the transfiguration itself as a liminal episode preceding Holy Week. Everything in this passage points either backward at transfiguration or forward to Palm Sunday.

Preachers can probably squeeze this much out of the text: Christian faith is a journey that leads to death. We can rebuke anyone who attempts to thwart our walking "on the Way" to Jerusalem. With Jesus, we can set ourselves toward Palm Sunday and await the shouts, "Blessed is the king who comes in the name of the Lord."

Luke 9:28-36 (37-43) (RCL alt.)
Luke 9:28b-36 (LFM)

Like the temptation of Jesus, the transfiguration might be among the most challenging texts for preachers. Both texts play with supernatural phenomena we're hard-pressed to deal with in a postmodern world. Our attempts to demythologize ultimately end up with sermons that domesticate the wildness of God's activity and God's vision for the world. Like Abram in this week's Genesis text, we're tempted to settle for something less. We've all heard sappy sermons scolding us for preferring "mountaintop moments" to ordinary Christian life "in the real world."

The transfiguration occurs in all three Synoptics, but it will strike some as odd that it's included in Lenten readings for the simple reason that typical interpretations associate it not with the temptation, but with the resurrection and ascension. I would argue that the temptation is the template for all of them in Luke's narratives, so I'm giving the transfiguration more attention than the primary RCL reading (Luke 13:31-35) for today. As Fred Craddock reminds us, Sundays in Lent are still supposed to be celebrations of the resurrection and are exempt from the forty days of Lenten reflection. And, as recently as the Last Sunday of Epiphany, the transfiguration narrative was a lectionary reading in the RCL.

The primary argument for including it in the Lenten reflections is a narrative one: it happened before Easter. Like the temptation, it features a supernatural and inexplicable encounter. Like the temptation, Jesus is lifted up to a high place. Whereas Jesus faced the devil in the desert and encountered three temptations, here he has face time with God, Moses, and Elijah and has three "confirmations" of his prophetic ministry. As the temptation marked the liminal space between baptism and the beginning of Jesus' ministry, the transfiguration marks another boundary for him: he is closing his ministry and turning his face toward Jerusalem.[8] During the transfiguration his face changes (v. 29) like Moses' face changed (Exod. 34:29), and barely thirty verses later he sets his face toward Jerusalem (v. 51). While there's no doubt that the transfiguration references the resurrection, we shouldn't overlook its symbolic partnership with the temptation.[9]

First of all, preachers should avoid any attempts at domesticating this narrative. There is no point in arguing whether it "really" happened. And preachers should avoid searching for analogous human experiences. Craddock reminds us, "Rather, the preacher or the teacher might be better advised to hold them before the listeners in their full extraordinariness rather than just reduce them to fit the contours of our experiences."[10] Preachers should present the transfiguration as a dazzling vision that makes theological claims.

The appearances of Moses and Elijah on the mountain not only constitute a powerful confirmation of Jesus' ministry to the poor and the oppressed, but their presence adds him to the ranks of the prophets and the beloved of God. John Petty writes, "Throughout scripture, mountains and clouds are 'windows into heaven,' as someone has put it. They signal the divine, the heavenly realm, the presence of God. The third major mystical sign is the appearance of angels. Angels are not needed in this story, however. Instead, we have a voice directly from God."[11]

Moses' own ministry was marked by mountaintop encounters with God, so we'll hear echoes of the law and the lawgiver, echoes of a great leader of God's people, and finally, the reminder that Moses didn't get to the promised land either. Jesus will die alone on another hill without seeing the kingdom of God completed. But he will, like Moses, be surrounded by clouds and glory.

Elijah was the long-awaited prophet of Israel, a raiser of the dead who had left the earth without dying, caught up in a whirlwind on a chariot of flame. Elijah has already appeared in Luke, first as Luke identified John the Baptist with Elijah (as the one who would prepare the way for Jesus, 1:17), then as Jesus presented Elijah as the example of a prophet who did great things outside Israel (4:25-26). Barbara Brown Taylor writes, "To see him standing there with Moses and Jesus was like seeing the Mount Rushmore of heaven—the Lawgiver, the Prophet, the Messiah—wrapped in such glory it is a wonder the other three could see them at all. But they did see that epiphany, and then they could not see anything anymore, because the cloud swallowed them up."[12]

Moses and Elijah speak with Jesus (the other Synoptics don't record any conversation) and refer to Jesus' departure using the word for "exodus" (departure) to refer to what lies ahead of him. Luke sees Christian faith as a journey, and particularly like the exodus journey, which is a wilderness journey full of temptation.

The "exodus" reference helps remind us what kind of glory and success lies ahead for Jesus. Mountaintop experiences could be heady episodes, and some preachers might be tempted toward Christian triumphalism by Jesus' being ushered into the Prophetic Hall of Fame. We know better. We know that in the days ahead, as he bears down on Jerusalem, he will have to remember his own conversation with the devil and reject all temptations to protect himself, to pursue political domination, or to dabble with religious superiority.

The transfiguration reinforces the Lenten themes of God's presence in times of liminality, reminding us that Christian life has occasional glimpses of glory which assure us we're on the same path with Moses, Elijah, Jesus, and all of God's chosen prophets. We know that the road leads to Jerusalem, so we join our exodus, our wilderness wandering toward the promises of God, knowing we're not alone. Where some preachers might scold and say, "Get off the mountaintop," today's narrative is more likely to teach us to "remember the mountaintop!"

Notes

1. David G. Buttrick, "Genesis 15:1-18," *Interpretation* 42, no. 4 (October 1988): 396.
2. Ibid., 395.
3. Walter Brueggemann, *Genesis*, Interpretation: A Bible Commentary for Teaching and Preaching (Louisville: John Knox Press, 1982), 146.
4. Peter L. Steinke, "Fear Factor," *Christian Century* 124, no. 4 (February 20, 2007): 20.
5. Elisabeth Castelli, *Imitating Paul: A Discourse of Power* (Louisville: Westminster John Knox, 1991). See also A. K. M. Adam, "Walk This Way: Repetition, Difference, and the Imitation of Christ," *Interpretation* 55, no. 1 (January 2001): 19–33.
6. Barbara Brown Taylor, *Home by Another Way* (Cambridge: Cowley, 1997), 139.
7. Amy-Jill Levine and Mark Zvi Brettler, *The Jewish Annotated New Testament* (New York: Oxford University Press, 2011), 110.
8. The extended RCL reading ends with Jesus performing a "reluctant" exorcism and indicating that he's ready to be done with this part of his ministry. The LFM reading ends before Jesus comes down from the mountain.
9. Craddock also argues that the transfiguration is analogous to the temptation. In Fred B. Craddock, *Luke*, Interpretation: A Bible Commentary for Teaching and Preaching (Louisville: John Knox, 1990), 133.
10. Ibid., 132.
11. John Petty, Lectionary Blogging: The Transfiguration: Luke 9:28-36, Progressive Involvement blog, February 8, 2010, http://www.progressiveinvolvement.com/progressive_involvement/2010/02/lectionary-blogging-the-transfiguration-luke-9-2836.html.
12. Barbara Brown Taylor, "Dazzling Darkness," *Christian Century* (February 4–11, 1998): 105.

March 3, 2013
Third Sunday in Lent

Revised Common Lectionary (RCL)
Isaiah 55:1-9
Psalm 63:1-8
1 Corinthians 10:1-13
Luke 13:1-9

Lectionary for Mass (LFM)
Exodus 3:1-8a, 13-15
Psalm 103:1-2, 3-4, 6-7, 8-11
1 Corinthians 10:1-6, 10-12
Luke 13:1-9

There's a fifteenth-century triptych by Nicolas Froment that shows Moses before the burning bush in its central panel. Moses is shielding his eyes with his right hand while he removes his sandals with the other hand. But, oh, what a burning bush! Moses seems stunned, not only by the angel appearing beside the bush, but by the fact that the bush is a flaming circle of rosebushes featuring the Madonna holding the Christ child. Art critics have interpreted the entire trio of paintings to refer to the Annunciation of Mary. As an imaginative exercise, the painting collapses several categories into one: Moses and God, annunciation or rising up (resurrection), the divine feminine, and incarnation.

The journey and wilderness themes continue with today's readings, along with images of banquets, food, drink, and fig trees. The Isaiah text conjures Lady Wisdom's banquet, Paul teaches about the universality of temptation, the psalmist hungers and thirsts for the Lord. There are strong vocational themes, including the call of Moses, and Lukan calls to repent and return to the Lord. The Lukan text poses the tricky theological problem of who deserves punishment and who deserves mercy.

First Reading
Isaiah 55:1-9 (RCL)

Food and meals are prominent in both testaments. Contemporary Christians may not be fully aware of how significant the idea of food and food sharing used to be, either in our own recent history or in the history of the Bible. The traditions of family Sunday dinners or neighborly potlucks have waned as we become busier and more mobile.

A quick Internet search will find statistics demonstrating how few families even sit down together regularly at the same table. This isn't a scold, just an observation. We've lost touch with the significance of table sharing and fellowship.

But in biblical times, food signified security from hunger and famine; it also signified divine favor. To be well fed wasn't taken for granted; it was a cause for celebration. Both testaments have religious classics that feature food. The Garden of Eden is well stocked with freebies; the exodus crowd finds manna from the sky and water from a rock; the Passover is marked by lamb's blood, herbs, and flatbread; Lady Wisdom throws a banquet; Jesus breaks bread, turns water to wine; Jews and Christians long for the messianic age of milk and honey. In the Bible, food is theological, as we see in Proverbs 9:1-6:

> Wisdom has built her house, she has hewn her seven pillars. She has slaughtered her animals, she has mixed her wine, she has also set her table. She has sent out her servant-girls, she calls from the highest places in the town, "You that are simple, turn in here!" To those without sense she says, "Come, eat of my bread and drink of the wine I have mixed. Lay aside immaturity, and live, and walk in the way of insight."

The Isaiah reading comes from Second Isaiah, just before the end of the Babylonian exile, addressed to a community that desperately needed assurance of God's favor and the hope of restoration. Today's text uses the metaphor of a banquet to explore the claims of divine abundance.

Drawing on imagery similar to the Lady Wisdom figure of Proverbs, Isaiah claims that God offers both literal food and spiritual food. In the first section (vv. 1-5) God speaks to Israel with a set of imperatives: "Ho, everyone who thirsts, come to the waters; and you that have no money, come, buy and eat! Come, buy wine and milk without money and without price" (v. 1). Freebies! A divine bonanza of abundance where you can buy what is priceless without paying for it. God offers abundant food, literal food, food that enables us to live the abundant life. There's an even more amazing claim in verses 3b-4; God isn't doing this because we (Israel) deserve it, but because of promises made through another. "For the love of David, with whom I made a covenant," says God. "I'm doing this because I made promises I'll keep, even if you haven't kept all your promises."

In the second section of the reading (vv. 6-11), God offers the spiritual fulfillment of mercy: "Seek the LORD while he may be found, call upon him while he is near; let the wicked forsake their way, and the unrighteous their thoughts; let them return to the LORD that he may have mercy on them, and to our God, for he will abundantly pardon" (vv. 6-8). God calls for repentance *after* the offer of the divine banquet and not before. Come, eat, repent.

In case we thought God behaved in another way, the Isaiah text reminds us that God is not a pay-for-play, *quid pro quo* kind of deity. Repentance is not the beginning of the relationship, but its finale. "My thoughts are not your thoughts, nor are your ways my ways" (v. 8).

In addition to the theme of food and repentance, there is also a powerful theology of the word operating in the Isaiah text. Behind the promises based on the covenant with David is the idea that God has spoken promises to which Israel should listen: listen carefully to me; incline your ear, and come to me; listen, so that you may live. This should remind us of the temptation story from the First Sunday of Lent. The devil tempted Jesus to turn stones into bread, but Jesus retorted, "One does not live by bread alone" (Luke 4:4b). In Matthew's Gospel the connection is more explicit: "One does not live by bread alone, but by every word that comes from the mouth of God" (Matt. 4:4b).

Finally, there is a universalism that permeates Isaiah as a whole and this passage in particular. Despite the fact that some Christians promote the claim that Judaism is exclusive and ethnocentric, there is a constant thread of universalism weaving through the story of Israel and pointing to the eschatological hope of both Israel and the church. The banquet invitation (like the great messianic banquet invitation in Luke 14:12-34) is for all who thirst for God (even the impoverished) to join in this divine open table. "When you give a luncheon or a dinner, do not invite your friends or your brothers or your relatives or rich neighbors, in case they may invite you in return, and you would be repaid. But when you give a banquet, invite the poor, the crippled, the lame, and the blind. And you will be blessed, because they cannot repay you, for you will be repaid at the resurrection of the righteous" (Luke 14:12b-14).

The other note of universalism comes in verse 5, at the pivot point between God's invitation to eat and God's call for repentance. "You shall call nations that you do not know, and nations that do not know you shall run to you."

Peter Steinke concludes his reflection on the Isaiah text like this: "God is not waiting for us to figure out everything, not hesitating to act until there is evidence that we will put our questions aside. 'Love bears all things,' even our questions and protests. God will come forward. We 'wait and see,' and in the meantime we 'take and eat.' The meal is free and holds the promise of freeing us from whatever holds us captive."[1]

Exodus 3:1-8a, 13-15 (LFM)

What do you say to a burning bush?

Moses has left Egypt far behind. He's settled in with Jethro's family in Midian, where he fled after he killed one of Pharaoh's men. He has, in common vernacular, returned to his roots as a wandering Aramean. His glory days as Pharaoh's right-hand man and project manager are over and we can only assume he's adjusted to his domestic life. He's a married man now; he and Zipporah have all the trappings of family life—kids, household, in-laws, and livestock.

He's out tending the flocks one day (beyond the wilderness!) when he notices some burning shrubbery. Moses turns aside (gets distracted from his task to look at the bush), the bush calls his name, and Moses answers, "Here I am." John Holbert reminds us that the biblical scene is pretty far from what the movies have given us: "To be sure, talking and blazing bushes are hardly the stuff of the everyday, but Moses, when confronted by the amazing sight, does not stare in stupefied religious silence but has a series of quite extraordinary things to say to the shrub, after the leafy plant commands him to act. In short, Moses is far less Charlton Heston here than he is Woody Allen."[2] Or maybe a character in a Monty Python skit.

The bush points out that Moses is standing on holy ground and needs to remove his footwear. Only then does the bush make divine claims. "I am the God of your father, the God of Abraham, the God of Isaac, and the God of Jacob." Now Moses is properly afraid; he hides his face.

The God of Abraham, Isaac, and Jacob gives Moses a mission, telling him that he's to go back to Egypt, back where Pharaoh lives, back where there's a price on his head, and convince Pharaoh to release the Hebrew captives. This is, of course, a theophany, a divine manifestation, not unlike the ones we've seen in the New Testament accounts of Jesus' baptism and transfiguration. It's also like the scene from Abram's covenant cutting where God is masked by darkness and smoke. The specific mission, to release the captives, resonates with Jesus' inaugural sermon in Luke 4:16-30.

Moses argues. If you notice, all the prophets resist God at first. Moses might be the first, although we could claim that Abram also argued, but he's not the last. Jeremiah will resist, Jonah will resist, Gideon, Ezekiel, and Isaiah will resist. Some might be right when they say that a sense of inadequacy or unworthiness is a prerequisite for being called by God.

Moses asks, "What are your credentials? When folks ask who authorized this mission, what am I supposed to say? Who are you?" And then God responds with something that scholars still can't decipher. God either says, "I am who I am," or "I will be what I will be," or "I am what I will be." None of the answers are particularly helpful or enlightening. God isn't about to be pinned down. God will adapt to whatever the situation requires. What scholars sometimes overlook in this naming issue is that in the ancient Near East there was a god for every little thing. For God to resist those narrow identifications was a testimony to radical monotheism. God's not about to let Moses go to Egypt and claim that the God of Prisoners or the God of Hebrews or the God of Burning Bushes sent him. YHWH is the only God, who is and will be everything and anything. God uses a verb form of "to be," which pretty much means God is the God of all existence.

We know, of course, that Moses eventually agrees to go. Just as the Lukan Jesus comes down from the mountaintop and sets his face toward his own exodus in Jerusalem, Moses comes down from the mountaintop and faces his own exodus in Egypt. As Holbert says:

God is forever calling persons to speak truth to power, to say things that most people have no desire to hear. And prophets have a way of dying at the hands of those to whom they have been called to speak. No, Moses is hardly Charlton Heston. He is, in fact, you and me—less than eager to speak the truth, more than eager to leave the task to someone else.[3]

Notice, please, that God's agency ultimately brings change, but God seems to work through reluctant human agents to make things happen.

Psalmody
Psalm 63:1-8 (RCL)

This is a short psalm, traditionally considered one of the psalms of David, written while he was fleeing from Absalom. The psalm also contains some of the features of a lament, and much of the language hints at nocturnal images and desert/wilderness images. The psalmist considers his current situation like being alone in the desert at night, hungry and thirsty, and hoping for contact with God. The psalm combines the food and feasting metaphors that we also found in the Isaiah text for today. The nocturnal character of the psalm is reminiscent of other nighttime scenes from the Hebrew Bible, including Abram's nighttime terror, the darkness of the temple where Samuel lay when God's voice confused him, and all the other times that night or darkness symbolizes God's absence or distance. In the New Testament writings, darkness is routinely contrasted with daylight and light, symbolizing the old age and the dawning new age.

Even though the psalmist feels separated from God, he still remembers God with nostalgia. He remarks that when he lies in bed at night and thinks of God, it's as if he's just completed a "rich feast." He remembers encountering God ("I have looked upon you in the sanctuary," v. 2) in all power and glory, suggesting that David speaks of looking upon God in the temple.

The language is intensely intimate: his soul "clings" to God, God has protected him with his "wings," and God holds him in God's "right hand." These could also be references to the ark of the covenant with its sculpted wings and the fact that the ark could be considered a sanctuary for those seeking refuge.

With the psalmist we can acknowledge what St. John of the Cross calls "the dark night of the soul," the sense of yearning for what is hidden and unseen, a spiritual crisis that journeys toward the dawn. Preachers might want to read about Mother Teresa of Calcutta, who was said to experience what she called "the dark night of the soul" lasting from 1948 almost up until her death in 1997, with only brief periods of relief: "Although perpetually cheery in public, the Teresa of the letters lived in a state of deep and abiding spiritual pain. In more than 40 communications, many of which have never before been published, she bemoans the 'dryness,' 'darkness,' 'loneliness' and 'torture' she is undergoing. She compares the experience to hell and at one point says it has driven her to doubt the existence of heaven and even of God."[4]

The lament psalms are like singing the blues, which is one reason they've endured and continued to be part of our religious heritage. They capture the same themes and experiences of Lent, the same sense of wandering, lostness, and abandonment, even as we cling to hope.

Psalm 103:1-2, 3-4, 6-7, 8-11 (LFM)

Today's LFM psalm response has the opposite tenor from the RCL psalm. Where Psalm 63 sings the blues, this section of Psalm 103 sounds more like the "Hallelujah Chorus." It's a blessed Sabbath relief from the somber tones of the penitential season, and it's theologically appropriate to the idea that the Lenten calendar exempts Sundays. If every Sunday is a celebration of the resurrection, this psalm captures that spirit.

The psalm is a psalm of thanksgiving, but since it's not addressed directly to God, it's not a prayer. It's a song of praise for all the mighty attributes and deeds of God. Part of the midrash commentary tradition of Judaism considers the psalm also for its anthropological dimensions and what it says about the human condition. The words of the psalm begin with self-exhortation to bless the Lord, and the tone is imperative, a kind of personal pep talk about how to orient toward God. The psalm moves from individual claims ("all that is within me") to broader covenantal claims. Rather than saying, "Remember," the psalm is a stronger reminder: "Do not forget." We know from personal experience that we tell ourselves, "Don't forget," only when forgetfulness is a powerful temptation. This is not a nostalgic stroll down memory lane; it's a powerful determination that stands almost as a self-warning.

"Bless the Lord, O my soul" turns the tables on petitionary prayer. Instead of asking for God's blessing, what if we blessed God for divine goodness? Blessings turn into a form of thanks and praise. Don't forget that God is the one who forgives, heals, redeems, and crowns with mercy. Don't forget it. You may not have everything you want, you may not be crowned as royalty in the world (something that would preoccupy David), but God provides what none other can provide. Don't you forget it.

Gratitude does something to us that's almost counterintuitive. Gratitude lifts our spirits. In verse 5, which isn't part of the response but should be included, the psalm speaks of renewed vigor. Gratitude is an antidote to self-pity or despair. One preacher, Lewis Smedes, writes:

> I can tell you for sure that nothing, nothing beats gratitude for sheer joy. It's the best feeling you or I will ever have. Better than a warm bed on a bad night, better than falling in love with the most beautiful person in the world, better than hearing the most beautiful music ever played. . . . Gratitude is the ultimate happiness. It comes down to this: gratitude is the best thing you can ever feel.[5]

The second half of today's reading (vv. 6-11) offers a broader vision of praise, shifting from the personal to the communal. The broader vision includes God's covenantal faithfulness and righteousness (*hesed*) not only to the covenant people, but to all who are oppressed. The postexilic dating of the psalm suggests that "the oppressed" are those who perceived themselves as being under God's wrath and punishment: disobedient Israel. Regardless of the original intention of the psalmist, we can expand God's vindication and justice to all who need to be freed from oppression. If we read and preach from a liberation-theology perspective, we should also bless the name of God who is surely at work in all the deeds of liberation in all places and in all times.

A sermon from this psalm should probably not take "points" from the first section alone. Many published sermons will follow three or four points (forgiveness, healing, redemption, renewal) and stop there. If we confine our sermons to a limited perspective on individual faith, we perpetuate a kind of piety that's more concerned with personal salvation than with social justice. An alternative sermon structure would be to follow the movement of the psalm itself, which moves from personal benefits, to communal benefits, to universal benefits. Praise God for all of God's mighty deeds. Don't you forget it.

Second Reading
1 Corinthians 10:1-13 (RCL)
1 Corinthians 10:1-6, 10-12 (LFM)

One of the best ways to begin sermon preparation is for the preacher to actually listen to the text being read aloud. While preachers might begin with commentaries, congregations begin their sermon encounter by hearing the reading. Martin Luther's bumper sticker, "Faith is an acoustical affair," should be plastered not just on pulpits, but on pastoral desks and computer monitors as well. It's a good idea to have someone read the text out loud to you. If that's not practical, listen to an online audio.

This reading starts in the middle of a long argument Paul is making, so the initial references and the warning tone will be jarring to us. If that's not enough, Paul seems to be using the story of Moses and the children of Israel as a scare tactic to rattle the church folk. The section starts off with Paul claiming he doesn't want the Corinthians to be unaware or confused, which is a typical Pauline rhetorical gambit that usually prefaces a "correction." Using the exodus metaphor as an analogy for the church, Paul compares the congregation to Moses' people who were all baptized by the same waters and who all shared the same spiritual food and drink, but continued "in idolatry." The sins of Israel that he catalogs were playing, sexual immorality, testing the Lord, and complaining. Then he points out that God wasn't pleased with them and punished them, leaving a trail of bodies on the way. He claims they serve as examples for us so that we don't think we're standing on solid ground when we're not.

Not only will the scare tactics be offensive, but the apparent theology of punishment/reward is seriously problematic. Is Paul actually slipping in some works righteousness and religious purity tests?

The best understanding of this letter comes from Pauline theology itself, especially the comments on wisdom and folly that come earlier in the epistle. The epistle is prompted by reports Paul has heard "from Chloe's people" that there's division at Corinth and that it's surfacing over disputes about Christian freedom and the nature of salvation. Apparently some of the folks think that being saved means they can behave any way they want to, including engaging in sexual improprieties and bringing lawsuits against one another.

Scholars who don't understand the eschatological/apocalyptic foundation for Pauline theology will be distracted by the specifics of behavior and will lead preachers down the wrong path. The theological problem for Paul isn't really that folks are behaving badly; the problem is that *their spiritual arrogance* leads them to behave badly. And if they're spiritually arrogant, they haven't understood the gospel Paul's been preaching. Paul sees the church as the advance guard of the coming new age when all will be ultimately reconciled in God. Those who have been baptized are already living in the new age, and their new way of living together is a witness of Christ's new creation. Humility is one of the virtues associated with the new age. Pride is not. The problem at Corinth is that some consider their salvation to be an excuse to act the way the unsaved act. They're glorying in their salvation.

In 1 Corinthians 1:26-30, Paul launches into his discussion of wisdom and folly, geared to give a wake-up call to the Corinthians:

> Consider your own call, brothers and sisters: not many of you were wise by human standards, not many were powerful, not many were of noble birth. But God chose what is foolish in the world to shame the wise; God chose what is weak in the world to shame the strong; God chose what is low and despised in the world, things that are not, to reduce to nothing things that are, so that no one might boast in the presence of God.

Neil Elliott claims that Paul is challenging an ideology of privilege or boasting rights.[6] It's the self-righteousness of the Corinthians that leads them to misbehave; they think they're exempt from moral and ethical standards.

Now his warnings make more sense. The Israelites thought they were safe but they weren't. God wasn't pleased with them and God won't be pleased with you, either. So if you think you are standing, watch out that you do not fall. Pride goeth before a fall. We can accept Paul's analysis even if we reject the idea of divine retribution. William Loader writes:

> So the rhetorical challenge needs to be seen in perspective. While the warnings about lust may apply to some, for most Paul is wanting to assert that they are no better, if they think spirituality is based on a wonderful past conversion and manifestation of wonders now. These people are just as much in danger of missing out as those who are flagrantly immoral. One might also argue that religion gone wrong is usually much more dangerous than the acts of immorality which it easily deplores.[7]

The best advice for preachers is to get straight to the heart of the Lenten theme: temptation. The temptations are not given by God in order to test us, but they come from worldly ways and devilish tricks. Christians who are still in the world but not of the world are living in liminal times, times when the tempter will show up and use the most seductive tricks to get us to think more of ourselves than we ought. When we are tempted to think better of ourselves, when we are tempted to boast in our salvation, when we consider ourselves beyond temptation is precisely when we are most vulnerable. Paul isn't offering a new list of rules and regulations; he's reminding us of the strength of the cross. If we don't understand the cross, we don't understand anything at all about Christian faith or Christian life.[8]

Gospel
Luke 13:1-9 (RCL, LFM)

"Everything happens for a reason." "What goes around comes around." For a Christian, there shouldn't be a more frustrating popular theology than the one that gives in to a fatalistic and deterministic worldview. American pop theology is not so different from the world described by one preacher writing about the first-century Lukan audience. Dave Ewart writes, "There was a widespread, taken for granted, deeply held, bedrock belief that EVERYTHING happened for a reason. God is just, and if bad things happen to someone, it has to be because—in some way—they deserve it. Or—in some way—something good will come from it and it only seems like a bad thing to us."[9]

This perspective is the same old reward-and-punishment scheme that operates in many religious expressions. It is, in fact, the same old reward-and-punishment scheme that operates in the classic notions of heaven and hell. The idea is so taken for granted, so automatically assumed, that to challenge it is considered blasphemous. When Rob Bell published *Love Wins: Heaven, Hell, and the Fate of Every Person Who Ever Lived* in 2011, many Christians of every stripe protested his challenge to the theology of punishment and reward.

Luke's Jesus would have loved Rob Bell.

The reading is peculiar to Luke and has no direct parallels in the other Gospels. Luke locates this call to repentance right before the pre-Holy-Week tension and controversies begin. At first the reading seems disjointed. Some scholars will even claim the sections *are* unrelated, but they actually make sense of each other. In the first section, Jesus is having the "When Bad Things Happen" philosophical conversation, and in the second section he tells the parable of the fig tree. The first section is the theological setup for the second section. And Luke's version of the parable is dramatically different from the cursing of the fig tree in Matthew and Mark: Luke's Jesus purposely delays judgment and allows more time for repentance. Fred Craddock calls it the parable of divine patience.[10]

In the first section Jesus raises the question of reward and punishment by piggybacking on an anecdote from some folks in the crowd. Preachers would do well to think as quickly on their feet as Jesus, so when someone says, "Everything happens for a reason," we'll be ready with stories and reflections. In the first instance, Pilate, the Roman governor, had killed some Galileans who were making sacrifices at the temple and then he mixed their blood with the sacrifices. No doubt this was a warning to other Jews to remember that Rome was in charge. But it could have signified more than that. There was a kind of "cross-town" Jewish rivalry between some Judean (Jerusalemite) factions and the hillbilly Galileans who were considered a little overzealous. Was someone in the crowd trying to get Jesus (a Galilean) to weigh in on the piety of the Galileans?

Jesus pokes back. "Do you think they deserved it? Do you think they were worse than others?" Then he answers his own question with a resounding "NO! And if you don't want to suffer their fate, you'd better repent."

In case they don't get it, Jesus offers an anecdote of his own, shifting the focus to some Jerusalemites who got killed when the Siloam tower fell over. "Do you think they deserved it?" Again, he says, "NO!"

In both cases, Jesus would have shocked his listeners, who were pretty sure that everything happens for a reason and that what goes around comes around. They also would have been exceedingly familiar with the bloodthirsty glee of folks who love to think that people deserve what they get. No matter how many times Jesus preaches that God doesn't act that way, people don't believe it. God is in the mercy business, not the retribution business.

Then Jesus gives them a parable, just in case they still don't get it. He tells them about a bum fig tree that doesn't bear figs. They've heard versions of this story before, maybe even the Markan and Matthean versions where Jesus curses the fig tree. In Luke's story the owner wants to cut the tree down, but the gardener intercedes and does everything he can to guarantee that the tree will produce. Ewart explains:

> In effect, Jesus is saying: *I've just dumped a lot of manure on you, and I'm giving you a year before I come back to see if you are bearing good fruit or not. So pay attention to what I've just taught you. Absorb it. Take it in. And let me activate in you what you are already designed for. You don't have to become completely different—become a whole new tree. Just bear the fruit that you already have been created for.*[11]

Why is it that the fundamental claim of Christian faith is still so routinely confused and misunderstood? Our explanations of salvation, our casual negligence of the theological problems with heaven and hell, and our ongoing incompetence as preachers have at least something to do with it. We have to preach the radicality of God's good news so that folks will think twice before they say, "What goes around comes around."

A few years ago there was a popular television show called *My Name Is Earl*. The main character was a petty criminal, hospitalized and under the influence of narcotics when he saw a television interview with someone explaining the idea of karmic retribution. He decided to turn his life (and his luck) around by making a list of all his wrongs so he could right them. Every episode of the show featured one wrong that Earl attempted to right and cross off his list. The show reinforced the idea of retribution and cosmic scorekeeping, or what one preacher calls "karma theology."

We want to be especially careful during Lent to avoid reinforcing the notion of retributive theology. We don't want people to repent so they can avoid karma or divine wrath, or so they can gain brownie points in heaven. We call people to repentance so that they will understand the radicality of divine mercy and become witnesses of that mercy in the broken and corrupt world.

Praise God! Everything doesn't happen for a reason. Shout hallelujah! What goes around doesn't come around. The holy gardener looks on the unfruitfulness of the church and the unfruitfulness of the world and says, "It's not a lost case yet. Let's give it another chance."

Notes

1. Peter L. Steinke, "Free Food," *Christian Century* 124, no. 4 (February 20, 2007): 21.
2. John C. Holbert, "It's Your Call: Reflections on Exodus 3:1-15," August 18, 2011, http://www.patheos.com/Resources/Additional-Resources/Its-Your-Call-Reflections-on-Exodus-3-John-Holbert-08-22-2011.html.
3. Ibid.
4. David Van Biema, "Mother Teresa's Crisis of Faith," *Time*, August 23, 2007, http://www.time.com/time/magazine/article/0,9171,1655720,00.html.
5. Lewis Smedes, "Things I've Learned on My Way to Eighty," radio message, December 17, 2000, http://www.csec.org/csec/sermon/smedes_4411.htm.
6. Neil Elliott, *Liberating Paul: The Justice of God and the Politics of the Apostle* (Sheffield, UK: Sheffield Press, 1995), 204.
7. William H. Loader, "First Thoughts on Year B Epistle Passages from the Lectionary: Lent 3," http://wwwstaff.murdoch.edu.au/~loader/CEpLent3.htm.
8. L. Susan Bond, "Preaching Paul," *Quarterly Review* 24, no. 3 (Fall 2004): 236–48.
9. Dave Ewart, "Luke 13:1-9," Holy Textures blog, February 22, 2010, http://www.holytextures.com/2010/02/luke-13-1-9-year-c-lent-3-sermon.html.
10. Fred B. Craddock, *Luke*, Interpretation: A Bible Commentary for Teaching and Preaching (Louisville: John Knox, 1990), 167.
11. Ewart, op. cit.

March 10, 2013
Fourth Sunday in Lent

Revised Common Lectionary (RCL)	Lectionary for Mass (LFM)
Joshua 5:9-12	Joshua 5:9a, 10-12
Psalm 32	Psalm 34:2-3, 4-5, 6-7
2 Corinthians 5:16-21	2 Corinthians 5:17-21
Luke 15:1-3, 11b-32	Luke 15:1-3, 11-32

Today's readings all capture hints of new beginnings. The long wandering in the wilderness is almost over for the exodus people as Joshua pauses on the brink of the promised land to mark the transition with Passover and circumcision. They leave behind the shame of their wilderness experience and celebrate with a feast. In Luke, the youngest son wanders in a different sort of wilderness, nevertheless lost in disgrace. In both stories, the wanderers make their way home out of the wilderness, but neither the nation nor the youngest son is able to shake the disgrace of disobedience on their own. It is only the pronouncement by the "other" that redeems them from their past. The psalmist sings of the joys of confession and being restored to God. The apostle Paul calls for expansive reconciliation that marks a new creation. New, new, new! This whole set of readings, especially when taken together, symbolizes the restoration and renewal of divine promises.

First Reading
Joshua 5:9-12 (RCL)
Joshua 5:9a, 10-12 (LFM)

We should start by assuming that the average congregation doesn't know much about Joshua or his place in the story of Israel. Some folks may have grown up listening to Mahalia Jackson or Harry Belafonte or even Elvis sing about the walls of Jericho, but beyond knowing that Joshua made the walls come tumbling down, they won't know much else. There's probably a giant memory gap between Moses giving the Ten Commandments and the battle of Jericho, and they might not even associate Joshua with that battle.

That memory gap is where today's story occurs. The Israelites wandered for forty years not because they were ignorant, but because they were being punished. Moses had died far behind them on Mount Nebo precisely because God said, "You won't get there, Moses. I'm going to punish you and your people for grumbling and making golden calves." Before Moses died, he deputized a strapping young warrior to make spy forays into the land that they would conquer. During the forty years between leaving Egypt and taking Canaan, an entire generation died. We don't know if they observed the Passover liberation feast during their time of wandering; the Bible is simply silent on that information. But we do know that they hadn't been circumcising their boy babies as part of the Abrahamic covenant.

So right before Joshua leads the tribes of Israel into the promised land, God instructs him to circumcise all the males. All the foreskins were piled up into a heap and each of the twelve tribal leaders placed a stone to form a stone circle around the heap. Removing the foreskins was associated with the removal of shame. "The LORD said to Joshua, 'Today I have rolled away from you the disgrace of Egypt.' And so that place is called Gilgal to this day" (v. 9). Scholars debate the precise name for the location, but it's not in dispute that the origins of the naming and the story behind the naming signify the Abrahamic covenant and the removal of shame. It's a story about how God reclaimed the wanderers and restored them to the promises. Howard Wallace writes, "It wasn't simply a matter of catching up on a requirement which in certain circumstances could not be fulfilled. In Joshua 5 there is the sense that the Lord is beginning again with a new generation of the people. A new generation now in the promised land makes a fresh commitment to the Lord."[1]

After they complete the circumcisions, they celebrate Passover. Even though we can't know if this was the first celebration since leaving Egypt, it makes a beautiful narrative bookend to their wanderings. Everything else in the Joshua text reinforces this symbolism; the manna from heaven (which had sustained them in the wilderness) ceases and they celebrate Passover from the bounty of the land: "The manna ceased on the day they ate the produce of the land, and the Israelites no longer had manna; they ate the crops of the land of Canaan that year" (v. 12). For them it was a feast of deliverance that celebrated the rolling away of their shame, the end to their wandering, and the brink of new promise. We can go all the way back in our lectionary readings and understand why Walter Brueggemann would associate the land with homecoming and resurrection (see the first reading for the First Sunday of Lent, above). The association is reinforced even more with today's Gospel story about the prodigal son.

It's important for preachers to keep in mind all the symbolism that's gathered into the Passover imagery so that we will have an expanded theological vocabulary for understanding the significance of the Last Supper. God is always the one who rolls away our shame, renews the promises, and starts a new generation. When we face difficult times, we remind ourselves of God's readiness and God's forgiveness and God's providence. When we break the bread and pour the wine, we remember all God's acts of deliverance, and Eucharist becomes for us a sign of our liberation and our meal of preparation.

Tissa Balasuriya, a Catholic theologian, wrote a wonderful book called *Eucharist and Human Liberation* where he explores the connections between the Passover symbols, the Lord's Supper, the eschatological future, and social justice:

> The Eucharistic table prefigures the ultimate stage of human liberation, the realization of the kingdom of God on earth as in heaven. It is eschatological. It signifies the stage promised in the scriptures when the lion and the lamb can lie together and share the same pasture; when every tear will be wiped from every eye; when God will be all in all. This is the Christian hope, the promised stage of human blessedness. This is also part of the Jewish tradition.[2]

The salvation and liberation for Israel have been a long time coming. On the brink of their new life, they celebrate a feast to remember God's providence and to ratify their forgiveness.

Psalmody
Psalm 32 (RCL)
Psalm 34:2-3, 4-5, 6-7 (LFM)

Psalm 32 is one of the penitential psalms and continues the themes of forgiveness and reconciliation and the sense of joy that comes from confession. The psalm begins and ends with joy, but in between we see the consequences of being separated from God by guilt. The overall metaphor for guilt is expressed in physical terms. The psalmist is heavy with guilt and silent: "While I kept silence, my body wasted away through my groaning all day long. For day and night your hand was heavy upon me; my strength was dried up as by the heat of summer" (vv. 3-4). The mercy that comes after confession is like a refuge, a safe hiding place where the threatening mighty waters cannot reach.

The double blessing at the beginning of the psalm serves to break the silence between the psalmist and God. This is a powerful way to think about prayer and worship, as a time when we break the silence that we ourselves have imposed. We all know what it's like to be locked in a pattern of silence or to receive the silent treatment. It's paralyzing. Reconciliation is impossible because the two parties aren't in communication. "Break the silence!" sings the psalmist. "Confess and move forward! Otherwise you'll be silent and wasting away." As in other psalms, there's an analogy between eating and being in communion with God. Those who are not in communion are starving and thirsting; those who are in communion with God received God's words of mercy, God's word, as sustenance. We don't live by bread alone, but by every word that proceeds from the mouth of God.

Breaking the silence allows the believer to break the stubbornness, to stop being like a mule, and to listen to God. There's also a teacher/student image system at work in the psalm, which hints at themes from wisdom literature. Clint McCann writes, "By defining happiness in terms of forgiveness, Psalm 32 functions as an important check against any tendency to misunderstand. That is, to be righteous is not a matter of being sinless but a matter of being forgiven, of being open to God's instruction."[3] McCann points out the different ways the psalmist refers to sin: transgressions, iniquity, and guilt.

Silence is a kind of wilderness, a drought of communion. The way forward, the eschatological hope, is to break the silence by blessing God, by confessing, by receiving God's life-giving mercy and divine wisdom.

Second Reading
2 Corinthians 5:16-21 (RCL)
2 Corinthians 5:17-21 (LFM)

This Pauline text is full of one-liners that are usually pulled out of context and used as punchlines. Conventional sermon approaches distort the sweep of Paul's call to reconciliation by reducing it to interpersonal relationships or to the intimate relationship between a believer and God. We'll recontextualize this portion of the letter within Pauline eschatology and ecclesiology, to see that Paul is talking less about personal piety and more about the vocation of the church as an agent of real sociopolitical change. Paul Hanson, a scholar of apocalyptic literature and theology, sets the stage for today's reading with this comment:

> For as the Apostle Paul explained to the Corinthians, only by being reconciled with God do God's people become ministers of reconciliation, capable of seeing the world not in terms of its fallen state, but in terms of what it can become by divine grace. That is to say, that even how the church looks upon the world is a gift of God, who has given it the mind of Christ, the heart of the New Creation, the perspective of the redeemed.[4]

The RCL reading starts with verse 16, which establishes Paul's cosmic and *kairos* theology of reconciliation: "From now on, therefore, we regard no one from a human point of view; even though we once knew Christ from a human point of view, we know him no longer in that way." As Hulitt Gloer writes:

> Christ's death is not merely an event which produces certain benefits for others (representation). It is not merely an event in which Christ acts as a substitute for others. It is rather an event in which others must participate. In short, one must die with Christ and in that death with Christ die to self, to the flesh, to the power of sin, to the powers of this world.[5]

To die to the powers of the world means that a Christian no longer measures the world by the world's measures of success, identity, or power. Jesus has redefined for us what it means to belong, what it means to be successful, and what power looks like. The worldly or human construct is one of domination systems, within which the primary tactics are those of domination and competition. Paul considers these the demonic powers, or the powers and principalities. The work of the church is to name, unmask, and redeem the powers and principalities, but the church cannot do that by dominating or competing.[6]

So Paul uses the genius vocabulary of "reconciliation" instead of sacrifice or justification or redemption imagery. Gloer explains:

> "Redemption" comes from the slave market of the first century and implies a release from bondage, yet many in our world have no particular sense of bondage. "Justification" comes from the world of the courtroom, and its juridical emphasis may have little impact where the sense of sin and any sort of accountability before God have vanished. "Sacrifice" evokes images of cultic ritual which have little meaning for moderns who are no longer plagued by a dread of the numinous. "Reconciliation," however, belongs to the sphere of personal relationships.[7]

In case we don't fully understand what "reconciliation" looks like, Paul reinforces it with the image of an ambassador. Speaking to a Hellenized audience under the Roman Empire, Paul uses the language of international diplomacy. He doesn't use the language of soldier sacrifices or Department of Defense bombers (which would be complicit with domination systems); Paul gives us the Department of State. Paul, who loves military imagery and notions of spiritual warfare, here gives us a diplomat.

And what a change of perspective that is! One of my pastor friends talks about folks who see Christian faith as an evangelistic hammer: "When you're carrying a hammer, everything looks like a nail." But Paul begs us to see the world and the role of the church differently: "So if anyone is in Christ, there is a new creation: everything old has passed away; see, everything has become new!" (v. 17). Most preachers will consider "new creation" to be analogous to personal salvation and the reformation of an individual's moral life, but that is way too small for Paul's claims. He doesn't say, "*You* are a new creation." He says, "*There is* a new creation." The whole world is changed for believers. The vocation of the church is reconstrued. Hanson says, "It is *in* the world *for* the world, and yet is not *of* the world, for it has become a part of the reality toward which the fallen world yearns, God's order of peace and justice. This makes it distinct from the world."[8] We no longer see the world in us/them terms; we see the world as a diplomat sees the world, as a place to make peace.

God, of course, is the initiator of this new creation as seen through the eyes of reconciliation. God's business in Jesus was the business of reconciling the world to the divine self. Again, Gloer:

In short, God reconciles and humanity is reconciled! For Paul it is never Jesus the loving son stepping into the gap to protect humanity from an angry father. It is God the Father who takes the initiative by sending Jesus the son to accomplish the work of reconciliation. "God is not an angry tyrant out to get" us, "but one whose reconciling love has taken flesh in the life and death of Jesus."[9]

Paul charges the church to be the advance guard manifesting the new creation and the ministry of reconciliation. As Hanson says, "Though in the popular eschatology of his day the new era of blessing was to come through a dazzling display of divine power in which the cosmos would be thrown into disarray, Jesus pointed out that in everyday human acts of reconciling and healing, the Kingdom of God was 'in the midst of you.'"[10] Lent calls us to reclaim our reconciliation. Since we see Christ from a different point of view, the whole vocation of the ministry of reconciliation takes on dramatically new meaning. We are the Peace Corps of God, the Red Cross of Reconciliation, and Ambassadors for Christ.

Gospel
Luke 15:1-3, 11b-32 (RCL)
Luke 15:1-3, 11-32 (LFM)

Robert Farrar Capon is the author of several stunning works on the parables. Capon types the parable into three categories: parables of the kingdom, parables of grace, and parables of judgment. In general, his approach to the parables is to disclose the left-handed, paradoxical, and indirect style of exercising power. The parables of grace are those told between the feeding of the five thousand and the triumphal entry, and all read as statements of radical, unmerited grace made possible by Jesus' death and resurrection and our own ongoing deaths to all attempts to live our own way into heaven.

In Luke's Gospel, we see the parables of grace between the transfiguration and Holy Week, once Jesus has begun his "exodus." Capon argues that once Jesus turns his face toward Jerusalem, his ministry changes from doing miracles and ethical teachings into something decidedly less "upbeat."[11] When dealing with the parables of grace, his approach for beginning the hermeneutical task is simple: look for the dead people. If there aren't any dead people, look for the closest thing to dead you can find. According to Capon, that's the God/Christ figure in the story. Because, says Capon, once we get to the parables of grace, we're only talking about death and resurrection.

Capon's approach is unorthodox and frequently outrageous, but it's always a way to open new insights. And if we ever needed novelty in sermon prep, we surely need it for the parable of the prodigal son, one of the most consistently misunderstood parables of American preaching. Barbara Brown Taylor calls it "limp from handling."[12]

But let's go with Capon and look for the dead people. If you think there aren't any, you're wrong.

The parable is an absolute festival of death, and the first death occurs right at the beginning of the story: the father, in effect, commits suicide. It took me years to notice this fact, but once you see it, it's plain as the nose on an elephant. The younger son comes to his father and says, "Give me the portion of goods that falleth to me." In other words, he tells his father to put his will into effect, to drop legally dead right on the spot. Obligingly enough, the father does just that. . . .[13]

The next one to die is the wastrel son himself. Not only does he spend his inheritance on gin and casinos, but he ends up working on a Gentile pig farm. We know it's a Gentile farm, because no Jew would run a pig farm. Barbara Brown Taylor writes:

Instead, the younger son loses everything, and he loses it to Gentiles—Roman citizens, pagan pig-owners, complete strangers to the God of Israel. He might as well have used his birth certificate to light an Italian cigar. What he does is so reprehensible that the Talmud describes a ceremony to deal with it—a *qetsatsah* ceremony, to punish a Jewish boy who loses the family inheritance to Gentiles.[14]

The *qetsatsah* ceremony was less like a formal disinheritance and more like an excommunication or a shunning. The offended family would take a jar of burned nuts and corn and vegetables and break it in front of the family home, between the front door of the house and the individual. In case busted crockery and inedibles weren't an obvious enough symbol of unwelcome, the family and the community would shout and chant something like, "George doesn't live here anymore. He is cut off from his people."[15] Ideally, this would happen when someone attempted to return home.

So, the body count stands at two. The wandering son, wandering in the wilderness, consorting with Gentiles, setting his face toward Calvary, has also committed suicide. As soon as he comes to his senses (in his own thinking), he decides to demote himself from beloved returning son to a hired hand. I would argue that the son has killed himself twice. Three deaths, two corpses.

Now it's time for the second suicide of the father. Capon describes the first death of the father and the two deaths of the son. Barbara Brown Taylor and David Mattson actually describe the second suicide of the father, but they don't fully understand the death and resurrection significance of the father's mercy. Kari Henkelmann Keyl gets closest in her online article, "God Is a Loony Dad (or Mom)."[16]

Yes, the patriarch of the family runs down the road to welcome his son, and that's where the second death happens. No respectable father would do something like that, so the father becomes a mother, clutching up her skirts and racing to meet her son. She should be smashing crockery and scattering scorched corn and making hex signs at him, but she doesn't. Certainly the kind of right-handed, direct, and dominating patriarchal God we keep Kabuki dancing with wouldn't do that. Only a woman in the ancient Near East would defy macho expectations and race down the road. So the father kills himself a second time, dying to his manhood to become not a father, but a mother.

In short order, we get a fatted calf and a big, embarrassing, overdone bash instead of vegetable crisps in the dirt. It would be easy to stop here, but it would be a mistake, says Capon. We should agree with Capon, too, or otherwise it's a lovely little story with a cathartic ending that asks absolutely nothing from us. You know how the New Testament is always talking about dying and rising in Christ? How Paul talks about the first death and the second death? The first death, in baptism, frees us to laugh in the face of the second death, which is the one most folks dread. But the first death frees you so the second death loses its sting.

The Loser Son and the Suicide Father/Mother have already died at least twice and they're full of joy and generosity. This is a good time to point out that the Loser Son never gets a chance to repent; he gets accepted back without a flinch. The only grump in the crowd is the guy who hasn't died yet: the other brother. As Capon points out, "The classic parable of grace, therefore, turns out by anticipation to be a classic parable of judgment as well. It proclaims clearly that grace operates only by raising the dead: those who think they can make their lives the basis of their acceptance by God need not apply."[17]

And we could add that by anticipation the parable becomes a call to repentance, a call to set our faces toward Jerusalem, ready for the big party, the big reconciliation that's coming, even if we know someone has to die first. Like the grumpy older brother, we're probably going to have to stop keeping count of who's doing things the right way. We'll have to die to the world.

Notes

1. Howard Wallace, Year C: Lent 4, Old Testament Lectionary Resources Blog, March 14, 2010, http://hwallace.unitingchurch.org.au/WebOTcomments/LentC/Lent4.html.
2. Tissa Balasuriya, *Eucharist and Human Liberation* (Sri Lanka: Centre for Society and Religion, 1977), 53.
3. J. Clinton McCann Jr., "Psalms" in *The New Interpreter's Bible* (Nashville: Abingdon, 1996), 4:805.
4. Paul D. Hanson, "The Identity and Purpose of the Church," *Theology Today* 42, no. 3 (October 1985): 349.
5. Hulitt Gloer, "Ambassadors of Reconciliation: Paul's Genius in Applying the Gospel in a Multi-cultural World: 2 Corinthians 5:14-21," *Review & Expositor* 104, no. 3 (Summer 2007): 591.
6. The work of Walter Wink echoes through my essay. See his trilogy, *Naming the Powers: The Language of Power in the New Testament* (Philadelphia: Fortress Press, 1984); *Unmasking the Powers: The Invisible Forces That Determine Human Existence* (Philadelphia: Fortress Press, 1986); and *Engaging the Powers: Discerning and Resistance in a World of Domination* (Minneapolis: Fortress Press, 1992).
7. Gloer, "Ambassadors of Reconciliation," 593–94.
8. Hanson, "Identity and Purpose of the Church," 346.
9. Gloer, "Ambassadors of Reconciliation," 594–96.
10. Hanson, "Identity and Purpose of the Church," 345.
11. Robert Farrar Capon, *The Parables of Grace* (Grand Rapids: Eerdmans, 1988), 12.
12. Barbara Brown Taylor, "The Parable of the Dysfunctional Family," April 17, 2006, http://www.barbarabrowntaylor.com/newsletter374062.htm.
13. Capon, *Parables of Grace*, 137.
14. Taylor, "Dysfunctional Family."
15. David R. Mattson, *Returning Home* (Lima, Ohio: CSS, 2001), 22.
16. Kari Henkelmann Keyl, "God Is a Loony Dad (or Mom)," By the Way blog, March 9, 2010, http://bythewaynashua.blogspot.com/2010/03/god-is-loony-dad-or-mom-by-kari.html.
17. Capon, *Parables of Grace*, 144.

March 17, 2013
Fifth Sunday in Lent

Revised Common Lectionary (RCL)
Isaiah 43:16-21
Psalm 126
Philippians 3:4b-14
John 12:1-8

Lectionary for Mass (LFM)
Isaiah 43:16-21
Psalm 126:1-2a, 2b-3, 4-5, 6
Philippians 3:8-14
John 8:1-11

This is the penultimate Sunday before Easter, and with Jesus and the disciples we're poised on the brink of Palm Sunday and the entry into Jerusalem. There's a sense of a "second wind" and forward movement in all the readings today. The Isaiah text is addressed to the exiles on the brink of returning to Jerusalem who are being reminded that God is about to do something new. They're instructed not to let the past do anything but inform them; it shouldn't hold them back. The psalmist sings of sowing in sadness only to reap in joy, while Paul urges the Christian communities to forget what lies behind and press upward. The Johannine readings provide us with the smell of anointing oil, a new beginning through death, and a circle of accusers who don't dare to cast the first stone, which allows an adulteress and the accusers to do something new.

First Reading
Isaiah 43:16-21 (RCL, LFM)

This section of Second Isaiah was probably addressed to the exiles while they were in Babylon or on the way home to Jerusalem after the edict of Cyrus. The reading is part of a larger trial scene in which God's sovereignty is being discussed. Preachers might want to peek at verses 22-28, which the lectionary designers left on the cutting-room floor; they complete the rhetorical section to speak of repentance, sacrifice, and forgiveness.

The whole of Isaiah 43 contains oracles that scholars consider classics of the literary genre "proclamations of salvation." The early church found a familiar home in Isaiah, and particularly the chapters that comprise Second Isaiah (40–55); they still provide more Hebrew Bible lectionary readings than comparable books. Today's reading, like many of the Lenten readings, has the exodus in view. The reading begins with reminders of God bringing Israel through the sea and defeating the Egyptian army. While the verses recall the past actions of God and Israel, they are meant as more than mere reminders; they're predictors of how God can do things that other gods can't do: create new life, new possibilities, and new people. As John Oswalt writes, "Yahweh is *not* one of the gods!":

> This idea that a god could do something new was very foreign to the ancient world. Of course the gods could not do a new thing. They are simply personifications of the world system. Can the thunderstorm be anything but a thunderstorm? Can autumn ever follow spring? The answer to both questions is, "Of course not." But, that is just the point that Isaiah is making in chapters 40–48 of this book. Yahweh is *not* one of the gods![1]

So the oracle works almost like a dare from God, who says, "You think I can't get you out of Babylon? You think I'm going to just leave you here among the pagans and the idolaters? You must not remember who I am. I'm the one who surprised everyone by getting you out of Egypt. In case you've forgotten, I told Moses to call me I Will Be Who I Will Be, which ought to remind you that I'm in the improvisation business when it comes to getting my people saved. Watch me do something new."

So even though it might seem like God is saying two contradictory things ("remember" and "don't live in the past"), the message for Israel and for Lent is simply this: the past is behind you not because it's worthless, but because God has even greater deliverance in the future. In the words of Alfred North Whitehead, God is the self-surpassing self-surpasser. God will continue to outdo the previous acts of God. Somewhere Karl Barth said, "When the sun comes up, all the lamps go out."

This kind of memory is what Johann Baptist Metz will call a "dangerous memory," which is more than a mere recollection of historic events. These dangerous memories echo through a community's specific historical past, their shared narratives, the stories of their predecessors and ancestors, and their own fragile victories. Such memories can continue to fund hope, project a better future, and empower communities to work for justice. Sharon Welch, along with others, claims that one of the enemies of justice-making is the death of the imagination, which gives rise to a culture of despair and a posture of resignation. "The death of compassion follows the death of the imagination" and leads to the inability to act or envision any better future.[2]

The prophet Isaiah wants Israel to use the exodus as a point on a trajectory that leads to something even greater. Like all of the Hebrew Bible and the New Testament, the people of God are future-oriented, anticipating promised lands and new creations and messianic ages and heaven on earth. The apostle Paul will capture this teleological impulse in his letter to the church at Philippi, urging them to shake off the dust and press forward. We'll see similar impulses in the John texts about a woman caught in adultery and a woman who anoints Jesus.

Letting go of the past is essential for any kind of repentance or forgiveness. We can remember the parts of the past that push us into the future, but we have to let go of the impulse to simply put down tent stakes and live there in the attic of old failures. Without that release, we cannot reach for the future. Look, here's the good news. For God to forgive us, God will have to let go of some of the past, too. "I am about to do a new thing; now it springs forth, do you not perceive it?"

Psalmody
Psalm 126 (RCL)
Psalm 126:1-2a, 2b-3, 4-5, 6

Today's psalm is one of the psalms of ascent, which were probably recited by pilgrims "going up" to Jerusalem. It's a good companion for this stage of the Lenten pilgrimage as Jesus turns his face toward Jerusalem and prepares for the Palm Sunday street theater. "When the LORD restored the fortunes of Zion, we were like those who dream" (v. 1). The psalmist captures not only the hope of David, but also the hopes of the exiles in Babylon who longed to see Zion restored.

In addition to the journey metaphor, there's also an agricultural/harvest metaphor: "May those who sow in tears reap with shouts of joy. Those who go out weeping, bearing the seed for sowing, shall come home with shouts of joy, carrying their sheaves" (vv. 5-6). The old hymn "Bringing In the Sheaves" draws its imagery from Psalm 126.

The backdrop for the psalm is the celebration of the harvest, the Feast of Sukkoth, which is also known as the Festival of Booths, or the Feast of Tabernacles. The Sukkoth booths or tabernacles were temporary tents that reminded the Israelites of the exodus wanderings. According to Zechariah, in the messianic era Sukkoth will become a universal festival and all nations will make pilgrimages annually to Jerusalem to celebrate the feast there. It's a homecoming that has exodus in its rear-view mirror and the messianic age in its future. Weeping in the past, laughter in the future.

Preacher Marjory Zoet Bankson writes about Michael Curry, an Episcopal priest friend who studies the slave spirituals to understand how people find joy in the midst of suffering.

> He says the biblical vision of peace and justice provides the basis for true joy out of gratitude. "Why didn't slaves go crazy?" Curry asks. "They had no doctors, no therapists or social workers. Even families were separated and sold. I believe it was their singing. Spirituals took away their shame, wiped away their tears and made them part of God's own family." Without the larger framework of God's purpose and promise, joy would have been absurd.[3]

"May those who sow in tears reap with shouts of joy. Those who go out weeping, bearing the seed for sowing, shall come home with shouts of joy, carrying their sheaves." Combined with today's readings, the psalm captures the sense of joyful movement toward divine promise associated with Jerusalem, even in the face of tears.

Second Reading
Philippians 3:4b-14 (RCL)
Philippians 3:8-14 (LFM)

This reading from Philippians comes right after the soaring Christ hymn in chapter 2, where Paul urges the church to know the mind of Christ in pursuing ministries of emptying, or kenosis. He cautions them to do nothing from ambition or conceit, but to empty themselves the same way Christ emptied himself on the cross. At the beginning of chapter 3, his tone shifts as he warns them, "Beware of the dogs, beware of the evil workers, beware of those who mutilate the flesh! For it is we who are the circumcision, who worship in the Spirit of God and boast in Christ Jesus and have no confidence in the flesh—even though I, too, have reason for confidence in the flesh" (vv. 2-4a).

While we don't know for sure if Paul has a specific group of "dogs" in mind or if he is just generally warning against folks who required circumcision for Christians, it's clear that he's frustrated again by the whole issue of who has the best credentials for teaching and practicing Christian faith. So today's reading starts there, where Paul says, "Credentials? You want to see credentials? Let me tell you who I used to be." And then, as soon as he's listed them, he dismisses them.

Paul refuses to take part in any scheme of score keeping or domination games. We've already discussed Paul's apocalyptic worldview and what it means to be an ambassador for Christ, so we know that behind this Philippians text is a whole domination system that he's rejecting. As one of my favorite preachers used to say, "You'll get to the top of that ladder only to find out it's leaning on the wrong wall." These worldly human systems are part of the fleshly world dominated by the powers and principalities. We're not playing that game.

Second, he reminds them that the priority is to increase in knowing Christ, the self-emptying servant from Philippians 2:4-8. In other words, we need to learn to empty ourselves. This sounds similar to his rant against the Corinthian church when he accused them of being "puffed up" (1 Cor. 4:6-7). "Yet whatever gains I had, these I have come to regard as loss because of Christ. More than that, I regard everything as loss because of the surpassing value of knowing Christ Jesus my Lord. For his sake I have suffered the loss of all things, and I regard them as rubbish, in order that I may gain Christ and be found in him" (vv. 7-9a). Lose it, says Paul. Empty yourself of any claims to special privilege or prestige.

Finally, he speaks of his own ongoing quest to pursue this knowledge himself. He doesn't claim to be perfect; he's still seeking Christ himself. The final three verses move me almost more than I can say. This was the text for my ordination sermon, and twenty-odd years later, it moves me even more than on that day. In an article titled "'The One Who Called You . . .': Vocation and Leadership in the Pauline Literature," Katherine Grieb discusses the kenotic nature of Christian vocation, and how so much of contemporary church life mitigates against kenosis for the clergy and the laity. In a section titled "The Upward Call for Downward Mobility," she writes:

> Paul describes God's humiliation of himself and of his co-workers as evidence that they are part of the Christ-pattern that he is commending to his churches for the ordering of their life together. This stress on the "downward mobility" of church leaders is particularly needed . . . where the Christian communities have become persuaded that success in church leadership means a high salary package, impressive credentials, and dramatic miracles.[4]

The pursuit of the heavenly call of God in Jesus Christ never ends while we're alive. We never get there. One of the themes we noted earlier in the Lenten readings was the idea of liminality, the in-betweenness of faith. Paul reminds us that the Christian life is never one of arrival, but one of never-ending pilgrimage and pursuit.

In his reflections on the reading, David Fredrickson discusses the way Greek artistic images could be similar to Paul's image of pursuing Christ.[5] My own reflections on his comments shouldn't be attributed to him, since I've taken a different imaginative flight. Typical Grecian urns pictured the lover pursuing his beloved. On one side of the vase was the young man stretching forward to catch her; on the other side was the young woman similarly poised to keep running. You could, depending on how you started, never be sure who was pursuing whom. I suggest that Paul is both chasing Christ and hoping to be caught. The lover is forever chasing his beloved.

Paul urges the Christian communities to forget what lies behind and press upward, forever.

Gospel
John 12:1-8 (RCL)

One of the drawbacks of the lectionary is that the three-year cycle tends to relegate the Gospel of John to the sidelines, hauling out his peculiarities mostly for special occasions. John is like the wacky uncle you can ignore most of the year, but shows up with a waxed mustache and a monocle for the holidays. Gail O'Day has pointed out elsewhere that John has a delight in irony and in letting the readers/listeners know more than the characters onstage. We've known since the prologue how this story ends, but we keep hoping the hero doesn't die. John tips his hand before he can get out of chapter 1: the hero is going to die. The advantage for preachers is that we can use Capon's strategy from last week to understand what's going on this week. The hero is a dead man walking.

The story of the anointing shows up in all four Gospels. In Matthew and Mark, the woman is nameless; Mark's Gospel emphasizes this namelessness. In Luke's Gospel, she's a "sinner" taken by many to refer to Mary Magdalene, subject of one of the worst negative propaganda campaigns in history.[6] In John's version, she's Mary, sister of Lazarus. Wes Howard-Brook notes that "only John attributes it to a known character and works it so completely into the fabric of the plot."[7] In some ways, it doesn't really matter which woman she is; it only matters that she's a woman, because as a woman, she doesn't belong at the dinner table any more than a dead man does. In other specifically Johannine ways, it matters that she's the sister of Lazarus (whose story only appears in the Gospel of John). But for John and the other writers, she's an exchange object who has no particular value for her own identity.

So it's really no wonder they recognize each other as extravagant losers.[8] He's going to pour out his blood on the world and she's going to pour out her costly, smelly unguent on him. Neither one of them is any good at bookkeeping, as Judas so helpfully notes. Judas, of course, is still operating in the nickel-and-dime business. Preachers, please don't get distracted by the poverty issue; this text isn't about taking care of the poor. Judas got distracted by it, too. That should be a hint.

The story is all about winners and losers and how the losers (women and dead men) form a lovely equation of death and resurrection. While the disciples hover in a circle, the spotlight focuses on Jesus and Mary. He lifts her up and claims she knows what she's doing. She lifts him up by anointing him for a burial that hasn't happened yet and for which he wouldn't otherwise be anointed. They crown each other, like Saul anointed David.

Can we talk about the anointing itself? Howard-Brook makes two significant points about the way John presents the story. First, Mary doesn't pour the oil on his head, which would be the typical symbolic action for anointing a king. Instead, she pours it on his feet (as predicted in John 11:2) and wipes it off with her hair, an intimate action that we might expect between husbands and wives in private, but not in public. This isn't a situation where we should focus on the question of whether "feet" is euphemistic for genitals, since it doesn't matter here. What matters is that she anoints the "wrong" part of his body and that she does foot washing before Jesus does foot washing in chapter 13. In discussing the foot washing that Jesus does, Howard-Brook notes that the practice has echoes of Moses removing his sandals to meet God barefoot and that there were some Hellenistic Jewish practices where foot washing was associated with sanctification.[9] Howard-Brook doesn't connect Mary's act with Jesus' act a mere chapter later.[10] If foot washing is associated in any way with death, as Mary's act signifies, then Peter's rejection of Jesus' foot washing takes on more drama. Was Peter denying Jesus and discipleship already?

The second point that Howard-Brook makes about the anointing is its smell. John's narrator reports that the whole house was filled with the smell of funeral preparation. None of the disciples present could have smelled the expensive substance without immediately thinking of embalming. "Nothing is more memorable than a smell. . . . Smells detonate softly in our memory like poignant land mines hidden under the weedy mass of years. Hit a tripwire of smell and memories explode all at once."[11] In ancient times, smells were considered as "exhalations of mist" associated with both life and death.[12] Howard-Brook speculates that the reference to "the whole house" might symbolize the entire community of the house-church itself. And finally, the excess of scent in the anointing story contrasts with the excess of death odor associated with Lazarus's own death a little later in the narrative. This is why it was important that it was Lazarus's sister who did the anointing; she can exchange this act for a "favor" and get her brother resurrected.

Mary's extravagance foreshadows Jesus' own extravagance. There is no ledger, no accountant, no nickel-and-dime budgeting. As Barbara Brown Taylor says, "This bottle will not be held back to be kept and admired. This precious substance will not be saved. It will be opened, offered and used, at great price. It will be raised up and poured out for the life of the world, emptied to the last drop."[13]

John 8:1-11 (LFM)

In the story of the woman taken in adultery, we have another of those particularly Johannine narratives and one of the most famous stories in the New Testament. The one-liner about casting stones is part of the cultural lexicon. Everyone knows the story is a rejection of religious hypocrisy and self-righteousness. But not everyone knows it's a story about radical mercy, the resurrection of three parties, and a challenge to sexism.

In Johannine narrative structure, this story is part of the Book of Signs that manifests Jesus as the incarnate God. The Book of Signs contains the "I AM" sayings and a series of miracles that will ultimately be so threatening that Jesus will be tried and executed for them. In John's Gospel, it's not a temple scene that provokes the authorities; it's the resurrection of Lazarus. The story of the woman taken in adultery is highly disputed among scholars since it didn't show up in manuscripts until very late (maybe as late as 900 CE).

The story is set in Jerusalem during the Feast of Tabernacles; the city would have been packed with pilgrims, booths, and first-fruits offerings. We know that Jesus has had multiple controversies with the religious authorities, but he hasn't yet been arrested. As Fred Craddock puts it, Jesus is "at large."[14] There's a sense that the authorities are following him around, looking for an excuse to arrest him.

They bring to him a woman "caught" in the act of adultery, which suggests that this was already a "gotcha" moment both for the woman and for Jesus. Gail O'Day will pursue her interpretation of the story by equating Jesus and the woman as analogous victims of the scribes and Pharisees. If we were stage-directing this scene, it would look very similar to the one from the previous reading: Jesus and a woman are the center of attention, surrounded by disagreeable folks. Father Robert Barron uses theories from René Girard to characterize the woman as a scapegoat: "Girard says in the course of human history there has evolved the scapegoating mechanism. A group finds a person or a group and they blame them for the crisis, they blame them for the tensiveness. What happens here is a kind of peace then reigns in the community because they have managed to vent their frustrations on this person or on this group."[15] Historically, the scapegoat was actually a goat offered for slaughter. The woman caught in adultery is (in Capon's approach; see p. 169f.) already counted as dead.

O'Day considers them both scapegoats, claiming that the story has been consistently misinterpreted in such a way that the woman continues to be erased by shifting the focus to the controversy between the authorities and Jesus.

> To summarize the story as sin (woman) and grace (Jesus) is to objectify and dehumanize the woman the same way the scribes and Pharisees do in v. 4. It is to define her away because of her sexuality rather than to treat her as a full person as Jesus does in vv. 10-11. It is to accept the scribes and Pharisees' definition of the woman (and the issues) rather than Jesus'. It is to ignore the invitation issued by Jesus in v. 7 and to cast a stone.[16]

She suggests a rhetorical analysis that pivots on the two speech-acts on either side of the act of writing in the sand. By doing this, we don't eclipse either saying; we don't reduce the story to one dimension or the other. We don't have to choose between the woman's sin and the authorities' sins; Jesus deals with both of them. "It is precisely the equality of the woman and the scribes and Pharisees before Jesus that is the heart of this story." O'Day claims that Jesus shows radical mercy on both the authorities and the woman, forgiving them both by not condemning them. The act of writing in the sand is not the point, other than the bracketing it provides.[17]

6b	Jesus bent down and wrote with his finger on the ground.
7b	Let anyone among you who is without sin/*be the first to throw a stone at her.*
8	And once again he bent down and wrote on the ground.
11b	Neither do I condemn you/*Go your way, and from now on do not sin again.*

O'Day argues that the parallelism of the portions italicized above and the parallelism of the unitalicized portions of 7b and 11b signify their equality and similarity. You could switch the italicized portions so that 7b would read, "Let anyone among you who is without sin go your way, and from now on do not sin again." Likewise verse 11b could be rewritten: "Neither do I condemn you, be the first to throw a stone." "Both the scribes and Pharisees and the woman are invited to give up old ways and enter a new way of life. Both stand under the power of old ways, the power of sin, to use the rhetoric of the text, but the present moment . . . invites both to a new way of life."[18]

Preachers are encouraged to read O'Day's article in its entirety. She addresses the issues of "writing on the ground," but her thorough discussion also probes the history of misreading that might have contributed to the canonical marginality of the story. She raises the question of whether or not early interpreters were more comfortable with Augustine's summary of the story as "*miseria et misericordia.*" Misery and mercy.

> There is no acknowledged shame among such interpreters, no sense of scandal about the way the story testifies against a male-dominated status quo. In fact, the narrative evokes men's fear of what Jesus' teaching might suggest to their wives, of what would happen if women's sexuality passed out of men's control. I submit that even when unacknowledged, these fears are real and have dominated both the canonizing process and the history of interpretation.[19]

In Capon's approach, all the dead folks have been resurrected. The scapegoated woman is released and forgiven to live a whole new life. Jesus has escaped to live another day, but will ultimately be condemned by the religious authorities and Rome, caught again in the center of their scapegoating. And the scribes and the Pharisees have also been resurrected to exercise mercy instead of their sexist applications of Levitical law.[20] The story of the woman taken in adultery is a dangerous memory indeed, but its telling could be redemptive for the church. George Eliot once said, "It's never too late to be who you might have been." The future can be better than the past.

Notes

1. John N. Oswalt, "The God of Newness: A Sermon on Isaiah 43:14-21," *Calvin Theological Journal* 39, no. 2 (November 2004): 386.
2. Sharon D. Welch, *A Feminist Ethic of Risk* (Minneapolis: Fortress Press, 1990), 60.
3. Marjory Zoet Bankson, "With Shouts of Joy," *The Living Pulpit* 5, no. 4 (October/December 1996).
4. A. Katherine Grieb, "'The One Who Called You . . .': Vocation and Leadership in the Pauline Literature," *Interpretation* 59, no. 2 (April 2005): 159.
5. David E. Fredrickson, Preaching This Week: Lectionary for October 5, 2008, Twenty-First Sunday after Pentecost, Philippians 3:4b-14: Commentary on Second Reading, http://www .workingpreacher.org/preaching.aspx?lect_date=10/5/2008&tab=3.
6. In 591 CE, Pope Gregory the Great preached a sermon on Luke's version of this story and suggested that Mary Magdalene was a prostitute. This perspective of Mary of Magdala has been perpetuated in sermons, literature, and film.
7. Wes Howard-Brook, *Becoming Children of God: John's Gospel and Radical Discipleship* (Maryknoll, N.Y.: Orbis, 1994), 269.
8. See my article on gendered readings of the anointing texts: "The Rhetoric of Gender and the Rhetoric of Folly: The Incompatibility of Two Feminist Approaches," *Encounter* 61, no. 3 (Summer 2000): 297–319.
9. Howard-Brook, *Becoming Children of God*, 295–96.
10. Barbara Brown Taylor does notice the connection in her sermon, "The Prophet Mary," March 21, 2010, http://day1.org/1760-the_prophet_mary.
11. Diane Ackerman, *A Natural History of the Senses* (New York: Vintage, 1991), 5.
12. Howard-Brook, *Becoming Children of God*, 269.
13. Taylor, "The Prophet Mary."

14. Fred B. Craddock, *John*, Knox Preaching Guides (Louisville: John Knox, 1982), 62.

15. Robert Barron, "Jesus and the Scapegoat," 30 Good Minutes, January 27, 2002, http://www.csec .org/csec/sermon/barron_4516.htm.

16. Gail R. O'Day, "John 7:53—8:11: A Study in Misreading," *Journal of Biblical Literature* 111, no. 4 (Winter 1992): 634.

17. You could argue that it was similar to the divine finger writing the Ten Commandments or the finger writing on the wall in Daniel 5. This would only support Johannine theology, but is *not* the point of the story.

18. O'Day, "John 7:53—8:11: A Study in Misreading," 637.

19. Ibid., 640.

20. Preachers will want to tread lightly in their interpretations of the scribes and Pharisees and to avoid the almost rabid anti-Judaism pervading John's Gospel.

Holy Week

Jonathan Linman

More and more, I find myself musing on the implied covenant between preachers and hearers. I marvel at the rare and precious gift those who listen give to those called to proclaim God's word, namely, their attention and time—ten, twenty minutes, perhaps more, depending on occasion and tradition. In this season of human existence, at least in Western cultures, we are ever more preoccupied with competing claims for our attention, overstimulating bits, nay bytes, of information swirling about us like the debris cloud of a tornado. Thus we seem to have ever less time on our hands. That people in our worshipful assemblies offer themselves to preaching ministers for such a comparatively extended and generous period is a wonder indeed. We who proclaim do well to take with utmost seriousness and appropriate gravitas the significance of this gift, and the needs of those who offer to us their listening ears. They desire a life-giving, sacred word. Our high calling, through the power of the Holy Spirit, is to feed them with the very bread of life, the Word that is Christ, and not just discourse *about* holy things, but sacred encounter itself in Christ. Proclamation is thus a matter of life and death, or to reverse the order for Holy Week, death and life.

The ministry of proclamation during Holy Week takes us to the very heart of Christ, to the very center of the message that is Christ, the Word at work in the world that subverts human business—and busyness—as usual. Proclamation, expansively understood in terms of the liturgical drama in play and not reduced to monologue sermons during this most holy of weeks, brings us to our senses quite literally. The story unfolds over the course of these days, employing all of our senses in multiple ritual enactments: processions with palms; dramatic readings of Passion narratives; foot washing; absolution; the Lord's Supper as remembrance of Last Supper; stripping of the altar; veneration of the cross; new fire at the Easter Vigil; baptismal washing and remembrance; and the Easter Eucharist as foretaste of the resurrection feast to come. In brief, Holy Week proclamation speaks and enacts a five-sense-oriented, confounding sanity that is the antidote to the crazy fever in human blood.

Pundits and social commentators of our age speak of the importance of framing the debate, as if to say the one who establishes the narrative framework and assumptions that predominate will likely emerge as the winner. Taking this insight from the realm of current civic discourse into reflections on the ministry of proclamation, the power of narrative to frame—indeed, to reframe—our sense of reality is profound. Narratives that break open conventional understandings of the world, our place in it, and God's role with it, have the power to take us to new realities, not just to inform and form us, but to reform and transform us. That is, such narratives, perhaps especially those of Holy Week, convey the emerging realities of God's reign expressed in Christ's victory over death and all death-dealing ways of life.

I am fond of saying of the human condition that we are "hermeneutically sealed," that is, we are trapped in our varied interpretive strategies that induce conditions of myopia, blurred vision, and shadows that interfere with our seeing with greatest clarity. Or as the philosopher Arthur Schopenhauer quipped in *Studies in Pessimism*, "Every man [*sic*] takes the limits of his own field of vision for the limits of the world." Holy Week proclamation at its best offers a word *extra nos*, from outside of ourselves, that breaks open the narrative strategies in which we find ourselves mired, and takes us to wider horizons of vision, namely, the vantage point of almighty God. In short, preaching ministry, especially during Holy Week, permits us to see with God's eyes, particularly as we tell and reenact the stories that contain the fullness of God's vision in Christ centered on cross and empty tomb.

Such new horizons can change human reality. Narrative frameworks, interpretive strategies, and ideas with their hosts of assumptions are part and parcel of how we live each day and are behind every social policy. In short, the stories we tell have much to do with the outcomes and quality of our lives, individually and communally. If we tell stories of scarcity and we live according to these stories' premises, then many will more likely live in poverty of one kind or another. If our story lines feature themes of terror, we are more likely to live in fear. If we otherwise proclaim God's abundance, we will more likely nurture confidence in the conditions of God's commonwealth. Holy Week proclamation, taking place during days of liminal transition between deathly fear in the poverty of the cross and the confidence in abundant life evidenced by the empty tomb, makes for the transformation for which our generous listeners yearn. Holy Week preachers are thus change agents in the power of the Spirit who conveys the living, transformative word. Trust this divine promise: "So shall my word be that goes out from my mouth; it shall not return to me empty, but it shall accomplish that which I purpose, and succeed in the thing for which I sent it" (Isa. 55:11).

But how, more particularly, does this work? Here is the wonder: each word of Scripture in its narrative context is like a seed that contains, as it were, the genetic narrative material that makes for God's reign of victorious love. Word-working ministers of proclamation both scatter and plant these seeds, and also nurture the soil of their own souls and that of their hearers. The Holy Spirit is active in the interplay between proclaimed word and hearers. The seed of the word breaks open in the soil, the humus—"remember that you are dust and to dust you shall return"—of our lives, our hearts and minds. The word then finds root in the deeper places where a new, life-giving, and life-altering story can more likely take hold with staying power as the Spirit guides us into all truth (cf. John 16:13a).

During Holy Week we are awash in words. The following pages of commentary will attempt to address some sixty or so readings from the Revised Common Lectionary if you also include Lutheran additions for the Easter Vigil (forty-five or so readings if you follow the Roman Catholic Lectionary for the Mass)—this in contrast to a mere four readings for any typical Sunday in Ordinary Time. Or, to employ the word-count feature of word-processing systems, there are some 21,000 words contained in these Holy Week passages. It is too much to take in, especially if one is poised to receive each word in the soil of each lesson as seed that has the potential to break open new insights into God's reign in Christ evidenced in Passiontide, particularly the Three Days.

Given this, and given the proclivities of our current Western culture to rush through our studied engagement with things to get to whatever the finish line happens to be, I hear, perhaps especially during Holy Week, the call to slow down, to savor scriptural engagement. I see an opportunity to offer as best we can our real presence to the one who, in word and in sacraments, offers us real presence, deep—*deus profundis*—speaking to deep. I hear the invitation to make space for, to be open to, the more contemplative dimensions of that which unfolds during these holy days, not just during the liturgies, but in preparation for preaching. Easier said than done during this busiest of liturgical seasons, amid a frantically busy season of human existence. But especially at such a time as this are we called to go deeper. To explore the contemplative aspects of Holy Week involves dwelling with the texts in quiet, studied reflection, savoring the word, soaking in it, letting the word reverberate in silence. Silence in close proximity to Scripture is not an empty void, but full of the echoes of God's living word in the power of the Spirit.

Contemplative engagement with the Scriptures is also subversive, especially when new or freshly remembered insights emerge that challenge the conventional wisdom of our contexts and days. The powers and principalities of our age want none of this. Nor did the same in Jesus' day. It is what got him crucified, after all. In Holy Week proclamation, guard against domesticating the stories of this week and minimizing their radical implications for life in this world. In your preparations, be mindful of the taboos extant in relation to the Holy Week passages. That is to say, what are the points in the passages that you might hesitate to preach on because they feel too risky? God give you the courage in the power of the Spirit faithfully and appropriately to go there. I believe that our hearers also, deep down and beyond the multiplicity of defensive strategies they bring to the act of listening, want such speaking truth to powers and principalities in love. The Holy Week texts are brimming to overflowing with such opportunities.

You are not going to preach on each day in Holy Week, nor touch on every passage included in the commentaries that follow. For those texts that do not receive your homiletical attention, I invite you to take those up in a more contemplative or devotional way. Take some time to dwell with those passages, for such dwelling will deepen your engagement with the Scriptures and will nurture the soil from which transformative and subversive insights will more naturally emerge. Such engagement is a great gift to your preaching ministry and to your hearers, and thus, ultimately, to our dying world in need of the life-giving word that has the power to slow us down, shake us up, and introduce the ways of God's commonwealth.

March 24, 2013
Sunday of the Passion / Palm Sunday

Revised Common Lectionary (RCL)

Liturgy of the Palms
Psalm 118:1-2, 19-29
Luke 19:28-40
Liturgy of the Passion
Isaiah 50:4-9a
Psalm 31:9-16
Philippians 2:5-11
Luke 22:14—23:56 or Luke 23:1-49

Lectionary for Mass (LFM)

Processional Gospel

Luke 19:28-40
Palm Sunday: At the Mass
Isaiah 50:4-7
Psalm 22:8-9, 17-18, 19-20, 23-24
Philippians 2:6-11
Luke 22:14—23:56 or 23:1-49

People on this festival day like to receive palms, a curious mirror to the increasing desire in recent years for ashes on Ash Wednesday, ashes traditionally made from burned palm fronds. Today, the palm branches are green and fresh, suggesting, among other things, new life in creation. The palm, as a symbol of this day, thus carries multiple meanings, as does this day itself. Children, glad songs, and a parade: it is tempting to jump from these festivities to the joy of Easter, skipping over entirely the darkness and gravitas of the intervening days of Holy Week. For those who will not attend liturgies during the Three Days, it is essential for them also to hear the stories about Jesus' last days before Easter. Hence the designation of this day also as Passion Sunday, as if in the telling of the narrative of betrayal and death we burn, reducing to dust, these green branches today even before they have a chance to dry before the next Ash Wednesday.

This is a day full of public spectacle, historically to be sure, as Jesus made his provocative entry into Jerusalem in regal humility, enacting a monarchical presence the people were not expecting. Our observances today are likewise laden with spectacle as our blessed branches make appearances on the sidewalks and streets of our communities as churchgoers leave for home. More than that, many congregations break with their usual, self-enclosed liturgical routines, taking to the streets, or at least the outdoors, for public procession. Do the work of evangelists and make the most of this breaking open, this going public, of the church in your settings.

Today is our grand entry into the Holy of Holies, which the story of Holy Week is for us, even as it was Jesus' grand entry into the holy city Jerusalem and its temple. It is a day replete with dizzying ranges of emotional responses, the passions that captivate the human spirit: exalting acclamation, a hero's welcome—"Hosanna!"—and the bitter, raging cry for death—"Crucify him!"—and this directed at one person by many of the same people in the crowds that gathered about him. We humans are fickle in our passions. It is a gladsome thing that *the* Passion anchors us, steadies us, claims us.

It is all so embodied and kinetic. Jesus' body endured so very much during the days described in the Passion narrative, moving in procession from place to place, station to station. So, too, in our assemblies, we can fully engage our bodies and passions. In your liturgical enactments, make the most of the embodied and kinetic qualities like processions, for we who are sacramentally constituted as Christ's current body for the world can be taken to the deeper places of this story through our holistic involvements in fleshly movement. If our members can walk the walk in the power of the Spirit, they will more formatively and transformatively via the Spirit incorporate the divine narrative into their witness and ministry in daily life. Moreover, through our direct participation in the liturgical drama, we will see ourselves variously in the many voices that cry out in conflicting ways, leading to cathartic confession and then a falling into the loving arms of our merciful God in Christ.

What is the purpose of preaching on this day? In brief, preaching serves to draw hearers and participants ever more deeply into the Holy of Holies contained in the Passion narrative and its reenactment, this for *anamnesis*, for the directly participatory remembrance and presence of Christ, thus subverting our human business as usual, breaking open new horizons of meaning. Preaching on the Sunday of the Passion is thus a profoundly spiritual undertaking. Let your ministry of proclamation, however you enact it, be an icon to your hearers, pointing away from yourself and focusing on the story, thus revealing the fullness of Christ and his life-altering presence for us.

Liturgy of the Palms

Gospel
Luke 19:28-40 (RCL, LFM)

In the Lukan narrative prior to the passage appointed as the processional Gospel for Passion Sunday, Jesus has just told the parable of the greedy and vengeful king (Luke 19:11-27), a stark contrast to the kind of monarchical reign he is about to introduce in his last days, the beginnings of which include his entry into Jerusalem riding on a colt. The streets of Jerusalem had seen numerous ceremonial processions of kings and military victors through its many years. To the people of Jerusalem, this is a familiar routine, a well-known ritual script. Jesus has an escort, the people offer up their cloaks, they give loud voice to praise. Expectations are high indeed. Yet no warhorse carries Jesus. Rather, "a colt that has never been ridden" (v. 30). Already something is amiss in this version of the script. Again, it is not the quality of claims to monarchical authority the people expect and have seen before. A young, untried colt? How unassuming is that? This is not "shock and awe," but an invitation to peace. Later in the story, in a handful of days, and unlike a victorious warrior, this thirtysomething young man's dead body will be placed in a grave. Even now our assumptions are being challenged, and will be the more so as we journey still closer to cross and empty tomb.

It is not that Jesus is without authority in this narrative depiction. To be sure, Jesus is no power broker in the common human experience of striving, ambitious people evident throughout history. He brings no trophies of successful, that is, body-strewn military conquests. Yet his actions are presumptuous and provocative, claiming an authority won only through the power of persuasion and demonstration, like preaching and teaching, eating with tax collectors and sinners, along with the working of some "deeds of power" (v. 37). Claiming the authority of a sovereign, Jesus instructs two of his disciples to commandeer the colt, not to negotiate for its rental, but simply to claim it. If confronted—and as it turns out, the two disciples are—Jesus' instruction is simply to tell them, "The Lord needs it" (vv. 31, 34). Quite a claim, and assumed title, *Lord*, indeed.

So let the parade begin. The crowds of disciples accompany him on the path descending from the Mount of Olives, and they offer their loud and joyful song of praise (v. 38; cf. Ps. 118:26, a psalm of welcome for pilgrims). In our liturgies, hear the echoes of our own familiar canticles, the *Benedictus* connected to the *Sanctus* during the Great Thanksgiving at the Eucharist; and this alongside echoes of the *Gloria in Excelsis*, the hymn of praise during gathering rites. This cry (v. 38b) further echoes the angel song to the shepherds at the birth announcement in the beginning of Luke's Gospel (cf. 2:14). Each and every Lord's Day assembly, not just Palm Sunday, is a remembrance, a reenactment of both the announcement of Jesus' birth and his provocative entry into the holy city, now our holy cities, and our holy temples.

How shall we greet this one? Also with loud, joyful praise, in company with the ancient voices. But "Crucify him!" is not far off. After all, Jesus' grand entry even now into our assemblies in our day persists in overturning (not unlike the tables in the temple; cf. Luke 19:45; Matt. 21:12) our own expectations, especially if we really listen to what he is up to and resist the temptation to domesticate this drama with only precious adornments and nostalgic enactments. The children are cute and integral to the story—"Let the little children come to me" (cf. Luke 18:16)—but even now, other voices in us, among us, also echo that of the ancient religious authorities: "Teacher, order your disciples to stop" (v. 39). But there is no stopping what has begun. If not these voices, then the very "stones would shout out" (v. 40; cf. Hab. 2:11a). With the playful ears of faith, I hear the noise of crashing stones at the temple's destruction, and the sound of building up again after three days as the temple of Jesus' body is raised (cf. John 2:19-22). I hear the rocks splitting as the earth shook at the time of Jesus' death (cf. Matt. 27:51b). I hear the muffled rumbling of the stone being moved away from the entrance at the tomb—how could that be silent (cf. Luke 24:2)?

Psalmody
Psalm 118:1-2, 19-29 (RCL)

A psalm to accompany a pilgrim's liturgical procession, perhaps on the occasion of national success (v. 25) and deliverance, particularly in recalling the exodus, these verses from Psalm 118 serve to set an appropriate tone for the procession with palms on Passion Sunday. Especially effective for procession is the repetition of thanks for God's "steadfast love [that] endures forever" (vv. 1, 2, 29). This psalm is long associated with Jesus' entry into Jerusalem as the Gospel writers themselves put the words of Psalm 118 into the mouths of those among the crowds (v. 26; cf. Luke 19:38). Likewise, Psalm 118 found its way into later Palm Sunday traditions in the church with its obvious references to Hosannas (v. 25), Palm Sunday refrains (v. 26), and "festal procession with branches" (v. 27). The church through the centuries has seen Jesus in this song of thanksgiving (v. 22; cf. Mark 12:10).

Liturgy of the Passion (RCL) / Palm Sunday: At the Mass (LFM)

First Reading
Isaiah 50:4-9a (RCL)
Isaiah 50:4-7 (LFM)

Here portions of the third servant song in Isaiah become the first reading on the Sunday of the Passion, functioning liturgically perhaps as an anticipatory interpretation of the events described in the Passion according to Luke. The suffering of the servant in contention and confrontation is the curricular raw material through which the servant as teacher learns to "sustain the weary with a word" (v. 4a). Or more colloquially, the "school of hard knocks" contributes much to meaning making amid suffering. But this is not garden-variety suffering that humans routinely encounter on life's way. Read christologically in the wider context of this day—how can we not, even as we give due regard to its more particular rooting in the history of Israel?—this reading anticipates the cosmic battle with forces of evil and death that is the meat of Jesus' last days before God's deeds of power raise him up, and all of us with him who are baptized into his death.

Indeed, God is the agent here. The Lord God "has given . . . the tongue" (v. 4a), and "wakens" (v. 4b), "has opened [the] ear" (v. 5), and "helps" (vv. 7 and 9), and "vindicates" (v. 8). Thus the confident tone of this passage, confidence that sustains amid the contention, the battle. God the immortal has the last word over enemies who "wear out like a garment," whom the "moth will eat . . . up" (v. 9b). Here is a curious thing, though: in this strife, brute force does not meet brute force to see which side has just a little more to win. Rather, it is a humiliating humility—giving the back to those who strike, the cheeks to those who pull out the beard (v. 6)—that wins the day and demonstrates the sovereignty and power of God.

Psalmody
Psalm 31:9-16 (RCL)

How quickly the mood turns, as these verses from Psalm 31 serve as a kind of fulcrum permitting the movement from "Hosanna!" to "Crucify him!" Psalm 31 is commonly considered a psalm of individual complaint or lament. It conveys both a sense of loneliness—our suffering is our own and others cannot ultimately know its depths and particularities—and an intimate familiarity made possible by being connected in relationship. This psalm likewise reveals dynamics of faith in the vacillation between petition of complaint and expressions of trust, this in keeping with the tone of the prophet Jeremiah who, like Jesus, suffers precisely because of his trust in God. One conjunction, "but" (v. 14), functions as the fulcrum, the verses prior expressing complaint, the verses following expressing a deep and abiding faith in God.

Psalm 22:8-9, 17-18, 19-20, 23-24 (LFM)

Psalm 22 has an ancient association with the Passion of Christ. Its first verse is on the lips of Jesus according to the Gospel writers (cf. Mark 15:34). Other verses of Psalm 22 appearing in this lection also find their way into Passion narratives (vv. 7-8; cf. Matt. 27:43; v. 18; cf. John 19:24). Not unlike Psalm 31, lament combines with praise in poignant juxtaposition, fitting for the confounding logic of the events surrounding Jesus' death.

Second Reading
Philippians 2:5-11 (RCL)
Philippians 2:6-11 (LFM)

Poetry and the singing of hymns have been employed throughout the Christian centuries to illuminate the faith to which we are drawn. Philippians 2:5-11 is commonly known as the great "Christ hymn." Whether or not this text was sung is left to historical speculation. If some Christian themes elude systematic categorization, poetry serves to evoke a sense of their meaningfulness. This particular poetic expression, which actually reads with creedal overtones, is brimming with rich and significant theological ideas, crucial to the emerging theological affirmations of the earliest centuries of our tradition: "mind" (v. 5), "form of God" (v. 6), "emptied himself," "form of a slave," "born in human likeness," "found in human form" (v. 7), and on it goes. This brief commentary cannot begin to attempt to unfold the riches of these theological themes. Suffice it to say that theological reflection can birth poetry and song; that is to say more particularly, it can bring us to our knees in worship (vv. 10-11). Rigorous thought and worshipful passion go hand in hand.

Gospel
Luke 22:14—23:56 or 23:1-49 (RCL, LFM)

I have always struggled with preaching on occasions when a whole Passion narrative is read. It is not so much that these readings take so much time. Rather, my struggle centers on this: What more can I say or add to this story? Doesn't it speak for itself with power, poignancy, and authority, the voice of the Holy Spirit like the rush of a violent wind (cf. Acts 2:2) accomplishing that which God intends (cf. Isa. 55:11)? As liturgy is commonly understood as the "work of the people"; it is a commendable thing also, so that proclamation is not solely the domain of the preacher, to give God's people work to do in participating in the dramatic reenactment of the Passion, perhaps assigning parts to many and certainly allowing the whole assembly to give voice to the crowd's refrains. What, then, is the role and place of the preacher and of homiletical commentary on the Passion narrative? Perhaps your liturgical tradition gives you some freedom to precede the reading of the Passion with a brief introductory homily that invites hearers and participants more deeply into the story. I have undertaken this to good effect, but I leave it to your musings about how best to engage this story homiletically, especially with an understanding that perhaps the preacher's first order of business on this day is to get out of the way of him- or herself, allowing the story to unfold and do what it needs to do in the power of the Spirit.

That said, now on to the Passion according to Luke. This story reads like a really bad dream, and it has that feel as well, as when one awakens with a sense of chaos and turbulence, and an inability to put all the pieces together again. But it was no dream. To put it in another but similar way, the Lukan account conveys the sense of a thunderstorm. The angry-looking clouds gather, as they did at supper (22:14-38) and during the prayer in the garden (22:39-46). Then the gust front with the first violent wind breaks forth, as Judas shows up with the crowds for the betrayal and the arrest (22:47-53), and all hell of thunder and lightning is unleashed. The storm continues as Jesus appears before the various authorities, religious and civil (22:54—23:25), and continues with the crucifixion (23:26-45), the damage done. Finally the storm ends and the earth grows calm again when Jesus dies and is buried (23:46-56). But oh, what hell has been unleashed.

The Lukan account, on first glance from our twenty-first-century vantage point, also reads like the twenty-four-hour TV and online news cycle in an age when the market clamors for the sensationalistic. Can you imagine the stories, the scoops, about conflict among Jesus' closest followers on display even at the supper (22:21-24)? What if, by the way, our eucharistic words of institution included Jesus' additional commentary in Luke, "But see, the one who betrays me is with me, and his hand is on the table" (22:21)? That addition might give a more accurate portrayal of what actually goes on in some of our churches. There are the swords (22:38) and their use (22:50), betrayal by an intimate associate, and with a kiss no less (22:47-48). There is the bird-dogging insistence of the servant girl who pursues Peter not unlike a reporter, "This man also was with him" (22:56), and Peter's subsequent denials (22:57-60). Religion and politics, local and imperial cultures and jurisdictions, get mixed up in some really ugly ways in this account. For instance, Herod and Pilate, in the spirit of strange bedfellows, somehow set aside antipathy toward one another and become friends amid the circumstances of Jesus' trial (23:12). It sounds like human world events and business as usual. The media pundits and late-night comedians would have a field day with this material.

Then there are the angry, fickle mobs of people, the crowd. Pilate was willing to be done with Jesus, but the crowd prevailed in insisting that he should be executed (23:23). It is as if something in the broken, captive-to-sin human spirit needs this kind of public, stormy catharsis with the people "beating their breasts" at the spectacle of it all (23:48). Our age, like many in human history, like that in Jesus' day, gives in to the seduction and indulges this, the worst of human traits.

But there is more. Fortunately for us, deeper things, more fundamental realities, are at work beneath this human *sturm und drang*. These are the divine realities expressed variously in the Lukan account. Quite significantly, all of the proceedings are contextualized by Jesus' communally worshipful observance with his disciples of the Passover holy day, which he "eagerly desired to eat" (22:15) with them. Even though this ritual observance is marred by dispute among the Twelve (22:24) and the communal meal is tainted by the presence of the one who would betray Jesus (22:21), the holy day is the sacred foundation beneath all the hellish claims that otherwise seek to mask the deeper sacrality, as if to assert that death and evil will have the last word. The Christian Eucharist, for which this account serves as one of the institution narratives, shares this sacred foundation. Let us not forget the sacramental bedrock that rests beneath the fever of our lives and days, rock that secured a cross and that served as the womb of resurrection, and which is our solid foundation as well, despite the storms that rage about us.

Moreover, beneath the stormy enactment of the ravages of human sin and rebellion and the presence of evil in both individual and collective behavior, a spirit of prayer is at the heart of this narrative and the reality it describes. Jesus had habits of seeking occasions apart for prayer, such as his customary spot, the Mount of Olives (22:39). His was no casual prayer life, but anguished with bloody sweat (22:44). This infrastructure of personal prayer, which expressed the union between Jesus and the one whom he addressed as Father, carried Jesus forward and, it might be said, was a vehicle through which God also ultimately won the day.

The content of Jesus' prayers is revealing and instructive for our own lives of prayer. His prayers to the Father focus on obedience to God's will (22:42), forgiveness (23:34), and commendation to God's hands (23:46), basic themes of our faith practice as evidenced by the one who teaches us to pray (cf. Luke 11:1). It might even be said that Jesus' dying breath (23:46b) was prayer in its most primary, wordless form, the very Spirit of God, as life-breath of God, praying with "sighs too deep for words" (cf. Rom. 8:26).

The Lukan Passion account begins with prayerful worship in the context of the Passover and concludes also with the traditional religious observance of resting on the Sabbath (23:56b), bookends that bracket and perhaps shed light on the rest of the Passion narrative. This Alpha and Omega of prayerful worship serves to drive home the point that whatever we humans unleash, whatever is at work in sin, evil, and death, something more profound, something sacred, is operative that precedes and follows the worst of what humans offer up. At this point in the story, the sacred meaning is hidden. We are not at the point, narratively in Luke and liturgically in Holy Week, of making sense of it yet. Moreover, the Gospel writer Luke promises an "orderly account" (cf. Luke 1:1-4) of what happened, not a finalized, systematized theology of the atonement. But as the Sabbath rest after Jesus' death was for his followers infused with wrenching bewilderment and grief, surely it was also filled with fervent, wordless prayer concerning what on earth and in heaven had just transpired. So we are left today with the women in that disquieting but sacred Sabbath rest (23:56b).

How does this preach? In your proclamation resist the temptation to tie up the loose ends, attempting to clean up theologically all of the narrative features. There is something to be said for leaving people hanging, wanting more. Holy Week is just beginning, after all, and the story still needs to unfold. Preach in such a way as to provoke a desire or even a need to come back for more on Thursday and Friday, Saturday and Sunday. Invite your participant hearers into the deeper, troubled waters. Don't leave it with the children's Hosannas—unless you emphasize the Hebrew meaning of the word, "pray, save us," the cry of all of God's children. Above all, lead your people through the troubled waters to the still-deeper places, waters so deep that they do not churn. That is the contemplative reality beneath this unsettling, terrible narrative as suggested by its beginning and ending in communal worship and prayer. It is from these depths, as from the void of a rock-hewn tomb (23:53), that resurrection vindication emerges, and this story of terror becomes a story of joyful victory, subverting human business as usual. Your capacity to lead your people homiletically to the deep suggests your having been there yourself. Hence the call to contemplative prayer and devotional engagement in the service of your homiletical preparations, especially amid the busyness of Holy Week.

March 25, 2013
Monday in Holy Week

Revised Common Lectionary (RCL)

Isaiah 42:1-9

Psalm 36:5-11

Hebrews 9:11-15

John 12:1-11

Lectionary for Mass (LFM)

Isaiah 42:1-7

Psalm 27:1, 2, 3, 13-14

John 12:1-11

Liturgies on Monday through Wednesday of Holy Week will not likely attract throngs of people. Those who have a practice of daily public worship may appear, and perhaps those who are unusually drawn to the deep and disciplined encounters that Holy Week affords. Maybe these days invite more personal and devotional engagement apart from scheduled liturgies. Given the riches before us during the Three Days, these days prior to the week's high points call for simplicity. Less is more. No full-blown sermons. Perhaps the appointed passages call for private devotion or conversation—for example, the group practice of *lectio divina* (sacred reading) or other methods of dwelling with God's word. In any case and through whatever means, here is opportunity to open space for deep spiritual engagement with the Scripture, less studied and exegetical, and freer, more playful, imaginative, meditative, and prayerful. The lessons for Monday through Wednesday in Holy Week may be seen as giving voice to themes of Jesus' preparations for what is before him beginning on Thursday. Likewise, we may view our observances on these days as preparation for our own participation with Jesus in the events of the Three Days. On Monday of Holy Week, the first reading focuses on the nature of servanthood, and the second, the nature of Jesus' priesthood. The Gospel features the story about the dinner party Mary, Martha, and Lazarus threw for Jesus after Lazarus was raised.

First Reading
Isaiah 42:1-9 (RCL)
Isaiah 42:1-7 (LFM)

In this passage from Isaiah, one of the servant narratives, the Lord's voice is heard as a kind of love song for the servant. The servant is the Lord's chosen and soul's delight, with the divine spirit upon him and upholding him (v. 1). These verses convey tenderness, as a parent who holds hands with a child (v. 6a). The beloved servant is called and sent, namely, to "bring forth justice to the nations" (vv. 1b, 3b, and 4a). Here is the wonder of it: justice will result from quiet, gentle persistence (vv. 2-4), not grand displays of force.

The Christian tradition, of course, sees Jesus in the servant, as the Son called by and beloved of the Father, even from the creative foundation of the world (cf. vv. 5-6). The particularities of the servant's ministry (v. 7) find echoes in Jesus' self-understanding of his ministry (cf. Luke 4:18-19, where he quotes the prophet Isaiah). The nature of the servant's presence (vv. 2-3) is how Jesus will present himself to the religious and secular authorities when later this week he will be arrested and put on trial. Again, it is a wonder: God's justice and righteousness, God's "light to the nations" (v. 6b), result from the gentle persistence seen on the cross and in the quiet of the empty tomb, and this despite the imperial display of force in state-sponsored murder.

Psalmody
Psalm 36:5-11 (RCL)

"Steadfast love," invoked three times in this portion of Psalm 36 (vv. 5, 7, 10), serves as a kind of mantra that sets the tone for this entire Holy Week. Here is a song of praise that marvels at the vast extent of the Lord's faithfulness, righteousness, judgments, and salvation. The Christian tradition views the psalms in part as Jesus' own prayers. Might Jesus in fact have given voice to this very psalm in his devotions, worship, and prayer during his last earthly days in Jerusalem?

Psalm 27:1, 2, 3, 13-14 (LFM)

Portions of Psalm 27 set a different tone than Psalm 36. Here is the expression of confidence (v. 3b) and courage (v. 14) in the face of adversity (vv. 2-3). What is there to fear when the Lord is our stronghold (vv. 1b, 3a)? Christians hear these verses also as Jesus' own emboldening prayer for what is before him during these days.

Second Reading
Hebrews 9:11-15 (RCL)

This passage from Hebrews conveys a developed theological perspective on the atoning nature of Christ's sacrificial death that is not so explicitly available in the Gospel Passion narratives. These verses particularly invite consideration of the Holy Place (v. 12a). The high priest in the temple in Jerusalem enters the Holy Place again and again in a perpetual cycle. Christ as high priest goes there once and for all. The Holy Place for Christ is not the temple building, but his bodily death, where he offered his own blood and not that of sacrificed animals (v. 12). How can death, particularly the way Christ died, in any way be considered a Holy Place, indeed, *the* Holy Place? Christ is the victim of injustice, an abuse of both religious authority and imperial power. The cross is an ugly sign of execution, of state-sponsored murder. All of this as Holy of Holies? Therein lies the confounding logic of the events of Holy Week and, indeed, of the whole Christian tradition. Rather than pursue answers, let these questions be rhetorical, and take the time simply to contemplate these perplexing holy mysteries that defy our religious and rational sensibilities.

Gospel
John 12:1-11 (RCL, LFM)

Prior to this passage in John's Gospel, Jesus has raised Lazarus (11:38-44), and as a result there is an active plot to kill Jesus (11:45-57). In thanks for what Jesus has done, however, Lazarus, Mary, and Martha throw a dinner party for him. That is the setting for this passage, John's version of the Mary and Martha story in Luke's Gospel (cf. Luke 10:38-42). In both John and Luke's account, Martha serves the dinner and Mary is the one who more directly engages Jesus. In Luke's account, Mary "sat at the Lord's feet and listened to what he was saying" (Luke 10:39), a rather staid expression of devotion. Here in John, and very much in contrast to the Lukan story, Mary engages in an act of ecstatic extravagance. She sits at Jesus' feet to be sure, but does far more. Mary offers up a full "pound of costly perfume," using it to anoint Jesus' feet, and then "wipes them with her hair" (John 12:3a). This over-the-top act fills the entire house with fragrance (v. 3b).

Intimate and sensual, an ecstatic expression in that she lost herself in the act, Mary's offering reflects a loving stance that would come to be associated with the love mysticism of the Christian tradition where the believer is cast as the bride and Jesus as the groom in a relationship of union as in marriage. This loving intimacy between Mary and Jesus also is characteristic of other portrayals of relationships in John's Gospel, namely Jesus and the beloved disciple (cf. 21:20-25) and the resurrected Jesus' appearance to Mary Magdalene near the tomb (cf. 20:11-18).

Such love is so very close to much human ugliness. This dinner party, the setting for loving exchange, is undertaken with Jesus' knowledge of the plot to kill him (cf. John 11:54). Judas, who is soon to betray Jesus, is at the dinner, complaining about Mary's extravagant waste of the costly perfume, and suggesting that it might otherwise have been sold with the proceeds going to the poor (John 12:5). Secretly, however, he desired to keep the money for himself (v. 6). Word got around that Jesus was at the home of Lazarus, so now there is a plot to kill Lazarus as well (vv. 9-11).

The experience of God's love, known in the nature of Jesus' relationship with us, does not happen in a pristine vacuum, a place and set of circumstances apart from and unspoiled by the ravages of human sin and betrayal, the very antitheses of love. No, the encounter between Jesus and Mary happens in the very thick of the hatred, the plots to kill encroaching, closing in. So it is that Mary's action prefigures the anointing associated with death. Jesus says as much in response to Judas's complaint (v. 7). Indeed, what follows on the heels of this story in John is the entry into Jerusalem, the beginning of the end, which then would initiate the fullness of life and love and joy. No human plot can snuff out the foundation of God's love known in Jesus. It is this reality into which we are invited to enter during Holy Week, and especially in the coming Three Days. Spend some time now contemplating the extravagance of Mary's ecstatic act, knowing that her action is but a mirror of even more extravagant love known in Jesus as the very face of God.

March 26, 2013
Tuesday in Holy Week

Revised Common Lectionary (RCL)
Isaiah 49:1-7
Psalm 71:1-14
1 Corinthians 1:18-31
John 12:20-36

Lectionary for Mass (LFM)
Isaiah 49:1-6
Psalm 71:1-2, 3-4a, 5ab-6ab, 15 + 17

John 13:21-33, 36-38

The readings for Tuesday in Holy Week further nurture us in preparation for deeper engagement with Christ in the Three Days. The first reading takes up themes of call and promise. The second reading focuses on the foolishness of the cross, which is God's confounding wisdom. The RCL Gospel keeps us in suspense as we wait with Christ for the hour that glorifies him. The LFM Gospel invites us to consider the nature of discipleship, using Judas, Peter, and the beloved disciple as types to reveal the range of responses to Jesus during his last earthly days.

First Reading
Isaiah 49:1-7 (RCL)
Isaiah 49:1-6 (LFM)

This passage from Isaiah contains both recollection of call (vv. 1-5) and promise of restoration (vv. 6-7). Who is being called? Perhaps more particularly, who is having God's call reaffirmed? The prophet as servant? All of Israel? As there is ambiguity about who is being addressed, it seems as though the voice of the Lord speaks simultaneously to both prophet and people (cf. v. 3). Despite suffering and exile (v. 7a) and a sense of vocational futility (v. 4), God's call is not in vain, for it extends back in time beyond the point of coming into existence (vv. 1b, 5a), and it is part of divine purposefulness (vv. 2-3, 5b). The aim of the call is the return and restoration of an exiled people. Moreover, the mighty act of God in bringing home the people of Israel will inspire the worshipful respect of other nations (v. 7). This blessing occurs because the Lord who is faithful has chosen to make it happen (v. 7b).

Especially during Holy Week, Christians identify features of this passage with Jesus' call and mission. The servant who glorifies God (v. 3) resonates in particular with John's Gospel, where the Father's glory is manifest in Jesus (cf. John 12:23, 28; 13:31-32). That the prophet and Israel are given as "a light to the nations" (v. 6b) also has parallel in Johannine themes, where Jesus is identified as the light of the world (cf. John 1:4-9; 8:12).

Psalmody
Psalm 71:1-14 (RCL)
Psalm 71:1-2, 3-4a, 5ab-6ab, 15 + 17 (LFM)

Psalm 71 is an individual lament from perhaps an older person (v. 9) who feels besieged by enemies (v. 10) and far from God (vv. 11-12). This experience gives rise to the plea for deliverance, rescue, and saving (vv. 2-4). Despite the lament, this psalm is full of hope and trust (v. 5), praise (vv. 6, 14), and the proclamation of God's saving deeds (vv. 15-17). During Holy Week, these words could be those of Jesus in both lament and praise, two dynamics of the spiritual life held together in paradoxical tension.

Second Reading
1 Corinthians 1:18-31 (RCL)

This passage from 1 Corinthians includes six references to foolishness (vv. 18, 20b, 21b, 23b, 25, 27a), thus a significant idea for Paul in connection with the proclamation of Christ crucified. The interplay between etymology and connotation helps drive home a sense of the strength of the word here. The Greek for foolish is *moros*, from which derives the word *moron*, which in popular usage in American English connotes a sense even stronger than being foolish. The message about the cross is viewed as moronic, stupid, insipid, and absurd. Christ crucified was nonsense to the Greeks who prized rational philosophical systems that led to wisdom (v. 22b). Paul suggests that for persons of Jewish heritage, the proclamation of Christ crucified is a stumbling block (v. 23), a scandal (*skandalon* in the Greek, a cause of offense), for the notion of a crucified Messiah is blasphemous. In the message about the cross, God is doing something radically different from rational philosophy, something that represents a major departure from inherited Jewish theological sensibilities.

Moreover, the people in Corinth would do well to put less prideful trust in their intellectual and other human capacities (vv. 26-29) and those of orators (v. 20). For in the proclamation of Christ crucified is the very power of God (vv. 18b, 24b) and wisdom of God (v. 24b) for life, salvation (v. 18b), righteousness, sanctification, and redemption (v. 30). If we are going to boast, we boast in Christ Jesus as Lord (v. 31).

These words from Paul echo through the centuries to our own day when we, even in the church, struggle with the interplay between our cruciform proclamation and the philosophical and religious assumptions and proclivities of our day. It is tempting to trust in messages and capacities other than Christ crucified when we attempt to translate the Christian story now, as was the case during Paul's time. The exhortation to discipline in preaching is the same: "but we proclaim Christ crucified" (v. 23a)—scandalous foolishness, but still the power of God for salvation through all ages.

Gospel
John 12:20-36 (RCL)

In Bethsaida, where Philip was from, Jews and Greeks intermingled. The Greeks worshiping at the festival in Jerusalem—perhaps Greek-speaking Jews of the dispersion—expressed curiosity to Philip about Jesus: "Sir, we wish to see Jesus" (v. 21b). Word of this reached Jesus, who then used the Greeks' curiosity as the occasion to speak again of his impending death, as if to say, "If these Greeks really wish to see me, have them look for God's glory in my death" (cf. vv. 23-24). The desire to see Jesus also occasioned Jesus' making the usual points in John's Gospel about the costs and benefits of discipleship (vv. 25-26).

These days in Jerusalem are Jesus' hour (v. 23), a significant theme in John (cf. John 2:4; 4:21-23; 5:25-28; 7:30; 8:20; 12:27; 13:1; 16:25, 32; 17:1). In an uncharacteristic moment of the Jesus portrayed in John, who normally proceeds with peaceful confidence, he acknowledges a troubled soul (v. 27a) and poses a rhetorical question, wondering if he should ask, "Father, save me from this hour" (v. 27a). In the portrayal of Jesus in Luke's Gospel, the concern is not rhetorical, but an expression of fervent prayer (cf. Luke 22:42-44). For John's Jesus, this hour is the whole purpose of his mission (v. 27b), which is all about glorifying God's name (v. 28a). At this moment in the narrative, a voice from heaven—thunder or an angel (v. 29)?—indicates that indeed God will glorify the holy name (v. 28b). This glorification will occur through Jesus' death, which ushers in judgment, driving out the world's ruler (v. 31), but which also "will draw all people to [him]self" (v. 32).

The heavenly voice and Jesus' elaboration on the "kind of death he was to die" (v. 33) produce confusion among those in the crowd hearing all of this (v. 34). Jesus continues by exhorting his hearers to walk in the light, as opposed to the world's darkness, that they "may become children of light" (vv. 35-36a). This discourse about light and darkness did not apparently clear things up for the hearers' understanding. Nor should it have, for the fullness of the hour has not yet come at this point in the Gospel narrative. So it is that Jesus "departed and hid from them" (v. 36b), thus maintaining the sense of mystery that will persist until Jesus has died, has been raised, and has ascended to the Father. So on this Tuesday in Holy Week, we like the Greeks and others in John remain in suspense as we await the fuller dramatic revelations of the Three Days. Today, devotionally, let yourself abide in this tension of unknowing.

John 13:21-33, 36-38 (LFM)

Holy Week is about Jesus, and with him our eyes are set to Jerusalem and what he will endure there. In this passage from John's Gospel, however, Jesus addresses his disciples and, by extension through the centuries, us as current-day followers: "One of you will betray me" (v. 21b). As the disciples gather about Jesus, they are confused and wonder who the betrayer might be (vv. 22-25). Jesus' provocative statement about betrayal invites us to examine the range of responses to Jesus on the part of his immediate followers.

An obvious starting point, of course, is Judas, whom Jesus singles out in this passage as the betrayer through a kind of anti-Eucharist: "It is the one to whom I hand the morsel after I have dipped it" (v. 26a NAB). This is perhaps a particularly odd moment in John, especially to those used to Christian sacramental practice, for example, when bread is dipped into the wine for distribution. Satan's entering Judas coincides with his receiving the dipped bread (v. 27a). Jesus' action here suggests hospitality, friendship, and the intimate familiarity he had with Judas. But giving the bread seems to occasion the moment when Judas is given over to the demonic forces that make for betrayal, forces to which Judas is lost, and powers that Jesus defeats when his hour fully comes. Concerning the response of discipleship, then, one option is to fall away irretrievably as Judas embodies by going out into the night (v. 30), lost to the forces of darkness (cf. 12:35).

Simon Peter reveals another stance in response to Jesus, who mysteriously speaks of his imminent departure (v. 33). In his bravado, perhaps, Peter expresses the desire to follow Jesus even to the point of laying down his life for him (v. 37). In reply to this, Jesus predicts that Peter will have denied him three times by cock crow (v. 38). Unlike Judas, however, Peter's denying Jesus is not the end of the story. Peter will come around as Jesus suggests, and Jesus says that later Peter will follow him (v. 36b; cf. John 21:15-19).

There is a third discipleship response in this passage, namely, that of the disciple whom Jesus loved, in John's Gospel perhaps the "type" of the ideal disciple, who in no way betrays Jesus. The beloved disciple's response to Jesus is one of intimacy, of union, of being joined at the hip, as suggested by his "reclining next to Jesus" (vv. 23, 25). The English translation in the NRSV does not do justice to the sense of what is going on here. The Greek in verse 23—*anakeimenos + kolpo*—suggests that the beloved disciple was lying back on Jesus' bosom. In verse 25 as portrayed by the NAB, the translation appropriately conveys a sense of the beloved disciple leaning back or, as suggested by the Greek, falling onto Jesus' chest (*epipeson + stethos*). In each case the beloved disciple's posture toward Jesus suggests a sensual kind of closeness—again, union—evocative of Jesus' intimate relationship to his Father (cf. John 10:30) and in keeping with Jesus' instructions in John's Gospel to abide in him (cf. 15:4-10).

The weekdays during Holy Week prior to the Three Days give us occasion to consider the range of our own responses to Jesus. Might we be tempted in the way of

Judas? Might we more likely be akin to Peter, both denying and following at various points in our journey of discipleship? And might our discipleship also reflect the union of the beloved disciple and Jesus, a dwelling with Jesus made possible by our eucharistic sharing in his body (cf. John 6:56)? In any case, the Son of Man and God are glorified amid all of the proceedings of this week (cf. 13:31-32), despite our discipleship responses.

March 27, 2013
Wednesday in Holy Week

Revised Common Lectionary (RCL)	**Lectionary for Mass (LFM)**
Isaiah 50:4-9a	Isaiah 50:4-9a
Psalm 70	Psalm 69:8-10, 21-22, 31 + 33-34
Hebrews 12:1-3	
John 13:21-32	Matthew 26:14-25

Traditionally known as "Spy Wednesday," Wednesday in Holy Week features Gospel readings that invite us to consider the storm of betrayal that is brewing, and to reflect again on our discipleship response and the extents to which we honor and/or betray Christ in our faith journey and ministry in daily life. The passage from Hebrews, appointed as the second reading for the RCL, further takes up the nature of discipleship, conceived as an endurance race that we run in the company of the saints and with our eyes focused on Jesus, who nears the completion of his contest during these days of Holy Week.

First Reading
Isaiah 50:4-9a (RCL, LFM)

For commentary on this passage, see the first reading for Sunday of the Passion/Palm Sunday, above.

Psalmody
Psalm 70 (RCL)
Psalm 69:8-10, 21-22, 31 + 33-34 (LFM)

Both Psalm 70 and Psalm 69 (selected verses here) share similarities as psalms of individual lament. Each psalm carries the voice of the suffering faithful one who bears the reproach of others (70:2-3; 69:8-10, 21-22) and who trustingly awaits God's saving acts, all the while praising God (70:4; 69:35 NAB), who identifies intimately with the circumstances of the poor and needy (70:5; 69:34 NAB). God has had many faithful suffering servants: the figure in Isaiah 53, Job, and Jeremiah, among others. Christians certainly count Jesus as chief among those suffering ones, and have used themes in these psalms in an attempt to make sense of what Jesus endured (in 70:3, cf. Mark 15:29; in 69:10 NAB, cf. John 2:17; and in 69:22b NAB, cf. Matt. 27:34 KJV).

Second Reading
Hebrews 12:1-3 (RCL)

The author of Hebrews here employs athletic imagery to describe the course of life for followers of Jesus. We are called upon to run a race (v. 1c), to engage a contest (*agon* in the Greek, from which is derived "agony"). We do not run alone, as the course is enveloped by "so great a cloud of witnesses" (v. 1a), that is, quite a crowd of martyrs (cf. *martyria* as witnesses), who have gotten to the finish line first and who, as in a stadium, cheer us on. We run the race single-mindedly focused on Jesus ("looking to Jesus," v. 2a; *aphorontes* in the Greek, "looking off, or away," having the sense of precise attention), the Alpha and Omega, our faith's pioneer (*archegon*, the original leader) and perfecter (*teleioten*, the one who makes for completion and maturation).

Appropriate for Holy Week, this passage speaks of Jesus "endur[ing] the cross" and "disregarding its shame," "for the sake of the joy that was set before him" (v. 2). Joy here is *chara*, the same Greek root for *charis* ("grace"), *charitoo* ("to bestow favor," "to bless"; cf. charity), *charisma* ("gift"), and *eucharistia* ("thanksgiving"; cf. Eucharist). In other words, Jesus can endure the cross and disregard its shame because the fullness of God's reign and its attendant features were before him—hence the joy for Jesus. And because of him, and because we look to him amid the saintly martyrs, we "may not grow weary or lose heart" (v. 3b), and can be free of the impediments that weigh us down (v. 1b).

Gospel
John 13:21-32 (RCL)

For commentary on this passage, see the Gospel (LFM) for Tuesday in Holy Week, above.

Matthew 26:14-25 (LFM)

This passage from Matthew focuses attention on Judas's betrayal of Jesus and precedes the institution narrative for the Lord's Supper (Matt. 26:26-29). The meal of the covenant that Jesus embodies and which points to the in-breaking of God's reign is deeply intertwined with the realities of human duplicity, greed, conflict, and, in short, sin. Judas visits the chief priests asking how much he might get for betraying Jesus (vv. 14-15a). They gave Judas "thirty pieces of silver" on the spot (v. 15b), a comparatively modest sum, an amount equivalent to compensation for an injured slave (cf. Exod. 21:32). Judas's ill-gotten gain contrasts sharply with the extravagant outpouring of generosity when, in the preceding passage, the unnamed woman pours costly ointment from an alabaster jar over Jesus' head (26:6-13). Is it simply paltry greed that motivates Judas's betrayal? Who can finally know? What is revealed here, however, is the reality that Judas cannot serve two masters, for example, God and wealth (cf. Matt. 6:24). In any case, Judas as opportunist seeks the context and means through which he will betray Jesus (v. 16).

Jesus commands the disciples to make preparations for their communal celebration of the Passover (vv. 17-19), a curious thing because Matthew's report of the supper (vv. 26-29) makes no mention of the typical features associated with the Passover menu—lamb and bitter herbs, for example. While the emergent Christian tradition, reflected in the Matthean account, may have interpreted the events of Jesus' last days in light of the Passover, there is a more significant sense in which Jesus' meal with his disciples is part of the inauguration of a new, eschatological reign (cf. v. 29).

During dinner conversation, Jesus names the reality that one of the disciples will betray him (v. 21). In a scene that is the basis for Leonardo DaVinci's famous depiction of the Last Supper, the agitated replies of one after another disciple ensue: "Surely it is not I, Lord?" (v. 22 NAB). Jesus indicates that the betrayer is one among the intimates, that is, one who shares the common bowl for dipping (v. 23; cf. Ps. 41:9). Jesus further suggests that all of this is part of God's plan for the Son of Man as it has been written, a reference not to specific Scriptures, but perhaps in keeping with the general depictions of the servant in Isaiah (cf. Isa. 53:1-12).

Judas's response contrasts with that of the other disciples. While the eleven exclaim, "Surely not I, *Lord*," an expression of allegiance and loyalty of closest allies, Judas replies, "Surely it is not I, *Rabbi*?" (v. 25 NAB), a more generic reference that does not reflect a devotion to Jesus as master. Clearly the author of Matthew sees Judas, who serves other masters, on the outside of the inner circle.

The events of Holy Week proceed apace. Tomorrow is Maundy Thursday/ Holy Thursday, which will include, in part, a dramatic focus on the Eucharist as our participation with Jesus in the Last Supper. Today affords the opportunity to consider our own eucharistic celebrations as they occur in the church that exists simultaneously as eschatological community and as a body comprised of finite, frail, broken, and sinful human beings. We, like Judas and, frankly, the other disciples, suffer divided loyalties and are prone to betraying the ones we love and cherish most dearly. Preaching and/or devotion on this day may explore the ways in which disunity and unity coincide paradoxically in the Holy Supper. Remember that betrayal does not have the last word, but rather Jesus' "blood of the covenant, which will be shed on behalf of many for the forgiveness of sins" (Matt. 26:28 NAB).

March 28, 2013
Maundy Thursday / Holy Thursday

Revised Common Lectionary (RCL)
Exodus 12:1-4 (5-10) 11-14
Psalm 116:1-2, 12-19
1 Corinthians 11:23-26
John 13:1-17, 31b-35

Lectionary for Mass (LFM)
Exodus 12:1-8, 11-14
Psalm 116:12-13, 15-16bc, 17-18
1 Corinthians 11:23-26
John 13:1-15

Some traditions call for confession and individual absolution to begin the Maundy Thursday liturgy, marking the conclusion of Lent, being a bookend to the penitential rite of Ash Wednesday, and echoing an early Christian tradition when Holy Thursday was the occasion for the return and reconciliation of those excommunicated. Many traditions include ritual foot washing in the liturgy for this day, either the washing of a representative few or everyone in the assembly who dares come forward, reenacting Jesus' own washing of his disciples' feet as recorded in John's Gospel. The Lord's Supper on this day has perhaps a special emphasis as the commemoration of Jesus' last supper with his closest followers, marking also the institution of the Eucharist. Some traditions further include a ritual stripping of the altar on this day, a practice that acknowledges the absence of the celebration of the Eucharist on Good Friday and calls symbolic attention to preparations for Jesus' death and burial.

The events of Jesus' life that this day recalls are intimate and familiar, conveying a sense of vulnerability that comes when people are in close proximity to each other. Palm Sunday/Sunday of the Passion–related readings are full of very public spectacle, recalling the grand entry into Jerusalem, Jesus' public trial, and his painfully displayed-for-all-to-see execution. In contrast, Maundy Thursday/Holy Thursday readings remember events that took place in one room, namely the Upper Room, and which involved only those closest to Jesus, his twelve disciples.

In keeping with the spirit of this day and its readings, liturgical enactments are thus also intimate and familiar, perhaps embarrassingly so. If it is part of your tradition, the absolution is individual, not plenary, and involves the presiding minister laying hands on each person's head, pronouncing for that person God's particular forgiveness for particular sins.

Foot washing is perhaps the most intimate of Christian liturgical enactments. I love to participate in a full range of ritual actions. However, foot washing is one I participate in, on the receiving end of things at least, reluctantly, perhaps grudgingly, with a sense of embarrassment, in keeping with Simon Peter's reaction to what Jesus was doing (cf. John 13:8). What if an odor is discernable? Or dirt or lint or calluses or blisters or other imperfections of unpedicured feet? Even in intimate relationships, how routine is it that we have our feet touched by others?

The Lord's Supper on this day does not have the tenor of a feast of victory for our God. The Eucharist is overdetermined in terms of its meaningfulness, and thus can encompass a wide range of moods. On Holy Thursday, it is a Last Supper, a commemoration of death, the Holy Day observance that marked the last night of Jesus' earthly life. As a memorial, the Eucharist today is very personal indeed, as the death of loved ones, of ourselves, is radically personal. Imagine the closeness of the space in that Upper Room, physically and psychically. Given that crowds may not be flocking to our churches on Holy Thursday these days, perhaps our observances have some of the sense of intimacy of that holy night centuries ago.

Consider the stripping of the altar that may conclude the liturgy in connection with Jesus stripping, tying a "towel around himself" (John 13:4) to wash his disciples' feet. The vulnerability of nakedness is constitutive of the atmosphere of this day, certainly Jesus' vulnerability historically, but also the vulnerability of all of his followers through the ages to our own day. Also mirroring Ash Wednesday— "remember that you are dust and to dust you shall return"—Holy Thursday is an occasion to follow Jesus' lead and to become naked in our own mortality, allowing ourselves to feel the vulnerability of having that to which we cling, that which otherwise covers us, adorns us, stripped from us.

In this way, Maundy Thursday is a dramatically enacted call to plumb the contemplative depths. It has the flavor of Thomas Merton's *New Seeds for Contemplation*, the reading of which in my experience makes for a sense of being stripped of the consolations even of theology, liturgy, and the traditions and structures of the church, driving us ever more deeply into a radical, more fundamental faith, a naked, vulnerable trust, and a falling into the arms of a merciful God.

If this is the mood of the day, thanks be to God that Maundy Thursday takes its Latinized name from Jesus' commandment, mandate (*mandatum*, hence Maundy), to love (John 13:34-35). Love undergirds everything today. It is love that gives us the freedom to be present to each other and to God, less defensive, less guarded, in the vulnerability of our mortality and, frankly, in our sin. The love of God in Christ is behind and makes possible the day's confession and forgiveness. This love also motivates Jesus' washing of feet, and is love's enactment in servanthood ministry. Moreover, this divine love is the wellspring of the Last Supper, the Eucharist. Finally, loving response, inspired by God's love, is expressed in the care with which members of our liturgical assemblies remove the appointments and adornments of the altars and chancels of our churches, even as the women at the tomb were prepared to lovingly anoint and otherwise care for Jesus' body.

This day, Maundy Thursday or Holy Thursday, however your tradition would have it, thus begins the Three Days, which also include Good Friday and Holy Saturday with its Easter Vigil, a seamless liturgy in multiple movements over the course of days. The Three Days allow the time and spaciousness for us to go ever deeper into the central stories of our faith. These days and their liturgical foci contain the fullness of the Christian tradition in concentrated and comprehensive form, a culmination of the whole liturgical year. It is the time when the faithful soak in the tradition for remembrance, *anamnesis*, the directly participatory reenactments for us and all time of salvation history. These days' events turned the world upside down, and continue to do so, particularly as the power of the Holy Spirit, carried in the liturgical drama rooted in the scriptural narratives, finds us and our world at the deeper places.

What is the nature of preaching on this day? Because the liturgy is heavy with dramatic action, today is a day not so much to talk, but to do. That is to say, the preacher is called upon once again to get out of the way, to be an inviting presence, particularly to lead people more deeply into the day's drama. Preach in such a way as to evoke a sense of worshipers' direct participation in Christ in the narrative and liturgical reenactments.

First Reading
Exodus 12:1-4 (5-10) 11-14 (RCL)
Exodus 12:1-8, 11-14 (LFM)

If you have the sense that this passage reads like rubrics or instructions for worship, that is because the majority of this passage is just that (especially vv. 1-11). Instructional manuals do not typically make for inspiring devotional reading. In books of liturgy, it is very easy indeed for worshipers to skip over or completely ignore rubrics, overlooking the instructions in the book or bulletin. It is also a seduction for worship planners and leaders to reduce liturgy to engaging rubrics rightly, thus creating a sense of rigidity and performance anxiety that can inhibit worshipfulness. Upon closer examination, however, instructions convey theological and devotional riches, as rubrics are rooted in theological affirmations and assumptions, and likewise serve to provide the kind of frameworks and guidance that make worship possible in the first place.

This passage is cast as instruction to Moses and Aaron, as if the original, historic exodus event was already itself an act of liturgical worship. This makes the important theological point that this pivotal historical event in the lives of God's people Israel remains alive and in the present tense in liturgical, devotional observance (cf. v. 14). Each detail of instruction includes fragments of historical memory, which, when woven together and enacted, make for the fabric of participatory remembrance.

Further conveying theological points, embedded in these instructions for the remembrance of the exodus is a focus on the worshipful observance of the whole community (vv. 3, 6b). Religious practice is, thus, not the domain of the solitary individual apart from community, arguably a countercultural claim in our day. That said, God's deliverance of the people of Israel from the hands of the Egyptians amid the sending of plagues nonetheless applies also to individual households. That the lamb's blood is put on the two doorposts and lintels of each house indicates this particularity of deliverance (vv. 7, 12-13). So the exodus is both for the whole community and at the same time for the individual households that comprise it. Likewise, there is concern for the just distribution of the meat of the sacrificed lambs among the households in the community, that all may have fair portions (v. 4). One might also see in this passage implications for good stewardship of the bounties of the earth entrusted to our care, that there would be no leftovers (v. 10).

Liturgical instruction gives guidance not just for what we do, but for how and in what manner we do it, hence serving the end of worship. In keeping with the spirit of the exodus, in that the people of Israel had to be at the ready to leave Egypt immediately upon word from Moses and Aaron, the instructions in this passage give a sense of urgency for the hurried eating of the lamb and unleavened bread and bitter herbs (v. 11a).

This story from Exodus has come to be associated with the Eucharist, thus its appointment as one of the readings for Maundy Thursday/Holy Thursday. Perhaps the associations between Passover and the Eucharist account, in part, for the brevity of the sending rites in current Western Christian practice. We eat our simple meal of bread and wine, Christ's body and blood, liturgical "fast food," and then are rushed out the door: "The Mass is ended; go in peace; serve the Lord." In the case of the people of Israel, they are delivered in a rush of divine activity, stripped of securities of food and shelter, the odd stability of their enslavement, only to enter into the long, faith-challenging sojourn in the wilderness on the way to the promised land. In the case of the church, we are propelled in the power of the Spirit to enter the wilderness of our lives and times in mission, bearing witness to a promised future in Christ, God's reign of loving peace in the divine commonwealth, a controversial claim in our time that challenges dominant narratives.

Psalmody
Psalm 116:1-2, 12-19 (RCL)
Psalm 116:12-13, 15-16bc, 17-18 (LFM)

With its origins as a song of thanksgiving for individuals who had experienced God's favor of deliverance, perhaps from death (v. 15), and for answered prayer (v. 1), this psalm came to be included in Passover observances (cf. v. 13, "lift up the cup of salvation," in connection with instructions in Exod. 29:40 and Num. 28:7). The lifting-the-cup reference along with offering the Lord a "thanksgiving sacrifice" (v. 17), and reference to "the death of faithful ones" (v. 15), may account for this psalm's associations with the Eucharist, and thus its inclusion among readings for Maundy Thursday/Holy Thursday.

Second Reading
1 Corinthians 11:23-26 (RCL, LFM)

Paul's eucharistic institution narrative is set within discourse about abuses of the Lord's Supper and conflict in the Corinthian community. In brief, it seems as though the more well-to-do members of the community come early to eat their fill and to overindulge in wine, while the less privileged come later only to have leftovers at best, thus dividing the community (cf. 11:17-22). This is the context for Paul sharing the heart of his understanding of the sacred meal that we now understand as the Eucharist. The sacrament of unity, even in its earliest expression, is marred by disunity in the community. The practice of the Corinthian community that Paul condemns, though, is in keeping with the quality of Jesus' own gathering with his twelve disciples at the Last Supper when they bickered among themselves about who was the greatest (cf. Luke 22:21-24). Perhaps we should not be surprised when our own sacramental celebrations in imperfect contemporary communities fall far short of their intended ideals.

In light of this conflict, and in relation to Paul's emphasis elsewhere in his writings about the church as the body of Christ (cf. 1 Cor. 12:12-27), Paul's reiteration of Jesus' words—"This is my body"—takes on an added texture of meaning. The bread communicates Christ's body, even as communicants also become that body as the church. Hence the centrality of "discerning the body" (11:29), a reference perhaps to seeing Christ in the many members that constitute the church as the body of Christ. Hence also the crucial importance of the communal, sacramental meal as being the occasion to "proclaim [*katangello*] the Lord's death until he comes" (v. 26b). While the Greek may translate "preach," it also has the sense that the whole fabric of our lives proclaims, as we carry in our actions the meaningfulness of the Lord's death and his promised return. In brief, Paul instructs that we do well to "practice what we preach," that the qualities of our communal life should be consistent with the significance of the sacred meal, characterized by unity and a just distribution of food, a living out of the sacrament in our wider community.

Gospel
John 13:1-17, 31b-35 (RCL)
John 13:1-15 (LFM)

In the Hebrew experience in the Greco-Roman world, there was nothing particularly unusual about foot washing, undertaken for reasons of cleanliness and hospitality and even for ritual purposes. Either guests would wash their own feet, or a servant would do it for them. What is unusual in this passage is that Jesus took on the role of both host *and* servant. As is often the case with Jesus portrayed in the Gospels, he employs the ordinary in the service of communicating extraordinary messages, and in this case, enacting a new reality through the foot washing. Jesus paradoxically subverts ordinary understandings of the roles of both host and servant, and in so doing conveys key characteristics of the reign of God he was called both to proclaim and to embody (vv. 13-17). Jesus, Lord and Teacher (v. 14), that is to say, host, becomes servant, dressing the part (v. 4) and acting the part (v. 5). For one who is regarded as Lord and Teacher, such servanthood as leadership was unheard of.

This enactment is about love (*agape*), a particularly prominent word in this passage and its addendum (used in one form or another six times, vv. 1, 34-35). *Agape* is a love that is not an abstraction, but demonstrated in the deed of washing the disciples' feet. It is a love characterized by servanthood, by the vulnerability of stripping off outer garments and getting up close and personal with members of his disciples' bodies that saw significant stress, the feet, punished by their constant contact with the earth. Moreover, this was an expression of love that took place at a liminal time, the eve of Jesus' death, opening the door to his return to the Father (v. 1). Quite significantly, the demonstration of love by Jesus took place amid conditions of profound betrayal of trust, with Jesus' full knowledge that his betrayer was at hand (vv. 2, 11). These features of the passage give a good sense of what *agape* means. The enactments are close to the heart of God, whom Jesus calls Father. The host becoming a servant glorifies God (vv. 31-32), as will Jesus' death (cf. John 12:27-28).

All of this is confounding to the disciples, represented by Simon Peter's reaction to Jesus: "You will never wash my feet" (v. 8a). Jesus makes it clear that at this point in the drama they cannot understand the meaning and significance of his actions: "You do not know [*oida*] now what I am doing, but later you will understand [*ginosko*]" (v. 7). *Oida* has to do with ordinary perception and awareness. *Ginosko* involves a kind of knowledge and understanding that is the fruit of a deeper participation and engagement in the very life of Jesus, and relates to his statement, "Unless I wash you, you have no share [*meros*] with me" (v. 8b). *Meros* conveys this sense of sharing, of direct communion with Jesus, which is constitutive of what we might now call contemplative encounter. Such knowledge born of relationship is in keeping with statements elsewhere in John, that understanding will emerge at the coming of the Holy Spirit, in John's Gospel the very breath of Jesus (20:22), which guides us into all truth (cf. 16:13a). This is precisely what the Holy Spirit is up to in our liturgies, the power of God carried in the drama of the scriptural narratives and our playing them out, a power to draw us into direct, contemplative sharing in Jesus, his life, his glory, his humility, his love, the stuff of true wisdom and knowledge so as to transform us and the world.

March 29, 2013
Good Friday

The Good Friday liturgy, the second day of the Three Days, continues where the drama left off on Maundy Thursday/Holy Thursday. That service may have concluded with the stripping of the altar, leaving it and the surrounding worship space unadorned, stark and naked in dimmed light, perhaps even darkness. This is the scene worshipers enter into on Good Friday. Because there is no need of greeting since the Good Friday liturgy is a continuation of the Three Days, worshipers and ministers may gather in silence. Silence also marks the solemnity of the occasion, in part because our response to the day's events is perhaps beyond words. Moreover, the silence creates the space for a deep attending to the voice of God offered up in the Spirit's power speaking in the scriptural narrative, taking us to the profound places that Good Friday—God's Friday—is all about. Good Friday silence, then, can nurture an atmosphere for contemplative encounter, which is such a prominent feature of Holy Week.

The Service of the Word centers on the reading or singing of the Passion according to John. This is preceded by passages from Isaiah and Hebrews and a psalm to help set the stage for the Johannine Passion narrative, traditionally used on Good Friday. A sermon or homily may follow the Passion story. Preaching ministers confront the same challenge and opportunity of Sunday of the Passion, and perhaps even Maundy Thursday: What can we say that adds anything more to the story and its dramatic enactments in the liturgy? With an abiding sense of humility, once again we simply invite our hearers more deeply into the narrative, letting its conclusions frame and claim us, form and transform us, getting out of the way of ourselves, letting the Spirit's wind blow where it will in taking hearers to new and/or remembered places.

A sermon or homily on Good Friday may also serve as a bridge between the service of readings and the liturgy to follow, namely, in many traditions, bidding prayers that rather comprehensively invite us to pray for the church, its leaders, those preparing for baptism, for other Christians and people of faith, for those who do not believe in God, for creation, those in authority, and those in need. Today is a day to dwell with the petitions of our prayers in a spirit of prayerful vigil at the tomb, not rushing through them, but offering up all our concerns, aspirations, and lamentations with "sighs too deep for words" (cf. Rom. 8:26).

The Good Friday liturgy may also include a procession with a large cross and provide occasion to reverence or venerate that cross while the solemn reproaches or other canticles are sung, which carry our adoration of the Crucified. Not unlike the kinetic participation of the Palm Sunday procession and the Maundy Thursday foot washing, worshipers may get up and move to the cross to bow or kneel before it, touch it, kiss it, or otherwise acknowledge it. Thus homiletical commentary on the day may also call attention to how best we might faithfully give reverence to the cross, a cruel tool of public execution.

The liturgy may end as it began: with silence, God's people lingering and then leaving the place of assembly in confounded, and perhaps confident, but speechless wonder at what has transpired, as the story of the Passion continues even in our day to hold the potential to turn our world upside down.

First Reading
Isaiah 52:13—53:12 (RCL, LFM)

This passage is the last suffering servant song in the book of Isaiah, a selection rich in texture, and made all the more complex by its use among Christians trying to make sense of Jesus of Nazareth, his death, and his role in salvation history. Adding to its play and place in Christian hearts, George Frederick Handel employed several verses of this section of Isaiah to elaborate musically on christological meanings in his masterpiece, *Messiah*. Peeling away the levels of meanings and associations is daunting. Even taking up this passage with Hebrew eyes apart from Christian interpretations reveals its complexity, nuance, and singularity. Is the suffering servant Moses, all of Israel, a prediction of the coming of a second Moses, some combination? Yes to all, in a word, as commentators have drawn varied conclusions. Traditional understandings of Moses, the place of the people of Israel, and their relationship to the nations combine in this passage to offer up a new synthesis, a new something that breaks open conventional views, and yet defies precise understanding. It is poetry after all, a servant *song*, and not a theological treatise, strictly speaking.

What is striking is that this servant, whoever it happens to be or represent, and what this servant suffers, gets the attention of the nations. They are "astonished" (52:14); he "startles many nations" (52:15); "kings . . . shut their mouths" (52:15).

They are provoked to consider, to contemplate this servant who is beyond conventional human understanding (cf. 52:14b), this servant whose punishment makes us whole (53:5). The silence of the kings is met by the silence of the servant, who "like a sheep that before its shearers is silent" (53:7). Who can believe this stuff (cf. 53:1), that the servant's bruises may heal us (53:5b)? What's more, all of this is somehow God's will, a will that "shall prosper" through the servant (53:10).

Astonished, startled, mouth-stopping silence, again a dimension of contemplative experience, is perhaps the best presence to bring to engaging the Passion narrative from John's Gospel on Good Friday. If we can but allow the peeling away of the layers of our own conventional understandings of this day and its stories, perhaps we can be confronted by the Passion as if for the first time, have our domesticated views overturned, and become overpowered by the story's claim that indeed God is doing something new. Even today, after some two thousand years of singing this servant song and rehearsing all the ways in which we think we have understandings about it settled, fresh meanings may be evoked. Whatever God is up to via the narratives of this day persists in being unsettling, but nonetheless also makes for our wholeness and healing.

Psalmody
Psalm 22 (RCL)
Psalm 31:2, 6, 12-13, 15-16, 17, 25 (LFM)
For comments on these psalms, see Sunday of the Passion/Palm Sunday, above.

Second Reading
Hebrews 10:16-25 (RCL)
Quoting statements (vv. 16-17) about the new covenant from Jeremiah 31:33 and 34b, and previously (vv. 11-12) suggesting that Christ, the great high priest, has made a onetime, sufficient sacrifice, the author of the letter to the Hebrews exhorts us to consider the qualities of true worship and faith life within the Christian community. First, because of Christ, we have "confidence to enter the sanctuary" (v. 19), unlike worship of old when only the priest entered therein, and worshipers waited beyond the confines of the Holy Place. Now the entire assembly is expected to participate boldly, unflinchingly in the fullness of the experience. It has taken various reform movements in Christian history to keep us true to this foundational exhortation to full worshipful participation. Moreover, we "approach with a true heart in full assurance of faith" (v. 22a), having been baptized (cf. v. 22b). That is, the baptized gather for worship with sincerity and integrity, abundantly confident, trustingly courageous, this in contrast to timid, halfhearted, or even two-faced participation. Further, even as we approach, we "hold fast to the confession of our hope without wavering" (v. 23a), our rooting, our stability in our confession of faith, and the foundation for our hope being Christ, the faithful one (v. 23b).

Finally, the author exhorts us "to provoke [incite, goad, or pester] one another to love and good deeds" (v. 24), being regular in our participation in community life (v. 25a) and holding each other accountable through encouragement and exhortation, ever mindful of the promised return of Christ (v. 25b). Good words for us in our day when we might be tempted to self-imposed exile and inaction with so much hate-filled, discouraging discourse and behavior about us. Consider this passage a set of rubrics for our own liturgical participation on Good Friday and always, as well as instruction for how we are to engage each other on the Christian journey throughout our lives in the communities of the church and world. This passage from Hebrews also serves as a fine segue to the encounter with the Passion from John, which, as you will read, takes up similar themes of confident approach. Moreover, this Hebrews passage sets the stage for the bidding prayers that may follow later in the liturgy when we confidently offer our prayers to God on this holy day.

Hebrews 4:14-16; 5:7-9 (RCL alt., LFM)

There is a twofold exhortation in this passage: "Let us hold fast to our confession" (4:14b) and "Let us therefore approach the throne of grace with boldness" (4:16a). To move and to stay put are not mutually exclusive, but express paradoxical tensions of the faith life. On the one hand is the call to stability, and on the other, activity. One supports and complements the other: contemplation and action. Each requires a great deal of spiritual energy. It is not just movement that expends energy; the effort to hold fast can be extraordinary, especially to the confession of faith in a world fraught with temptations to stray.

The source for both holding fast and approaching with boldness is Christ, our high priest, whose qualifications for effective and faithful priesthood are centered precisely on his being one of us, "sympathiz[ing] with our weaknesses," knowing that which tests us, yet remaining sinless (4:15). In Christ we have the picture-perfect priest, "Jesus offer[ing] up prayers and supplications, with loud cries and tears" (5:7a). Such is the role of the priest as fully engaged intercessor, a model for our own priestly ministries, this Jesus to whom we look as "the pioneer and perfecter of our faith" (cf. Heb. 12:2). With loud cries and tears, we see Jesus the high priest fully at worship —especially instructive for our liturgical leadership on this Good Friday— whose reverent submission, that is, devout or pious self-offering, got the attention of God (5:7b).

Even as God's Son, Jesus "learned obedience through what he suffered" (5:8). This suffering on the cross, remembered today, made him "perfect" (5:9a), that is, consecrated and complete. Our obedience (*hypakouo*; see the English word *acoustic* in the root, having to do with hearing) to him (cf. 5:9b) on this day centers on hearing with rapt attention his voice carried on the words about him in the Passion narrative.

Gospel
John 18:1—19:42 (RCL, LFM)

Holy Week affords us the opportunity to engage two Passion narratives in close chronological proximity, this year Luke's account on Sunday of the Passion, and today, the Passion according to John, traditionally read or sung on Good Friday for centuries. Studying one sheds light on the other, and thus may contribute helpfully to homiletical preparations.

While John stands apart from the Synoptics in that it does not explicitly draw on the same textual material, all Passion accounts nonetheless share traditions of the basic elements of the story, such as the betrayal and arrest of Jesus, his appearance before religious and secular authorities, and the crucifixion and death. That said, each Gospel emphasizes different features of the essential narrative building blocks, makes different theological points, and, quite significantly, offers the narrative with distinct moods.

In commentary on the Gospel for Passion Sunday, I suggested that Luke's account reads like a bad dream or thunderstorm or the twenty-four-hour news cycle, full of the heaving mess of human religious and political maneuverings. In contrast, while the religious and political intrigue is very much present, John's account conveys a tone of serene confidence on the part of Jesus, and claims a kind of leisure and spaciousness to offer explicit interpretations of the events, often suggesting ways in which the incidents of Jesus' last hours were fulfillments of Scripture (18:9; 19:24b, 28, 36-37).

It is interesting to note that in both Luke and John, the post-supper story begins in a garden, a place of prayerful convening, and each account concludes in the garden where the tomb is located. In connection with the Lukan story, I emphasized the importance of the infrastructure of worship and prayer for understanding the narrative. I suggested that this worshipful, prayerful foundation carries Jesus forward in the divine power that ultimately wins the day. I would make similar points concerning John's account, except that John conveys a different sense of this prayerfulness, especially as it reveals the nature of Jesus' relationship to God the Father, a relationship that features a present-tense and full participation in God's eschatological realities.

In Luke, Jesus' prayer is agonizing (Luke 22:44), it is a time of trial or temptation (22:40), and Jesus asks to be delivered from this hour (22:42). In John, there is no time of prayer in the garden across the Kidron valley (18:1-2). However, it may be that Jesus' long prayer for his disciples, which immediately precedes this passage (17:1-26) and which may function rhetorically as the bridge between the supper and the betrayal and arrest in the garden (18:1a), is the prayerful foundation for proceeding into this hour. Jesus does not seek to escape this hour in John, but embraces and refers to it again and again (cf. 2:4; 7:30; 8:20; 12:23, 27; 13:1; 17:1).

An essential angle, then, for understanding the nature of Jesus' presence in the Johannine account of the Passion involves looking closely at this series of conversational and prayerful proceedings at the supper, which include chapters 13–17. John's Gospel devotes five full chapters to the supper-related sequences, in contrast to two chapters for the events of arrest and trial, death and burial, and two for resurrection-related stories. This significant amount of narrative material sheds light on how it is that Jesus can be portrayed in John's Gospel as one confidently serene. Recall that these chapters include the foot washing and related discourse (chap. 13); the farewell discourse, including the promise of the Spirit (chaps. 14–16); and the prayer known traditionally as Jesus' high priestly prayer (chap. 17).

Since what you are reading is commentary on John's Passion in chapters 18 and 19 and not a focused exploration of chapters 13–17, I cannot go into detail about these pre-Passion encounters. Suffice it to say that the Spirit of these chapters—and indeed, much of the focus there is on the coming of the Holy Spirit as Advocate—reveals the source of the nature of Jesus' confident presence in the Passion account. Distilling essential features of chapters 13–17, key words there convey the sense of this Spirit that also characterizes the quality of Jesus' presence: love (13:1; 14:21-24; 15:9-17; 17:26); glory (13:31-32; 17:1-5); believing (14:1, 12, 29; 16:27; 17:8, 20-21); abiding (14:17b; 15:4-7, 9-10); dwelling (14:2, 10); joy (15:11; 16:20-22, 24; 17:13); peace (14:27; 16:33); knowing (14:4-7; 17:6-8); truth (14:6, 17; 15:26; 16:13; 17:8, 17-19); keeping the word (14:23-24; 15:7); eternal life (17:2-3); and bearing fruit (15:2-8). Constellated together and found throughout chapters 13–17, these words, as they reveal dispositions associated with the intimacy of Jesus' participation in the Father, capture the essence of what Jesus brings to his betrayal, arrest, trial, death, and burial.

These same qualities will also mark the lives of Jesus' disciples and their life together once the Holy Spirit, the Advocate, comes. For Jesus, however, the eschatological future is a present-tense reality dating from the foundation of the world in his oneness with the Father (cf. 1:1-18). For the disciples, that eschaton will also be a present-tense and significantly realized reality in the life of the Spirit. In brief, however, it is Jesus' participation with the Father that results in a presence characterized by love, glory, believing, abiding, dwelling, joy, peace, truth, and eternal life. It is these qualities that make for Jesus' confident, controlled serenity in John's Passion.

Returning to that story, Jesus enters the garden with knowledge of what is to transpire (18:4a), conveying a sense of confident control. When the soldiers and police appear (18:3), Jesus "[comes] forward," a bold move, and he, not they, utters the first words, "Whom are you looking for?" (18:4). When they say they are looking for Jesus of Nazareth, twice he says without hesitation, "I am he" (18:5a, 8a), furthering this sense of confidence and being in control that Jesus' divine presence embodies in John's account. This stance is very much in contrast to the portrayal of Peter in John, who in parallel fashion to Jesus was also on trial of a sort in the casting of this narrative. Peter says three times in denial, "I am not" one of Jesus' disciples (18:17, 25, 27). Clearly, Peter does not yet have the gift of the Spirit that would enable the kind of faithful confidence Jesus embodies.

Furthermore, Jesus has no apparent fear of the soldiers and police. In contrast, shattering conventional expectations, it is they who appear to fear Jesus of Nazareth when they fall to the ground at the announcement of his presence (18:6). When Jesus might have encouraged further use of the sword (cf. 18:10), he instructs Peter to put it away (18:11), his confidence transcending the seduction of an escalation of violence, which is itself an overreaction to fear. Jesus' appearance before Annas is likewise bold and confident (18:20-23). Pilate cannot intimidate Jesus (18:33-38a). Despite flogging (19:1) and the mocking display with purple robe and crown of thorns (19:2), insults and striking on the face (19:3), and the cries to crucify him (19:6), it is Pilate who fears Jesus, especially concerning claims to sovereign and divine sonship (19:7-8). Jesus gives no answer to Pilate's query about where Jesus is from (19:9). When the interrogation turns to questions of power (19:10b), Jesus concludes that Pilate has no power over him because the source of Pilate's authority is not from God (19:11a).

There is something about the quality of Jesus' presence that, while it is what we would commonly associate with a deeply religious person, was nonetheless so threatening to both religious and civil authorities that execution was the inevitable outcome. Moreover, the Gospel writer John makes a lot of Jesus' kingship (18:33-39; 19:2-3, 12-15, 19-22). But it is a sovereign reign that is not sourced in human business as usual: "My kingdom is not from this world" (18:36a). There is little more threatening to powers that have been and powers that are than the kind of presence Jesus embodied.

This transcendent, sovereign, confident, and serene presence is carried over also in Jesus' behavior on the cross where he offers words that are, on the face of it, quite matter of fact. Looking beyond himself to the needs of his mother and the disciple whom he loved, he says, "Woman, here is your son. . . . Here is your mother" (19:26-27a). John has Jesus saying, "I am thirsty," more in order to fulfill Scripture than to express the wrenching nature of his condition (19:28). Jesus' final word from the cross in John is the simple but profound utterance: "It is finished" (19:30a). That is to say, Jesus' work of this eschatological hour is done, complete. Jesus reigns in glory, but a glory unrecognizable to and not received by the world (cf. 15:21; 16:8-11).

How does all of this preach on Good Friday? This day's solemnity is about Jesus, not about us. Preach in such a way as to unfold the nature of Jesus' presence as conveyed in John, perhaps in the spirit of John the Baptist, who was called to point to Jesus the Lamb of God (cf. 1:26-27, 36). That said, there may be occasion to suggest in a Johannine way that what Jesus embodies is ours also in the power of the Spirit (cf. 17:6-10, 22). Our abiding in Jesus and thus also in the Father is made possible through the Eucharist (cf. 6:53-58). Our participation in Jesus through the Spirit he imparts after his resurrection (cf. 20:19-23) does not remove us from the travails of the world's hatred (15:18-27). Rather, the Spirit of Jesus will infuse us with the very qualities—love, glory, belief, peace, keeping his word, truth, joy, abiding in him, fruit bearing—that will likewise empower us to witness to the world in serene confidence. Here again is a call to the kind of deep spirituality that Jesus modeled, which opens up the greater experience of our abiding with Jesus and thus bearing fruit in the Spirit as he did. In this Spirit, the assembly can confidently approach God in the bidding prayers. In this Spirit, members of the assembly can adore the monarch Christ on the throne of the cross. In this Spirit, worshipers can linger wordlessly with faith that the silence is not a terrible void, but full of glorious, cruciform, divine presence.

March 30, 2013
Holy Saturday

Revised Common Lectionary (RCL)

Job 14:1-14 or Lamentations 3:1-9, 19-24
Psalm 31:1-4
1 Peter 4:1-8
Matthew 27:57-66 or John 19:38-42

Known from ancient times as the "Great Sabbath," the hours of Holy Saturday prior to the Easter Vigil occasion a possible refrain from activity, making room to reflect on Jesus' death and, as we confess in the Apostles' Creed, Jesus' descent to the dead. In the frantic activity of this week, and given the human proclivity to avoid confronting mortality, it can be easy to proceed quickly from Good Friday to celebrations of Easter. Today, if you can carve out the space for fasting amid the preparations for feasting, take some time to dwell with the texts appointed for Holy Saturday, texts that provoke us to take seriously the reality of Jesus' death and, by extension, our own mortality. Jesus really did die, and we will, too. Spending spiritually imaginative time at the sepulcher can build anticipation for the festival at hand, when the tomb becomes the place of resurrection and rebirth. There is no Eucharist during the hours of the Great Sabbath. If there is a liturgy, it would be a simple Service of the Word. A traditional prayer for Compline focuses the meditative imagination for the themes of Holy Saturday:

> O Lord Jesus Christ, Son of the Living God, who at this evening hour didst rest in
> the sepulchre, and didst thereby sanctify the grave to be a bed of hope to thy people:
> make us so to abound in sorrow for our sins, which were the cause of thy passion, that
> when our bodies lie in the dust, our souls may live with thee: who livest and reignest
> with the Father and the Holy Spirit, one God world without end. Amen.[1]

First Reading
Job 14:1-14

Conveying the poetic tone of a psalm of lament, this passage is a prayerful interlude amid Job's discourse with his "friends" about the horrific lot that has befallen him. Here Job laments the brevity and troubled nature of human existence (vv. 1-2). The fate of a tree, which can regenerate itself after it is cut down (vv. 7-9), may be preferable to human mortality. Indeed, Job is on the brink of concluding that death is final (v. 12). Yet in hopeful faith he prays: "Oh that you would hide me in Sheol" (v. 13a) and "that you would appoint me a set time, and remember me!" (v. 13c).

When it is all said and done, perhaps this is the most primary prayer at the time of death: "Remember me!" That is to say, "Oh, that we would not be forgotten." On the despairing side of the equation, Jesus prayed as much: "My God, my God, why have you forsaken me?" (Matt. 27:46b). The prayer of the criminal crucified with the Lord is our prayer: "Jesus, remember me when you come into your kingdom" (Luke 23:42). Job waits prayerfully for his release (v. 14b). We wait prayerfully, too, on this day, close to the tomb where Jesus' body lay in death.

Lamentations 3:1-9, 19-24

A passage from Lamentations makes perfect sense on Holy Saturday when in the present moment of the Three Days drama we may suspend belief and let ourselves entertain the possibility that suffering, darkness, and death, not light and life, have the last word. The individual lament of the voice in this passage speaks of great physical (v. 4) and spiritual suffering (vv. 1-3, 5-8). Yet faith is implied in the acknowledgment of God as the source of the suffering, his agency indicated by the repetition of "he has" (eight times in vv. 2-9). That is to say, at least God has done these things that make for suffering, and they are not the result of human whim or natural causes.

Features of this passage evoke thoughts of Jesus in the tomb (vv. 7a, 9a). Worshipful utterances lie close at hand to the lament here (vv. 21-24), even as the vigil at the tomb occurs in close proximity to the first celebration of resurrection. In temple worship, lament expressed liturgically is answered after a period of vigil keeping, with the announcement of God's saving acts. So it is during the liturgy of the Three Days that the lament of Good Friday and Holy Saturday is answered with the *Exsultet* and other resurrection proclamations of the Easter Vigil.

Psalmody
Psalm 31:1-4

These verses from Psalm 31 give voice to the cry for deliverance, surely an appropriate prayer at the tomb on this day. The psalmist describes the Lord as a "rock of refuge" (v. 2b, 3a), a curiously appropriate designation on Holy Saturday when in faith we acknowledge as holy the rock that entombs Jesus, a place of refuge for Jesus and us. (For additional commentary on Psalm 31, see Sunday of the Passion/Palm Sunday, above.)

Second Reading
1 Peter 4:1-8

Christian tradition has it that Jesus' mission in death was to embody God's reign even in the place of the dead, suggested by the affirmation in the Apostles' Creed: "He descended to the dead." Likewise, that same creed affirms Jesus as the one who "will come again to judge the living and the dead." This passage from 1 Peter serves as a biblical foundation for these traditional affirmations (vv. 5-6a). Because Jesus' death and resurrection usher in a new reality, serving as a fulcrum between the old order and the new way, the author of 1 Peter exhorts hearers to live now according to the new way in Christ (v. 2). Moreover, because of the immanence of the consummation of God's reign in Christ (v. 7a), we are called to "be serious and [to] discipline [our]selves for the sake of [our] prayers" (v. 7b). Above all, these end times call for "constant love for one another" (v. 8a). The passage concludes with an acknowledgment that has guided the best practices of the church for two thousand years of end times: "Love covers a multitude of sins" (v. 8b). Indeed, love is that which most characterizes the new age in Christ, and it is God's love, made known by Jesus in laying down his life, that will have the last word as God raises him from the dead.

Gospel
Matthew 27:57-66

People respond to death variously, and they grieve in different ways. Such reality is perhaps reflected in this passage from Matthew describing the characters who attend to Jesus' body and his burial. First, Joseph of Arimathea responds with a practical kind of piety. Knowing that unburied bodies are unclean and thus compromise the Sabbath, he arranges with Pilate to retrieve Jesus' body so that he can place it in his own tomb, wrapping the corpse in "a clean linen cloth" and securing the tomb by placing a large stone at the entrance (vv. 57-60). Indeed, some people in the face of death respond by being practical and observing commonly held religious and cultural customs.

In contrast, Mary Magdalene and the other Mary are also present, "sitting opposite the tomb" (v. 61). Their response here in Matthew's account is to refrain from activity. They choose to just be there, keeping a kind of prayerful, perhaps contemplative, vigil. They wait, not knowing what if anything might come next. Certainly, the stance of simply being present is part of the repertoire of human response to death and to grief.

Then there are the chief priests and Pharisees, whose reaction can be characterized as defensive and fearful. In particular, they fear the word from Jesus who said, "After three days I will rise again" (v. 63). These religious leaders ask Pilate to secure the tomb lest Jesus' followers steal the body and then make the claim that he rose from the dead (v. 64). Pilate puts the concern back on the chief priests and Pharisees (v. 65), who then go with guards to the tomb to seal it (v. 66). Surely fear and reactive, defensive posturing, and the desire to guard and seal off uncertainty and the unknown, are also dimensions of the human response to death and to the mystery of what lies beyond that finality.

As people go through the stages of grief, they may find themselves responding variously, sometimes in the manner of Joseph of Arimathea, sometimes as Mary Magdalene and the other Mary, and other times as the chief priests and Pharisees. Where are you on this continuum today in response to the reality that Jesus died, and as you come to terms with various experiences of grief in your own life?

John 19:38-42

The depiction of Jesus' burial in John is nothing short of luxurious and noble, or, to employ a term common in Johannine theology, glorious. His body is attended to both by Joseph of Arimathea, a secret disciple, and by Nicodemus, the religious leader who visited Jesus at night (cf. John 3:1-21). Having gotten permission from Pilate to receive Jesus' body, together they wrap him according to Jewish custom in linen cloths along with one hundred pounds of a spiced mixture of myrrh and aloes (vv. 38-40), quite an extravagant amount of burial spices. Joseph and Nicodemus place Jesus' body in a tomb in close proximity to the garden place where Jesus was crucified (v. 41). Betrayed and crucified in a Garden setting, and buried in a garden in a brand-new tomb that had never before seen a corpse, the Gospel writer makes a point about a kind of return to the Garden of Eden, to pristine paradise, made possible by Jesus' glorification in death. All of this is in keeping with the dignity of Jesus in betrayal and death that is a significant feature of how Jesus is portrayed in John (cf. my commentary on the Passion according to John for Good Friday, above).

Death, particularly horrific circumstances that lead to death, can rob us of dignity. If we die ignominiously, surely at least we can expect a decent burial. That Jesus died and was buried in such a way as to show God's glory has bearing on Christian death. We who have been baptized are, according to Paul, baptized into his death (cf. Rom. 6:3). Baptism is our decent burial, where we are buried with Christ (cf. Rom. 6:4a). The baptismal font is our garden tomb in which we luxuriate in God's glory as we are also raised with Christ, "so we too might walk in newness of life" (cf. Rom. 6:4b). May this awareness prepare you for the first celebration of resurrection at the Easter Vigil.

Note
1.   *Cuddesdon College Office Book* (New York: Oxford University Press, 1961), 51.

March 30/31, 2013
Resurrection of Our Lord / The Great Vigil of Easter

Revised Common Lectionary (RCL)

Genesis 1:1—2:4a
Psalm 136:1-9, 23-36
Genesis 7:1-5, 11-18; 8:6-18; 9:8-13
Psalm 46
Genesis 22:1-18

Psalm 16
Exodus 14:10-31; 15:20-21
Exodus 15:1b-13, 17-18
Isaiah 55:1-11
Isaiah 12:2-6

Proverbs 8:1-8, 19-21; 9:4b-6 or
Baruch 3:9-15, 32—4:4
Psalm 19
Ezekiel 36:24-28
Psalm 42 and Psalm 43
Ezekiel 37:1-14
Psalm 143
Zephaniah 3:14-20
Psalm 98
ELW adds:
Jonah 1:1—2:1
Jonah 2:2-3 (4-6) 7-9
Isaiah 61:1-4, 9-11
Deuteronomy 32:1-4, 7, 36a, 43a
Daniel 3:1-29
Song of the Three 35—65

Romans 6:3-11
Psalm 114
Luke 24:1-12 or John 20:1-18 (*ELW*)

Lectionary for Mass (LFM)

Genesis 1:1—2:2 or 1:1, 26-31a
Psalm 104:1-2, 5-6, 10 + 12, 13-14, 24 + 35 or Psalm 33:4-5, 6-7, 12-13, 20-22

Genesis 22:1-18 or 22:1-2, 9a, 10-13, 15-18
Psalm 16:5 + 8, 9-10, 11
Exodus 14:15—15:1
Exodus 15:1-2, 3-4, 5-6, 17-18
Isaiah 55:1-11
Isaiah 12:2-3, 4bcd, 5-6
Isaiah 54:5-14
Psalm 30:2 + 4, 5-6, 11-12a + 13b
Baruch 3:9-15, 32—4:4
Psalm 19:8, 9, 10, 11
Ezekiel 36:16-17a, 18-28
Psalm 42:3, 5; 43:3, 4 or Psalm 51:12-13, 14-15, 18-19

Romans 6:3-11
Psalm 118:1-2, 16-17, 22-23
Luke 24:1-12

A most ancient liturgy and day three in the Three Days, the Great Vigil of Easter has it all: new fire; procession with paschal candle; singing of the *Exsultet*, the Easter Proclamation; a full service of readings covering key points in salvation history; the sacrament of baptism and/or affirmation of and thanksgiving for baptism; the celebration of the first Eucharist of Easter with the return of alleluias. When it is all said and done, worshipers on this night come away steeped in the fullness of the stories of salvation, having also been participants in the principal ritual enactments of our tradition. Included in this rich liturgy may be preaching, though a sermon or homily needs to be seen in light of all of the proceedings, especially as every feature of the liturgy ultimately points to and otherwise proclaims good news focused on Christ's resurrection.

The Vigil of Easter is a feast of contrasts, as suggested by a phrase in the *Exsultet*: "This is the night in which heaven and earth are joined—things human and things divine."[1] The darkness of both the night and the church in which we gather contrasts with the light of new fire, the illumination of individual candles held by worshipers, and the flood of lights returning during the singing of the Hymn of Praise at the Eucharist. Silence in keeping vigil at the beginning of the service along with time for quiet reflection after each reading contrasts with a liturgy that is full of sound and speech in the many readings, the joyful songs, the church bells pealing during the *Gloria in Excelsis*. In terms of categories of classic understandings of Christian spirituality, the Easter Vigil contains elements that are apophatic, that is, sacred experience born of wordless mystery, darkness and void, as suggested in another phrase from the *Exsultet*: "O night truly blessed which alone was worthy to know the time and hour in which Christ rose again from hell!"[2] These features contrast with aspects that are kataphatic, sacred experience that is sensate and sensual, richly elemental, drawing on symbols of creation: fire, water, oil, bread, and wine.

There is also the stark contrast between death and life taking place in worship space that functions both as tomb and, if you will, as womb for springing to life in resurrection. Moreover, the Easter Vigil makes much of contrasts ancient and contemporary, beginnings and endings, as in the words the presiding minister uses in connection with praying at the paschal candle, tracing the sign of the cross, Alpha and Omega, and the year of our Lord: "Christ, yesterday and today, the beginning and the ending. To Christ belongs all time and all the ages; to Christ belongs glory and dominion now and forever."[3] Amid the tensions of these contrasts, we "celebrate the divine mysteries with exultation."[4]

Tonight we get pretty much all that word and sacraments have to offer. Consider again readings that start at the beginning of creation and proceed through the centuries of salvation history, addressing us in our current year, as a living word for us is carried on the winds of the Spirit blowing through these ancient narratives. With new fire and candlelight in mind, think of a village gathered around the central communal fire, a campfire setting, the revered village storytellers captivating an enraptured audience as if we are hearing the old, old story for the first time. Tonight new Christians are made in the waters of baptism, entering and emerging from the tomb and womb of the font with Christ, even as we all participate with them in remembrance of and thanksgiving for our own baptism, our own death to resurrection. While the Eucharist on Maundy Thursday/Holy Thursday had the sense of commemoration of the Last Supper, tonight's celebration conveys the tenor of feast of victory for our God who in Christ gives us a taste of the heavenly banquet that knows no end.

Yet again, like Passion Sunday and the other Three Days liturgies, this night presents the preacher with challenges and opportunities. What might we say alongside the menu of liturgical and textual riches that the Easter Vigil offers up? One piece of practical wisdom is this, and it is obvious: less is more. Tonight is arguably not the night for a full-length sermon. I once, to good effect, preached a brief homily during an Easter Vigil that focused on a single word from the mouth of the resurrected Christ: "Greetings," that is, "Rejoice," or *chairete* in the Greek (cf. Matt. 28:9), which I suggested contained in a word the fullness of the gospel, even as a seed contains all the genetic material to become a flowering bush. For its root relates also to the Greek words for joy, grace, gift, generous spirit, thanksgiving, and ultimately Eucharist. An approach that allows a part to reveal the whole could enable preaching at the Easter Vigil to unfold meanings further alongside all of the other dimensions of the liturgy. The Easter Vigil also affords the great opportunity to enact proclamation in expansive ways not limited to a monologue sermon. Perhaps tonight is the time to try your setting's hand at doing dramatic readings of the passages appointed for the day, using the gifts of a company of lay readers. Perhaps the Easter Vigil is also the occasion to employ visual arts, maybe via PowerPoint or other technologies, in the service of artistically exploring the meanings of the many readings.

Old Testament Readings
CREATION
Genesis 1:1—2:4a (RCL)
Psalm 136:1-9, 23-26
Genesis 1:1—2:2 or 1:1, 26-31a (LFM)
Psalm 104:1-2, 5-6, 10 + 12, 13-14, 24 + 35 or Psalm 33:4-5, 6-7, 12-13, 20-22

God's creating activity, perhaps related to the divine wind "that swept over the face of the waters" (1:2b) amid the "formless void and darkness" (1:2a), was to bring order, demarcating natural distinctions: day and night; evening and morning (1:3-5); sky (1:6-8); earth and seas (1:9-10); vegetation (1:11-13); sun, moon, and stars; seasons, days, and years (1:14-19); birds and sea creatures (1:20-23); animals of the earth and human beings (1:24-27), who were given a special place in creation (1:28-30). God's creative energies also importantly distinguished between work and rest (2:2-3), a feature of natural order forgotten in our productivity-crazy, 24/7 age.

God's creative energies are located in the verbs "said" and "let" (cf. 1:3-5; note how this verbal pattern repeats in Genesis 1). God's word makes things happen in creative ways, and it is unambiguously "good" (cf. 1:4, with repetition in Genesis 1). The Easter Vigil liturgy calls us back to creation basics, featuring aspects of the natural world: darkness and light, water, and fruits of the earth like oil, bread, and wine, along with focus on God's word in the readings, which still contains for us creative power and divine goodness.

Psalms 136 (RCL), 104, and 33 (LFM) each serve as worshipful responses in thanksgiving for God's creative work, appropriate in connection with the Genesis 1–2 creation story.

THE FLOOD
Genesis 7:1-5, 11-18; 8:6-18; 9:8-13 (RCL)
Psalm 46

Water makes life possible and nourishes it for continuance, thus participating in the dynamics of creation. Water can also kill and destroy. Here is the scriptural story of the great flood, waters that purged the earth of life, aside from those, human and animal, chosen by God to ride out the destruction on Noah's ark. The ark and its passengers make way for re-creation, as when Noah and descendants and animals are commanded by God to leave the ark after the flood to "be fruitful and multiply" (8:17), thus echoing the same creative command in Genesis 1:28. The church sees allusion to baptism in the story of the flood, as suggested by reference to this event in a thanksgiving over the water used at baptismal liturgies: "Through the waters of the flood you delivered Noah and his family."[5] Features of this Genesis reading set the thematic stage for the focus on baptism at the Easter Vigil: the church as ark (cf. 7:17-18); the simultaneously destructive and re-creative waters in which we baptismally drown to sin and are reborn to life and restored to wholeness; the appearance of dove and olive leaf (8:11), which we might associate with the Holy Spirit (cf. Luke 3:22); the covenant established by God that promises that one flood is enough (cf. 9:8-11), even as baptism occurs only once in a lifetime. Flooding the baptismal font with a rainbow of light (cf. 9:12-13) would reinforce the covenantal themes of promise in this passage.

A fitting response to the story of the flood, *Psalm 46*, especially 3a, "though its waters rage and foam," reminds us that despite earthly destructive forces of many kinds, "God is our refuge and strength, a very present help in trouble" (v. 1) in whom we can "be still," knowing that the Lord is God (v. 10).

THE TESTING OF ABRAHAM
Genesis 22:1-18 (RCL, LFM)
Psalm 16
Genesis 22:1-2, 9a, 10-13, 15-18 (LFM alt.)
Psalm 16:5 + 8, 9-10, 11

Many today ask, "How can our merciful God command Abraham to sacrifice his son Isaac?" A fine question with which we would do well to struggle as God's ways persist in being mysterious to us. This concern bracketed for purposes here, however, it is true that the story turns out well and that Abraham's obedience of faith makes possible the increase of God's chosen people and opens all nations to blessing (vv. 17-18). We can also pursue a christological reading of this passage where we hear echoes of Jesus' sacrificial, unique, and divine sonship (v. 2). It is an imperfect symmetry—God and Abraham and Isaac, and God and Jesus—but the church on this night during these Three Days cannot help but hear christological resonances. We may also see ourselves in this story in baptismal ways. Parents present their children, and sponsors their candidates, for immersion into Christ's sacrifice, saying in effect, "Here I am" (22:1b, 7a, 11b). We may call the place of the bath "The LORD will provide," because we like Abraham suddenly see in the thicket of our mind's eye a ram, a lamb, Christ, to be sacrificed on our behalf (cf. 22:8, 13-14), which makes for increase of the faithful and for blessing.

It is said that Abraham and Isaac journeyed to the place for worshipful sacrifice (22:5). Given what happened, that indeed the Lord provided and promised blessing, *Psalm 16* (especially vv. 1-2, 9-11) is a fitting response to this narrative.

ISRAEL'S DELIVERANCE AT THE RED SEA
Exodus 14:10-31; 15:20-21 (RCL)
Exodus 15:1b-13, 17-18
Exodus 14:15—15:1 (LFM)
Exodus 15:1-2, 3-4, 5-6, 17-18

God's intervention on behalf of the people of Israel in delivering them from slavery in Egypt and creating passage for them through the Red Sea is a centerpiece of the exodus event. This is a core story in Judaism that also serves as a focus for the celebration of Passover. In keeping with many of the readings for Easter Vigil, we Christians again cannot help but see our own tradition's themes in this passage. The winds of the Holy Spirit cleave the waters of our fonts as the baptizing minister lifts the hand (cf. 14:16). Our own spiritual enemies, whom we renounce in the liturgy, pursue us into these waters, only to find themselves drowned like the Egyptians (cf. 14:23-28). Like the Israelites, we find ourselves full of faith on the other side of the waters (cf. 14:30-31), and we may wish to erupt in song and dance (cf. 15:1-21, which constitutes the response to this reading in the Vigil liturgy). In the paschal candle, we even have our own pillar of cloud and fire that lights up the night (cf. 14:19b-20, 24). While baptism happens to us individually, it is also helpful to view it communally, especially in light of this story of the deliverance of the whole people of Israel, acknowledging that the collective horses and riders of communal foes are likewise vanquished in these waters that save us as a people, a church.

SALVATION OFFERED FREELY TO ALL
Isaiah 55:1-11 (RCL, LFM)
Isaiah 12:2-6 (RCL)
Isaiah 12:2-3, 4bcd, 5-6 (LFM)

In this beloved and well-known passage, the promises of the prophet Isaiah expand the covenant with David (55:3b-5) and reverse the threat of judgment to make for abundance (vv. 1-2). These blessings result from the performative nature of God's word (v. 11). This selection can function as a kind of call to worship for us. "Come to the waters" (v. 1a) is a final invitation to the catechumens to be baptized this night. That which quenches thirst and fills us is free (v. 1b), *sola gratia*, grace alone. "Incline your ear, and come to me; listen, so that you may live" (v. 3a): here is an invitation to still deeper listening in this liturgy's service of readings. In this passage is also a call to repentance (vv. 6-7), a pointing to divine mystery (vv. 8-9), and finally, the promise that things are really going to happen (v. 11), features of which help further to set the tone for fuller participation in this liturgy.

The response to this passage (*Isaiah 12:2-6 [RCL]; Isaiah 12:2-3, 4bcd, 5-6 [LFM]*) reinforce the call-to-worship themes, verses 2 and 4-6 serving as a kind of entrance hymn of praise.

Isaiah 54:5-14 (LFM)
Psalm 30:2 + 4, 5-6, 11-12a + 13b

This passage from Isaiah speaks to deeply personal aspects of the Lord's relationship to the people of Israel, as it is akin to the covenant between husband and wife (vv. 5-6). The prophet suggests that the Lord promises a gathering-in despite a moment of abandonment (v. 7), an outpouring of compassion in everlasting love despite an overflowing of wrath (v. 8), and an everlasting covenant of peace (vv. 9-10). There is the promise of a bejeweled future for the Lord's spouse (vv. 11-12), prosperity for the children (v. 13), and the removal of oppression and terror (v. 14). We may likewise hear this as God's promise to the baptized who are united with Christ.

Portions of *Psalm 30* serve as the response to this passage from Isaiah in the form of a reply of the spouse to the Lord, as mourning turns into joy.

THE WISDOM OF GOD
Proverbs 8:1-8, 19-21; 9:4b-6 (RCL)
Baruch 3:9-15, 32—4:4 (RCL alt., LFM)
Psalm 19 (RCL)
Psalm 19:8, 9, 10, 11 (LFM)

The author of Proverbs casts wisdom as calling the simple ones to deeper encounter with prudence and intelligence (8:5), with noble things and rightness (8:6), and with truth and righteousness (8:7-8). We may hear via the voice of wisdom in this passage another call to worship, an invitation to gather (8:1-4), to listen for God's word (8:6-8), to share in the Lord's Supper (9:5), and to "walk in the way of insight" (9:6b).

Before this encounter with wisdom, that is, with Christ via baptism and our walk of discipleship, we were the simple, imprudent ones. On the other side of this holy sojourn, we find ourselves wiser, more mature, and able to live (9:6a).

The passage from Baruch also is a call to Israel for entry into wisdom (3:9-15), into the commandments (4:1), and thus into deeper encounter with the Lord (3:35-36). An invitation to proceed from folly to prudence, here also is a call to repentance, another resonance with the baptismal themes of this night, when we soak deeply in the wells of wisdom in the sacramental waters.

Psalm 19 (RCL) or portions thereof (LFM) serves as the response to the Proverbs or Baruch passages. This psalm reports how creation itself tells of God's glory (vv. 1-6), and it extols the virtues of the commandments (vv. 7-12).

A NEW HEART AND A NEW SPIRIT
Ezekiel 36:24-28 (RCL)
Psalm 42 and Psalm 43
Ezekiel 36:16-17a, 18-28 (LFM)
Psalm 42:3, 5; 43:3, 4 or Psalm 51:12-13, 14-15, 18-19

The word of the Lord that Ezekiel reports (vv. 16-20) is an angry, wrathful word indeed, expressing judgment for the house of Israel's defiling and profaning the holy name through their idolatrous behavior. For the sake of honoring that holy name (vv. 21-23), the Lord promises a return and forgiveness (vv. 24-25). Moreover, a new heart and spirit are promised that will make for obedience and a restoration of covenantal relationship (vv. 26-28). Christian ears will hear in this passage still more baptismal themes in reference to cleansing waters (cf. v. 25). This cleansing also regenerates in the giving of a new heart and spirit, making possible the keeping of God's commandments (cf. vv. 26-27) and solidifying the covenant we have with God in Christ in baptism (cf. v. 28b).

Psalms 42, 43, and 51 (or portions) are the response to this Ezekiel passage and offer the voice of God's plaintive, longing children in counterpoint to the voice of God's promise and call.

THE VALLEY OF DRY BONES
Ezekiel 37:1-14 (RCL)
Psalm 143

The valley of dry bones, a metaphor for exile and lament, perhaps a recollection of a battlefield filled with dismembered body parts, is a horror too readily known in the millennia of human existence, and particularly vivid for the people of Israel. A divine vision takes Ezekiel to this place. Then the Lord gives the command to prophesy (vv. 4b, 5a). God's speech carried on the lips of the prophet effects a re-creation, parts of the bodies coming together in the opposite order of decomposition. This divine word makes for new life, for enspirited flesh, that the whole house of Israel (cf. v. 11) may return to their homeland (v. 12b), and that they may know that the Lord's word generates mighty deeds (v. 14b). To Christian ears this rings with the echoes of the promised resurrection at the last day, when the valleys of human desolation will be filled with the living, breathing bodies of the ones Christ calls to new life.

The plea for deliverance from enemies in *Psalm 143* makes a fitting response to this passage from Ezekiel, where the tone is in keeping with the exiles' lament, especially when the psalmist speaks of the soul's thirst for the Lord (v. 6) and expresses fear that the Lord's hiding the divine face will result in the dreaded experience of going "down to the Pit" (v. 7b).

THE GATHERING OF GOD'S PEOPLE
Zephaniah 3:14-20 (RCL)
Psalm 98

This passage from the final verses of the brief book of the prophet Zephaniah is a celebratory hymn of joyful deliverance, as if it, like the psalms, might be used in ritual observances. These verses promise homecoming and restoration to a remnant in exile (v. 20), along with salvation for the oppressed, lame, and outcast (v. 19). The NRSV uses the English word *exult* (vv. 14, 17), alongside "sing," "shout," and "rejoice" (v. 14), to invite the people to sing in joyful song. On this night we cannot help but think of our song of rejoicing, the *Exsultet*, the Easter Proclamation, sung at this liturgy's beginning. A christological hermeneutic applied to this passage suggests themes of Immanuel, God with us in our midst (vv. 15b, 17a). The command to not fear (v. 16a) suggests the angelic announcement to the shepherds in Jesus' birth narrative (cf. Luke 2:10). God's saving the oppressed, the lame, and the outcast is likewise suggestive of Jesus' appearance at the synagogue at Nazareth at the beginning of his ministry (cf. Luke 4:18).

Psalm 98 as a response to this reading continues the theme of joyful praise for God's victory in judgment. Here the very earth praises the Lord (vv. 7-8).

THE CALL OF JONAH
Jonah 1:1—2:1 (ELW)
Jonah 2:2-3 (4-6) 7-9

As a story about a prophet, Jonah is a unique work in biblical literature that defies categorization in terms of purpose, origin, genre, dating, and even message. It thus lends itself to multiple interpretations and themes. In this passage we see the call of Jonah, a call that he actively seeks to flee (1:3). It is a common thing to resist God's call for various reasons and in varied ways, as suggested by the biblical greats Moses (cf. Exod. 3:1-12), Elijah (cf. 1 Kgs. 19:1-18), and Jeremiah (cf. Jer. 1:4-10). Jesus himself wants out of what is before him, but ultimately prays that God's will be done (cf. Luke 22:42). Even today, stories of calls to ministry commonly include tales of fleeing. But God will not have it, as indicated by the sending of the great wind to interrupt the escape to Tarshish (1:4-11), and the rescue by the great fish, despite Jonah's being thrown into the sea (1:12—2:1). God will insist on sending us on our way to do the work we have been called to do. Defying precise exegesis, Christians might make baptismal themes out of the tempestuous waters that are calmed by sacrificing one, Jonah (Christ), to their deathly raging, likewise seeing resurrection in the emergence from the womb and tomb-like belly of the great fish after three days and nights (1:17—2:10). Perhaps more parallel allusions to Jonah in Gospel literature are evident in Jesus' stilling-of-the-storm sequences (Mark 4:35-41; Matt. 8:24-27).

Jonah 2:2-3 (4-6) 7-9, comprising Jonah's psalm-like praying (cf. portions of Psalm 69) from the belly of the fish, is the response to this Easter Vigil reading. In these verses we hear the call of distress and the acknowledgment that the Lord listens and ultimately delivers.

AN EVERLASTING COVENANT
Isaiah 61:1-4, 9-11 (*ELW*)
Deuteronomy 32:1-4, 7, 36a, 43a

This passage from Isaiah suggests a call narrative for the prophet to proclaim the day of the Lord's salvation to those who mourn in Zion (vv. 1-3a). It is verses 1-2 that Jesus stands to read when he is given the scroll of the prophet Isaiah at his hometown synagogue in Nazareth, making the claim of this Scripture's fulfillment in that assembly's hearing (cf. Luke 4:16-19). Verses 3-4 and 9 in this Isaiah passage speak to the mourners, whose mood will turn to rejoicing. Verses 10-11 give voice to the prophet's celebratory rejoicing and praise for the magnificent things God is up to, all of this in keeping with the spirit of the resurrection feast soon to be celebrated during this Easter Vigil (cf. v. 11).

Deuteronomy 32:1-4, 7, 36a, 43a, from the Song of Moses, furthers the tone of praise for the Lord's vindication as the response to the Isaiah 61 reading.

DELIVERANCE FROM THE FIERY FURNACE
Daniel 3:1-29 (*ELW*)
Song of the Three 35–65

The Hebrews Shadrach, Meshach, and Abednego, officials appointed in the province of Babylon, refuse King Nebuchadnezzar's order to worship before his idolatrous golden statue (v. 12), thus enraging the king, who then orders that the three be thrown into the furnace of blazing fire (vv. 19-23). As signs of his monarchical power and wealth, Nebuchadnezzar had his phallus-like statue of gold (v. 1), his company of bureaucrats (vv. 2-3), his plenteous court musicians (vv. 5-10), and the threat of execution by fiery ordeal, with the heat of the furnace turned up so hot (vv. 19b) that it killed his strongest guards who attended it (vv. 20-22). All of this, fire included, did not overcome Shadrach, Meshach, and Abednego (v. 27). This, of course, astonishes the king (v. 24), who acknowledges the God of the three (v. 28) but continues in his ways of violence unchanged (v. 29). Faith in the God who delivers, expressed in the three's statement to the king (vv. 16-18), is far more powerful than the idolatrous trappings of empire. God is God, a great comfort to those who suffer oppression under colonial occupation. Earthly empire, wielding all its might in execution, also ultimately held no power over Jesus, whom God raised from the dead, astonishing imperial figures and likewise comforting the oppressed in those days of Roman occupation. This is good news for us in our day as well.

The apocryphal *Song of the Three 35–65*, long understood as the song that Shadrach, Meshach, and Abednego sang upon their deliverance from the fiery furnace, is the response to the Daniel passage. A song directing all of creation to sing praise (*Benedicite, Omnia Opera*, "All you works of the Lord, bless the Lord"), it is a fitting conclusion to the liturgy of readings with the refrain sung again and again, "Praise and magnify God forever."

Epistle Reading
Romans 6:3-11 (RCL, LFM)

In Romans 6, Paul addresses the reality that the human propensity to sin continues after baptism (cf. vv. 1-2). Paul's response to this dilemma focuses on our baptismal sharing with Christ in his death and resurrection. Via baptism, "we have been buried *with* him" (v. 4a—*synthapto*, "we were entombed together"); we "have been united *with* him in a death like his" (v. 5a—*symphytos*, as if to say we were planted together with him in death); we "will certainly be united *with* him in a resurrection like his" (v. 5b). Our "old self was crucified *with* him" (v. 6a—*systauroo*). We have "died *with* Christ" (v. 8a—*synapothnesko*), and we "will also live *with* him" (v. 8b—*syzao*). *With* (cf. the Greek prefix *syn-*) is a word easily overlooked, but crucial for Paul and for us in its theological significance. Baptism bonds us with Christ, uniting us with him and to the events of his death and resurrection. In short, we are with Christ, and Christ is with us. It is the reality of this intimate participation with Christ baptismally that makes possible a genuinely new life that frees us from enslavement to sin (v. 6). That is to say, our efforts at trying harder will not make the difference when we are tempted by the old ways of sin and death. Rather, it is the symphony of Christ with us that makes for new life on this other side of the resurrection. Paul here wakes us to this reality and exhorts us to live accordingly (vv. 12-14), a fitting call to remembrance on a night so focused on baptism as the foundational reality for the Christian life.

Psalmody
Psalm 114 (RCL)

Psalm 114 is one more remembrance of the exodus event, when God made possible the people of Israel's flight from Egypt. The particular divine attribute that the psalmist invokes in these verses is that of God who has power over creation (vv. 7-8). It is this power of God that also divided the waters of the sea (vv. 1-3) and will usher in the day of judgment (v. 7), even as this same power raised Jesus from the dead.

Psalm 118:1-2, 16-17, 22-23 (LFM)

These verses from Psalm 118 speak to God's victory of life over death, which inspires the psalmist to utter twice that the Lord's "steadfast love endures forever!" (vv. 1-2). Christians see Christ in the rejected stone becoming the chief cornerstone (v. 22), and hear resurrection themes in the marvel we behold in God's action of raising Jesus from the dead (cf. v. 23).

Gospel
Luke 24:1-12 (RCL, LFM)

I suggested in my Passion Sunday commentary (above) that the Lukan Passion narrative leaves us hanging. The loose ends are not tied up, unlike the Passion from John's Gospel where the theological ducks are more in a row. Before us now is Luke's account of the empty tomb. The story continues to unfold, but alas, even here we are left wanting and needing more. In short, the encounter with the empty tomb and with the "two men in dazzling clothes" (v. 4b) does not result in the experience-based knowledge and belief that Christ has been raised. The empty tomb evoked perplexity (v. 4a) on the part of the women who dutifully visited the grave to attend to Jesus' body. The dazzling heavenly beings provoked in them terror and "bow[ing] their faces to the ground" (v. 5a). When the several women eyewitnesses report the empty tomb and the message of the angelic figures—"He is not here, but has risen" (cf. vv. 5b-7)—to the other disciples, they dismiss it as an "idle tale," or nonsense, and "they did not believe them" (v. 11). Peter ran to the tomb to see things for himself, but Luke reports only that "he went home, amazed at what had happened" (v. 12). Perplexity, terrified bowing of the faces, an idle tale, and amazement, but neither belief nor the proclamation of the resurrection.

We need to go further in the Lukan narrative for the confession on the part of the disciples that Jesus has been raised. Namely, it is the encounter on the road to Emmaus (Luke 24:13-35), where the risen Lord opens the Scriptures to the two disciples and is finally recognized and known in the breaking of bread, that results in the disciples' exclamation, "The Lord has risen indeed" (Luke 24:34). But let us not go there quite yet. There is more to consider in the empty-tomb narrative.

The dazzlingly clad men instruct the women to "remember," namely, to remember Jesus' own words about his death and resurrection (vv. 6-7). This instruction recalls the various Passion predictions in Luke's Gospel (cf. Luke 9:21-22, 43b-44; 18:31-33) and begins the process of connecting the dots that will lead to faith and to the proclamation, "He is risen." With the creedal-like words—"be crucified, and on the third day rise again" (v. 7b)—the women "remembered [Jesus'] words" (v. 8). "Remember," a key ingredient of faith, is appropriately invoked at the tomb, which in the Greek, *mnemeion*, is a memorial vault, a place of remembrance. At this point, however, theirs is not a living memory, a seamless whole of participation in the one remembered. That would come on the road to Emmaus and at the table (cf. Luke 24:30-32). Living memory that births the confession of faith comes to us in our day in the same way, namely, in breaking open the word of Scripture and dining at the eucharistic table: "Do this for the remembrance [*anamnesis*] of me." Luke's account, where the empty tomb does not produce faith in the resurrection, but the sacramental encounter does, preaches this night and always, as if to say that the way the resurrected Lord was made known to his original followers is the same way in seamless continuity through the centuries that he is made known to us even now.

John 20:1-18 (*ELW*)

For commentary on this text, see the Gospel for Easter Sunday, below.

Notes

1. *Evangelical Lutheran Worship: Leader's Desk Edition* (Minneapolis: Augsburg Fortress, 2006), 647.
2. Ibid.
3. Ibid., 644.
4. Ibid., 646.
5. *Evangelical Lutheran Worship: Pew Edition* (Minneapolis: Augsburg Fortress, 2006), 230.

March 31, 2013
Resurrection of Our Lord / Easter Day

Revised Common Lectionary (RCL)
Acts 10:34-43 or Isaiah 65:17-25
Psalm 118:1-2, 14-24
1 Corinthians 15:19-26 or Acts 10:34-43

John 20:1-18 or Luke 24:1-12

Lectionary for Mass (LFM)
Acts 10:34a, 37-43
Psalm 118:1-2, 16-17, 22-23
Colossians 3:1-4 or 1 Corinthians 5:6b-8

John 20:1-9

If your setting offers a full complement of liturgies for Holy Week and the Three Days, the preaching minister may come to Easter Day, the festival of the Resurrection of Our Lord, quite exhausted. Preachers and liturgical ministers may wish to occupy for a time of rest the tomb that Jesus just vacated. Yet the spiritual and actual adrenaline is still high for this day.

The character of the assembly on Easter Day is likely quite different from the gatherings for the other liturgies during Holy Week. Unless there are baptisms that draw large numbers of extended family members, the Easter Vigil congregation, for example, may resemble a faithful remnant. On Easter Sunday, in contrast, you behold perhaps large throngs of people you do not normally see, among them seekers or "cultural Christians" who have little knowledge of the Christian faith and limited commitments to discipleship. Like many of the days of Holy Week, then, preaching on Easter Sunday presents challenges and opportunities. In the Revised Common Lectionary, the choice of Gospel readings for this day are the same as for Easter Vigil. Given the likely differences in the qualities of the assembly, an Easter Sunday sermon may well have a very different flavor from proclamation at the Easter Vigil, even when drawing on the same textual material.

Consider the challenge and opportunity embedded in the popular name for this day, Easter, deriving from archaic forms of English and German, having to do with the "East" and also having association with a pre-Christian deity, the goddess of the dawn. What might the preacher make of this? Recognizing that Christianity is not immune from influences of other religious traditions and is, in fact, indebted to some, especially Judaism, we may well claim the religious melting-pot dynamics of this day to make distinctively Christian claims, especially that the Son's rising is not simply the same as the sun's rising.

Moreover, the day is likely rather overstimulating in sensate ways. The worship space may be filled to overflowing with flowers, a feast for the eyes and for our noses. Think of the competing claims of the symbols. Blossoming flowers are signs of fertility, as are Easter eggs and bunnies that may decorate the homes of the people in church this day. These fertility symbols convey a sense of life from life, not life from death. Resurrection is more than the natural life cycle. Yet signs of fertility may tend to overpower other symbols in our worship spaces, especially ones like crosses unadorned by depictions of Jesus' corpus. In preaching, then, focus on the signs and themes that more fully point to life from death, a singular victory in which we now share via the sacramental life of the church.

The resurrection-day preacher may also know the challenge of being heard amid the competing claims that also include perhaps multiple selections of choral and instrumental music—for example, featuring the overpowering sound of the trumpet. As is the case on Sunday of the Passion, when people may want more palm than Passion, people in the assembly today may come with preconsciously held cultural expectations to have more Easter than resurrection. Your calling as a minister of proclamation is to seize the opportunity to cut through this thematic noise to get to the heart of it: Jesus Christ has been raised from the dead, and this changes everything.

First Reading
Acts 10:34-43 (RCL)
Acts 10:34a, 37-43 (LFM)

Prior in Acts, Peter had just experienced the shared but remote vision with the Gentile Cornelius and had journeyed to him for a face-to-face encounter as instructed by the Spirit (Acts 10:1-33). This passage features Peter's inspired, prophetic utterance to Cornelius and his friends and relatives, along with some of Peter's believing companions from Joppa. The Peter who appears before Cornelius and others is not the Peter of the Good Friday Passion narrative who denies three times that he even knew Jesus. No, here is the post-resurrection and post-ascension, and particularly the post-Pentecost Peter, who in the power of the Spirit proclaims a Christ-focused message as boldly as he did, for example, in the immediate aftermath of the Spirit's coming (Acts 2:14-36).

What Peter says sounds like the rudiments of our ecumenical creeds (cf. esp. v. 36—"he is Lord of all"—and vv. 38, 40, 42b). In addition to these basics of the emerging Christian kerygma, Peter here has an awakening in light of his vision and this encounter with Cornelius, namely that the message of Christ extends not just to the Jewish people, but to people of all nations (vv. 34b-35, 43). The message is the same: Jesus died on the cross, "but God raised him on the third day" (v. 40a). Peter and the other apostles endure the privileged calling of bearing witness to, of being martyrs (*martyria*; cf. vv. 39a, 41, 42) for, this Christ and the message about him. This apostolic calling has been passed on through the generations of the church to our own day. Thus, who are the Corneliuses to whom we are sent now to proclaim, "Christ is risen"?

Isaiah 65:17-25 (RCL alt.)

Coming very close to the conclusion of the book of Isaiah with its final judgment and vision, this passage speaks of the blessed effects of the vindication of the servant figure who is featured so prominently in much of the latter parts of Isaiah (cf. Isa. 52:13—53:12). The prophet speaks of "new heavens and a new earth" (v. 17a), and a new creation of Jerusalem, a holy city formerly characterized by "weeping" and "distress" (v. 19), but which is now marked with gladness, joy, rejoicing, and delight (vv. 18-19). The prophet envisions not just God's restoration of Jerusalem, but a genuinely new way that may really be a return to the paradise of the original circumstances of creation, where humans enjoy lengthy life spans (v. 20), where labor and child bearing are not in vain (v. 23), and where predator and prey eat together (v. 25a). The serpent remains accursed, however (v. 25b; cf. Gen. 3:14). In brief, this new creation, in sharp contrast to usual human experience, is summed up thusly: "They shall not hurt or destroy on all my holy mountain, says the LORD" (v. 25c). Christians see in the resurrection of the servant Jesus the inauguration of the envisioned age of "new heavens and a new earth" (v. 17a).

Psalmody
Psalm 118:1-2, 14-24 (RCL)
Psalm 118:1-2, 16-17, 22-23 (LFM)

For commentary on this text, see the Psalmody (LFM) for the Great Vigil of Easter, above.

Second Reading
1 Corinthians 15:19-26 (RCL)

The context for this passage from 1 Corinthians is the dispute in the community at Corinth about the resurrection of the dead, not a widely held belief among people of faith in that day. The faithful at Corinth did not deny Christ's resurrection as a onetime miraculous occurrence. It is the general resurrection of others that they found problematic. Paul's rhetoric is powerful, if not stinging, suggesting that we are to be pitied if we do not also embrace our promised resurrection (v. 19). For Paul, Christ's resurrection is inseparably linked to a general resurrection, and vice versa. If Christ is raised from the dead, then we who belong to Christ will also be raised. If the Corinthians have trouble with the general resurrection, then surely they must struggle with Christ's resurrection.

Paul's argument here centers on the theme of "first fruits," that Christ's resurrection is the first harvest among all those who have died. In keeping with biblical tradition (cf. Exod. 23:19a), giving over to God the first fruits of the harvest makes holy the entire crop. Thus Christ's death and resurrection sanctify our own death and make possible our own resurrection. In Adam, the natural human, we know death (vv. 21a, 22a). In Christ, a new Adam, we will experience new life (vv. 21b, 22b). All of this proceeds according to the order in which God has appointed it (vv. 23-24), until all Christ's "enemies [are] under his feet" (v. 25; cf. Ps. 110:1) and death at last is destroyed (v. 26). In short, Paul's message to the people at Corinth, and to us in our own day, is that we are not ones to be pitied at all, if indeed we cling by faith to the hope that is in us, that as Christ was raised, "so all will be made alive in Christ" (v. 22b).

Acts 10:34-43 (RCL alt.)

See comments on the first reading, above.

Colossians 3:1-4 (LFM)

In the letter to the Colossians, the author addresses dualistic philosophical systems that are at odds with the proclamation about Christ's death and resurrection. In the paradigm of thought that is argued against in this letter, that which is above (vv. 1-2) is immaterial and thus good; that which is on earth (v. 2b) is material and thus bad. The author of Colossians uses these philosophical categories to make a christological point, namely, that Christ dwells above, that is, in the heavenly place that marks the new age inaugurated by his resurrection. That which is of earth is of the old age, that is, the old ways that held sway prior to the victory of Christ having been raised. Access to "what is above" is made possible because the risen Christ is already there, "seated at the right hand of God" (v. 1b NAB). Our access to Christ is through baptism, for which "being raised with Christ" (v. 1a NRSV) is a kind of code language (cf. 2:12). While this new reality is not yet fully available either to the hearers of this letter or to us in our own day, and thus our "life is hidden with Christ in God" (v. 3), we all nonetheless cling to the totality of Christ's claim on us, he "who is [our] life" (v. 4a NRSV), and trust the promise that with the fullness of the revelation of Christ will come our revelation also "with him in glory" (v. 4). Our task now is to "set [our] mind on [these] things" (v. 2a NRSV), that is, to think on Christ being raised with intentionality, reframing our narratives, telling new stories, thus improving our ability to struggle creatively and faithfully against the continuing claims of the old earthly ways.

1 Corinthians 5:6b-8 (LFM alt.)

The context for this passage from 1 Corinthians is Paul's concern for the unwarranted arrogance of people in the church at Corinth, unwarranted because of the flagrant sexual immorality of some in the church there (addressed throughout 1 Corinthians 5). Here he essentially says that a few bad apples ruin the whole bunch (cf. v. 6b NAB: "A little yeast leavens all the dough"). Hearkening to the Passover ritual of removing all yeast from the household during this festival (v. 7a; cf. Exod. 13:7), Paul exhorts his hearers and us to live according to the new reality that results from Christ's death and resurrection, Christ being "our paschal lamb [cf. Exod. 12:21] . . . [who] has been sacrificed" (v. 7b). Our celebration of the festival of post-sacrifice and post-resurrection life is characterized by "sincerity" and "truth" and not "malice" and "wickedness" (v. 8 NAB). The unleavened bread we take in the Eucharist, conveying to us Christ's very body and blood, and thus our participation in his death and resurrection, makes possible this new way of celebrating life, that is, with sincerity and truth.

Gospel
John 20:1-18 (RCL)
John 20:1-9 (LFM)

This passage from John's Gospel contains two scenes: the empty-tomb narrative (vv. 1-10) and the resurrected Jesus' appearance to Mary Magdalene (vv. 11-18). Unlike the Lukan account, where the empty tomb provoked mainly perplexity and fear, and not faith, John's version has the encounter with the tomb result in belief on the part of the disciple "whom Jesus loved" (v. 2). In this scene, Mary Magdalene runs to tell Simon Peter and the other disciple that the stone has been removed from the tomb (v. 1b), the presumption being that Jesus' body has been stolen or misplaced (v. 2b). Simon Peter and the other disciple then run together to the tomb (v. 4a). The beloved disciple gets there first (v. 4b), looks into the tomb to see the grave clothes (v. 5), but defers to Peter, who enters and sees that the grave clothes are neatly arranged apart from where the body was (vv. 6-7). Then it is the beloved disciple's turn to enter the tomb. John reports that "he saw and believed" (v. 8b), despite the fact that the disciples "did not understand the scripture, that he must rise from the dead" (v. 9).

What is the significance of the beloved disciple, first of all, and of his belief upon seeing the tomb? In brief, the beloved disciple carries in himself the love, the familiarity, the intimacy that are the ideal of discipleship in John (cf. my commentary on the LFM Gospel for Tuesday of Holy Week, above). It is this loving intimacy that allows the beloved disciple also to get there first in faith, as it were, and to believe without the benefit of, as yet, a firsthand encounter. Such faith is born of love and not evidence, and itself is a mark of our discipleship on this side of the resurrection and ascension: "Blessed are those who have not seen and yet have come to believe" (John 20:29b).

Mary Magdalene's encounter with the risen Lord, which results in her becoming the apostle to the apostles as the first to proclaim the resurrection (20:18), echoes the themes of intimacy seen in the beloved disciple's response to the empty tomb. Mary is found weeping at the tomb, testifying to the depth of her feelings for Jesus and what he represents to her. She encounters the angels situated where Jesus' body had been when she looks in the tomb, and they inquire about her weeping (vv. 11-13). Hearers and readers of John's narrative, that is, we who believe though we have not seen, know that Jesus has been raised, and thus may see the ironic humor in the case of mistaken identity when Mary supposes him to be the gardener (v. 15). In fact, it is the Lord himself who also inquires about her weeping. Mary again offers up her interpretation of what has happened, namely, that Jesus' body has been misplaced or, worse, stolen. Then Jesus calls her by name, "Mary" (v. 16a). Immediately she, the disciple, recognizes her teacher: "Rabbouni!" (v. 16b). Here is an intimate encounter, a recognition of the risen Lord born of a long history of knowing each other by name and title, and recognizing the voice of the familiar: "He calls his own sheep by name and leads them out" (John 10:3b); "My sheep hear my voice. I know them, and they follow me" (John 10:27). It is this knowing and being known in the flesh that births recognition in faith, and presumably Mary's impulse to embrace her beloved teacher (cf. Jesus' instruction to her, "Do not hold on to me," v. 17a).

I suggested in my Good Friday commentary that the Passion in John's Gospel is perhaps best seen in light of Jesus' farewell discourse that precedes it. I would make a similar point here, that Mary's resurrection encounter is likewise a reflection and fulfillment of themes of the farewell discourse. Mary's weeping turns to joy, as Jesus had suggested before his death (cf. John 16:20, 22). Likewise, explaining why Mary should not hold on to him, Jesus says that he has "not yet ascended to the Father," echoing similar statements made in the context of his discourse with the disciples prior to his death (cf. John 14:28; 16:5-11, 16-17, 28). Jesus further elaborates with Mary, expecting that she will communicate this message to the other disciples: "I am ascending to my Father and your Father, to my God and your God" (20:17b). Jesus' prayer during the farewell discourse (John 17:1-26), in the context of which he prays that his disciples will know the same unity he shares with his Father, acknowledging that the disciples have a full share with him and thus also with the Father, renders intelligible "my Father and your Father" and "my God and your God." The resurrection is the down payment on this intimate relating in John, the fullness of which will immanently be known when Jesus imparts to them the promised gift of the Holy Spirit in another resurrection encounter behind locked doors, which follows on the heels of this passage (cf. 20:19-23).

So what is the good news of these readings that transcends the clamor of this festival day that we may preach? Each reading makes the point in its own way that the resurrection of the Lord is not business as usual in any way. We are talking about new heavens and a new earth, a new age of peace and joy (cf. Isa. 65:17-25). Breaking open religious boundaries, the message is for the nations and not just the Hebrew people (cf. Acts 10:34-43). Resurrection is for all and not just for Jesus (cf. 1 Cor. 15:19-26). Philosophically, old dualisms disappear in Christ (cf. Col. 3:1-4). In terms of the ethical life, we can put away our old immoral ways because of Christ's resurrection (cf. 1 Cor. 5:6b-8). Finally, it is our intimacy with Christ in faith, our sharing in the divine life, that makes it possible for us to believe the unbelievable and to proclaim that which defies explanation (cf. John 20:1-18). The flowers adorning our worship spaces may be beautiful, and the festive music on this day a delight to the ears. The new life of spring may be breaking out of the cold ground. But none of this captures the heart of resurrection. God is up to something different today that subverts both human and natural business as usual. This is the good news we are called to shout above the clamor of competing signs and symbols today.

Luke 24:1-12 (RCL alt.)

For comments on this passage, see the Gospel for Easter Vigil, above.